I0822048

PROMOTING THE WAR EFFORT

MEDIA AND PUBLIC AFFAIRS

Robert Mann, Series Editor

PROMOTING THE WAR EFFORT

Robert Horton and Federal Propaganda 1938–1946

MORDECAI LEE

Louisiana State
University Press
Baton Rouge

Published by Louisiana State University Press

Manufactured in the United States of America
First printing

DESIGNER: Michelle A. Neustrom
TYPEFACE: Chaparral Pro, text; Futura BT, display
PRINTER: McNaughton & Gunn, Inc.
BINDER: Acme Bookbinding

Frontispiece: Robert Horton at his desk, Spring 1942. Prints & Photographs Division, Library of Congress.

Charts and map created by Mary Lee Eggart

LIBRARY OF CONGRESS CATALOGING-IN-PUBLICATION DATA

Lee, Mordecai, 1948–
Promoting the war effort : Robert Horton and federal propaganda, 1938–1946 / Mordecai Lee.
p. cm. — (Media and public affairs)
Includes bibliographical references and index.
ISBN 978-0-8071-4529-6 (cloth : alk. paper) — ISBN 978-0-8071-4530-2 (pdf) — ISBN 978-0-8071-4531-9 (epub) — ISBN 978-0-8071-4532-6 (mobi) 1. Horton, Robert (Robert Wyman), b. 1902. 2. World War, 1939–1945—Propaganda. 3. World War, 1939–1945—United States. 4. Propaganda, American—History—20th century. 5. United States—Politics and government—1933–1945. 6. Public relations and politics—United States—History—20th century. 7. Politics and war—United States—History—20th century. 8. United States. Office for Emergency Management. Division of Information—Officials and employees—Biography. I. Title.
D810.P7U396 2012
940.54'88973092—dc23

2011051747

The paper in this book meets the guidelines for permanence and durability of the Committee on Production Guidelines for Book Longevity of the Council on Library Resources. ♾

To my grade-school teachers at Cumberland and Lydell Schools (1953–59) of the Whitefish Bay, Wisconsin, public school district, who nurtured my curiosity and joy of learning—along with giving me a monthly iodine pill and lessons in how to duck and cover in case of an atomic sneak attack by the Commies

CONTENTS

PREFACE

One thing leads to another. Researching a book on FDR's Office of Government Reports (OGR), I often ran across references to OGR's sister agency, the Division of Information (DOI) in the Office for Emergency Management. Both were within the new Executive Office of the President. Trying to keep my focus on the subject at hand, I skipped lightly over the references to DOI. Still, it kept popping up. The two agencies were largely complementary and worked closely together. OGR focused mostly on the civilian side of the executive branch, while DOI focused on the temporary agencies created to ramp up production of armaments for national defense and Lend-Lease. OGR had almost no media relations activities, distributing its information directly to individuals and groups. DOI, on the other hand, focused largely on disseminating information indirectly to the citizenry through the news media. The two agencies were often mentioned in the same political breath when conservatives criticized the unprecedented scale of FDR's public relations activities. The close interrelationship between the work of OGR and DOI was confirmed when, in June 1942, FDR consolidated federal information agencies into the new Office of War Information (OWI). OGR and DOI were two of only three agencies that were wholly abolished in the reorganization. The short-lived Office of Facts and Figures (October 1941–June 1942), headed by Archibald MacLeish, was the third. OWI also received portions of the foreign broadcast activities of the Coordinator of Information agency (renamed the Office of Strategic Services, later still the CIA), which continued in existence. There seemed to be a gap in the literature, with book-length histories of OGR and OWI, but none on DOI.[1] So, this study, something of a companion volume to my earlier examination of OGR, treats the second of the three agencies that were eliminated in their entirety to create OWI.[2]

Still interested in the history of government public relations after finishing the OGR book, I wrote a short piece a few years later about the World War II public information work of Bruce Catton, who in the 1950s and 1960s was a best-selling and award-winning popular historian of the American Civil War.[3] Catton's first book (before he began writing about the Civil War) is a memoir of his service as an information officer in the federal government during the war. It is a paean to Robert W. Horton, Catton's initial boss and head of DOI.[4]

Catton begins his book with a vivid and gripping description of a formal dinner in Washington, DC, just days before Pearl Harbor. (A reminder that at this point the war had been going on—without the United States as a combatant nation—for more than two years, beginning with Hitler's and Stalin's invasion of Poland in September 1939.) The dinner was hosted by Donald Nelson, then heading the prewar armament buildup that was partly for national defense purposes, partly for export through Lend-Lease. Before joining the government, Nelson had been executive vice president and vice chairman of the executive committee of the giant retailer Sears, Roebuck. The guest of honor at the dinner was Vice President Henry Wallace, also (typically) tasked by President Roosevelt to help in that production effort. Other pooh-bahs included Secretary of the Navy Frank Knox and two other major figures in the arms production effort, William Knudsen (former president of General Motors) and Edward Stettinius Jr. (former chairman of the board of U.S. Steel). Also present, but much lower on the totem pole, was Horton, the director of information for the defense production effort. When the meal was over, all the high-ranking men there were invited by the host to give short after-dinner talks. According to Catton (who never says if he was present or not; probably not),[5] Knox was very reassuring in his comments, including saying: "But I want you all to know that no matter what happens, the United States Navy is ready! Every man is at his post, every ship is at its station. The Navy is ready. Whatever happens, the Navy is not going to be caught napping."[6]

Horton, so junior in status compared to the other guests, was not scheduled to be one of the after-dinner speakers. According to Catton, after hearing Knox's comments, Horton quietly asked Nelson, if he, too, could be called on to make a few remarks. Horton proceeded to tell of his recent experience on a cruise down the Potomac in a small motorboat with friends. It demonstrated extremely lax security at several Navy installations near the capital. For example, even though the presence of the British aircraft carrier *Illustrious* at the Norfolk Navy Yard was considered a major military secret, Horton and his friends had entered the waters of the navy yard and cruised past the British carrier, which was being repaired by American workers from combat damage it had sustained. Also, the vessel had been openly flying the Union Jack. There was no mistaking that the United States was actively helping the United Kingdom fight the Germans notwithstanding its legal status of peace with Germany. Even though this was a secret, there was no water-based security around the carrier, and no one stopped Horton's boat as he and his friends came close to it. According to Catton, during this recounting, "Knox leaned over to Nelson and whispered savagely, behind his hand: 'Who *is* this son of a bitch?'" When he finished telling his story, "Horton paused, and looked coldly at Knox, who by now was painfully close to apoplexy. 'Mr. Secretary,' he said, 'I don't think your Navy *is* ready.' This was the night of December 4, 1941."[7]

This anecdote is no mere glancing mention of Horton's truth telling. A continuing thread running through Catton's book is Horton's approach to honest public information and how it was gradually trumped by public relations, eventually pushing Horton out of power entirely. Catton reiterates his admiration for Horton on several subsequent occasions. Right after the book was published, Catton sent Horton (by then out of government service and back in his home state of Vermont) a copy. In a cover letter, Catton wrote that the book highlighted Horton and his information principles so much because of Catton's "profound admiration" and "very deep and permanent human affection" for "the finest guy I ever worked for."[8] More than twenty years later, by now famous for his Civil War books, Catton was asked to select a passage from any of his writings that he considered his best. Skipping all his Civil War books, he selected this opening scene in his World War II memoir, which highlighted Horton's flinty commitment to honest communication. Writing a new short introduction to the passage, Catton wrote, "I *still* feel a grim fascination with the way in which an outspoken ex-newspaperman, Robert Horton, bluntly told the Secretary of the Navy, three days before Pearl Harbor, that the Navy did not seem to be entirely prepared for what might soon happen to it."[9]

As it turns out, Catton's penchant for melodramatic storytelling included taking some liberties with accuracy to make the story better. The dinner that he claimed had occurred on Thursday, December 4, 1941, three days before Pearl Harbor, actually occurred on Friday, November 28, nine days before the Japanese attack. This is a major error that a reputable historian—whether popular or academic—should not have made. Subsequent histories have accepted Catton's version at face value and repeated it.[10] Given the importance and vividness of the incident, for this inquiry I sought independent confirmation of Catton's story. I could not find any accounts of the dinner from other participants, but Vice President Henry Wallace's appointment book documented that the dinner occurred on November 28. Wallace attended a different dinner on December 4.[11]

Even though wrong about the date, if Horton had left such a strong impression on Catton, then surely it was worth knowing more about his work in government public relations. Horton's professional career as a public information officer (PIO) began in 1938, when he resigned as a Washington-based journalist to head public relations at the US Maritime Commission. Then, from mid-1940 to mid-1942, he headed the Division of Information in the Office for Emergency Management. He was its only director. Notwithstanding Roosevelt's frequent tinkering with the organization of the national defense production effort, DOI was remarkably stable. The government "holding company" it was within changed several times, but not DOI itself and not Horton's leadership of it. DOI began in mid-1940 as a division within the National Defense Advisory Commission, then was within the Office of Production Management, finally was an independent agency within the Office for Emergency Management. That final incarnation straddled two important historical eras. For the first eleven months of 1941, while a world war was raging, the United States continued in its status as a noncombatant nation. Then, after Pearl Harbor, the United States joined the war. DOI's activities before and during the war provide a case study of potential differences in the norms of government PR in peace versus war.

At its peak, DOI was the largest information agency in Washington, with more than 500 employees, including about 160 in forty field offices, and an annualized budget of $2.6 million. As mentioned, in June 1942, FDR abolished DOI and merged it into the new Office of War Information (OWI). In short order, from mid-1942 to spring 1944, Horton headed OWI's Press Bureau, was deputy administrator of the Office of Price Administration for public relations, and then director of information for the Interior Department. His last posting began in spring 1944, when he returned to the Maritime Commission to run its PR office, as well as that of its wartime sister agency, the War Shipping Administration. In the summer of 1946, during the postwar demobilization, he resigned from government service and moved back to his home state of Vermont. Horton's career as a PIO provides a lens that illuminates the practice of government PR, especially because it occurred when the context of such PR work changed so much: from peace, to a twilight zone of neither peace nor war, to war, and, finally, to demobilization and peace.

In part, the research question is whether the "rules of the game" of government PR are fixed or whether they vary based on external circumstances. The plain question is: What's OK and what's not? With PR having become a permanent element of modern public administration, what are the normative rules governing its practice? In a separate study, I examined Congress's efforts throughout the twentieth and early twenty-first centuries to define those rules, including formal legal prohibitions on propaganda, on the use of PR to lobby Congress indirectly, on hiding the source of "news" coming from an agency, and banning employment of publicity experts.[12] Horton's career occurred at about the midpoint of these congressional activities. How did Horton and DOI maneuver to stay out of relatively major trouble with Congress, but still practice a robust PR program?

Historians and researchers are a bit like oil wildcatters, playing hunches and mostly finding dry holes. But once in a while, and enough to justify keeping at it, we hit a gusher. In the mid-1980s, Richard Ketchum was in the midst of researching what became *The Borrowed Years,* a history of the United States from 1938 to 1941. After some difficulty and with great persistence, Ketchum located Horton, still in Vermont, then eighty-six years old. Horton agreed to be interviewed for the book, and Ketchum found him to be "sharp as a tack." Ketchum quotes from it in his book. On a hunch, in 2009, I wrote Ketchum to ask if he still had his notes from that conversation. To my delight, he called back and kindly directed me to the papers he had recently donated to the University of Vermont Library. They included six pages of typewritten notes of his interview with Horton on December 30, 1987. I felt fortunate to have located them. As far as I have been able to determine, this was the only time Horton reminisced about his Washington experiences. My thanks to Mr. Ketchum for his generosity and help. In the interview, Horton confirmed the general accuracy of Catton's account of the dinner, but he did not mention that Catton got the date wrong. The only substantive detail Horton added to Catton's version was that not only had he cruised past the British aircraft carrier without being stopped by security, but he had actually *boarded* it, again without any challenge.

In terms of the context regarding the dinner, Horton said he "didn't care for Frank Knox." During Horton's career as a reporter in New England, he had known Knox in two capacities, first when Knox was founder and publisher of the nearby *Manchester (NH) Union-Leader.* A few years later, when Knox was a senior executive for the Hearst newspaper chain, he was sent to Boston as a kind of "efficiency expert" to turn around its three money-losing papers there. Horton claimed that to cut costs at the papers, Knox had removed free Kotex from the women's restrooms and insisted that reporters produce the stub of a pencil before getting another. In general, Horton felt "Knox wasn't very bright." But the straw that broke the camel's back, Horton told Ketchum, was the contents and tone of Knox's after-dinner talk. He "just couldn't let Knox get away with the bullshit about how well prepared the navy was."[13] Politics also lurked in the background. Knox was the Republican Party's vice-presidential candidate in 1936, chosen as the conservative to balance the ticket with the moderate governor of Kansas, Alf Landon. During the campaign, Knox made slashing attacks on the New Deal.[14] Horton, on the other hand, supported the New Deal even before joining the administration in 1938. This probably contributed to Horton's frank and confrontational tone toward Knox that evening and why it was so memorable.

My desire to know more about the hero of this specific anecdote and, more generally, about Catton's strong admiration for Horton's work in the federal government led to my writing this book. Its successful completion was partly due to the extraordinary efficiency and persistence of the Inter-Library Loan staff at my university's Golda Meir Library. Amazingly, they were able to obtain practically every item I was seeking. My thanks to all of them. Additional nearby libraries holding materials I examined included the central branch of the Milwaukee Public Library, Marquette University's Raynor and Law Libraries, Memorial Library at the University of Wisconsin–Madison and the government documents collection at the Wisconsin Historical Society. The major field research occurred at the National Archives II site in College Park, Maryland, which possessed DOI's office files, located in OWI's records (Record Group 208).

From personal visits and from afar, many other librarians and information professionals helped me. Additional federal sources were the library of the US Forest Service's Forest Products Lab, the Historical Office of the Tennessee Valley Authority, the Naval History and Heritage Command at the Washington Navy Yard, the Roosevelt and Eisenhower Presidential Libraries, the Pacific Regional Archives of the National Archives in San Francisco, and three divisions of the Library of Congress: its Reading Room, the Prints and Photographs Division, and the Manuscript Division. Other library and archival sources were the Martin Luther King Jr. downtown branch of the District of Columbia Public Library (which has the morgue of the *Washington Star*), UCLA Film and Television Archive, University of Wyoming's American Heritage Center, Vermont Historical Society, special collections of the University of Vermont's Bailey/Howe Library, and the Briscoe Center for American Heritage at the University of Texas–Austin. Archivists at the National Gallery of Art in Washington, DC, and the Museum of Modern Art in New York City helped me locate records on their exhibition of the winners of DOI's art competition in early 1942. My gratitude to all these dedicated professionals who helped me. I regret that there were so many that I cannot name them individually. I hope they will accept this appreciation as personally addressed to them. It was a pleasure working with LSU Press bringing the book to print, especially series editor Bob Mann and Acquisitions Editor Alisa Plant. Finally, my continuing appreciation to Andrea Zweifel, a Program Associate at my school, for applying her incredible proofreading skills to my manuscript. She saved me from dozens of embarrassments.

Even though scores of people made constructive contributions to the manuscript when it was in progress, ultimately an author is deservedly responsible for the final product. Therefore, I heartily declare that any and all remaining mistakes in this book are mine alone.

ABBREVIATIONS

BOB: Bureau of the Budget, an agency within the Executive Office of the President

CSC: Civil Service Commission, an independent agency in the federal executive branch

DOI: Division of Information; initially within the National Defense Advisory Commission, then an independent agency within the Office for Emergency Management

EOP: Executive Office of the President

FY: fiscal year (At the time of the events recounted here, the federal fiscal year began on July 1 and ended on June 30. It was named by the year it ended in, for example, FY1942 began on July 1, 1941, and ended on June 30, 1942. In the 1970s, the federal fiscal year (sometimes FFY) was advanced by a quarter of a year, to run from October 1 to September 30.)

GPO: Government Printing Office, an agency within the legislative branch

MC: Maritime Commission (see also US MC), an independent agency in the federal executive branch

NDAC: National Defense Advisory Commission

OEM: Office for Emergency Management (sometimes incorrectly referred to as the Office *of* Emergency Management), an agency within the Executive Office of the President

OFF: Office of Facts and Figures, an agency within the Office for Emergency Management

OGR: Office of Government Reports, an agency within the Executive Office of the President

OPM: Office of Production Management, an agency within the Office for Emergency Management

OWI: Office of War Information (sometimes incorrectly referred to as the Office *for* War Information), an agency within the Office for Emergency Management

PIO: public information officer (usually a generic term, sometimes a position classification or a title)

US MC: US Maritime Commission (Note: USMC, without a space between the two pairs of letters, is commonly the acronym for the US Marine Corps)

WPB: War Production Board, an agency within the Office for Emergency Management

PROMOTING THE WAR EFFORT

INTRODUCTION

GOVERNMENT PUBLIC RELATIONS

What's OK and What's Not?

The collective American historical consciousness and folk memories about World War II often include images of salvage-collection drives for aluminum pots and pans to be recycled for military uses, newsreels of America as the arsenal of democracy, shuttered factories springing back to life, posters and civic pageants promoting patriotism, families gathered around the radio to listen to programs about national defense, and recruiting drives for Civil Defense and other volunteers. However, all these occurred *before* Pearl Harbor, when the United States was not yet a participant in World War II. They were conducted by an obscure government agency called the Division of Information (DOI), headed by an equally obscure bureaucrat, Robert Horton. Given that these kinds of persuasive and exhortative PR campaigns occurred when the United States was at peace with Germany and Japan, they raise a basic question of what forms of public relations in public administration are OK in general, are acceptable only in war, or are somewhat permitted in the twilight between peace and war? What is the boundary—whether temporal or based on content—between propaganda and information?

Public Information versus Government Propaganda

Propaganda. The spoken word sounds harsh and ominous, with a hard-sounding consonant beginning each of its first three syllables. The unpleasant sound of the word is somewhat onomatopoeic; it is most definitely not euphonic. Propaganda had largely meant a form of communication that was untruthful and manipulative, usually used for sinister purposes.[1] The ultimate embodiment of the evilness of the term was Hitler's Reich Ministry of Public Enlightenment and Propaganda, headed by Joseph Goebbels.

After World War II, the word gradually took on a somewhat blander and less ominous connotation.[2] In the 1970s, Senator William Fulbright (D-AR) condemned what he called the Pentagon Propaganda Machine. Based on contemporary usage, he suggested, propaganda involved "some degree of subterfuge."[3] Jeffrey Berry calls it "a rather inflammatory word that suggests manipulative and dishonest communication."[4] It is now generally used with two related meanings. The first is as a political attack word to criticize persuasion-oriented or promotional communications with which the attacker disagrees.[5] When the word is used in this pejorative sense, anyone can call anyone else's public messages propaganda. The other common meaning is descriptive, conveying a major and dedicated public relations effort to advocate for something. For example, in a 2010 work, Daniel Okrent describes the PR output of a pro-Prohibition group urging Congress to adopt a constitutional amendment as "forty tons of prohibitionist propaganda each month." The lack of an automatically negative meaning of the word is apparent when, discussing a different topic, he precedes it with a negative adjective: "George Creel, whom Wilson had placed at the head of a *malignant* propaganda body officially called the Committee of Public Information."[6] A prominent political consultant suggests, in a 2011 college textbook, an even more benign usage: "promoting 'news' with an agenda—or by another term, propaganda."[7]

Regardless, politicians know they don't like it, especially when it comes from the bureaucracy. The rough consensus of American political culture has generally been that government agencies can and should disseminate neutral and helpful information, but cannot engage in propaganda, roughly meaning persuasive and advocacy communications.[8] The difficulty, of course, is that this meaning of propaganda is largely in the eye of the beholder. One person's propaganda is another's information. Generally, American politicians denounce as propaganda public relations efforts by executive branch agencies with which they disagree, while they praise as helpful information similar activities by agencies they support.[9] Congress has enacted various prohibitions against agency PR, in particular an explicit across-the-board ban on engaging in propaganda as well as a separate prohibition on the bureaucracy using external communications to influence legislative debates indirectly.[10] Given this general pattern, public administrators in the United States have been somewhat timid about the use of external communications programs, hoping to avoid the criticism of engaging in propaganda. It is understandable that they would choose to avoid controversy rather than to come close to the line.[11]

Still, this political consensus tends to accept, however grudgingly, three somewhat vague exceptions to the propaganda taboo. The first relates to widely held values. In that case, propaganda by government agencies—in the sense of trying to influence and mold public behavior—becomes acceptable. These are sometimes called public service or public education campaigns.[12] Some common examples include: Buckle your seatbelt! Stay in school! Don't drive drunk! But, some values are more widely held than others. The accusation of propaganda lurks close to the surface of all government public relations. "Use a condom" can be denounced as promoting sexual activity. "Don't reuse needles" can be criticized as condoning drug use. Even "Only you can prevent forest fires," the signature line of the US Forest Service's longtime Smokey Bear campaign, was criticized because sometimes the agency itself engages in controlled burns. That's a double standard confusing to the citizenry, critics argued. Indeed, in reaction to such criticism, the agency changed the slogan to "Only you can prevent *wildfires.*"

The second exception relates to presidents. That the president—an elected official, head of the executive branch, and coequal of Congress—would engage in persuasive communication such as trying to convince the public to support a particular program that the administration has proposed, trying to persuade Congress to enact legislation requested by the White House, or explaining and justifying major policy decisions is viewed as inherent to the presidential office.[13] In the context of external communications, a key factor is that presidents are *politicians.* When in their first term, they generally seek to maximize their prospect of being reelected. Then, if reelected, they seek to maintain their popularity as a way to build political capital (usually vis-à-vis Congress) and then expend that capital to accomplish their political goals. Whether motivated by politics or not, what a president says and does is interpreted and analyzed through this filter. *Everything* a president does is political.

The prerogative of a president to engage in external persuasive communication is assumed to extend beyond the president personally and the Oval Office per se. Certainly, the president's White House staff would be permitted to do so. Since Richard Nixon's presidency, every White House has had an Office of Communications as well as the traditional news secretary.[14] The presidential exemption from limits on persuasive communication ("propaganda") does not end at the White House fence, either. Members of the president's official family, specifically cabinet secretaries, are expected to promote the administration's agenda and advocate for it publicly. While less clear, the propaganda exemption extends also to the subcabinet, which consists of hundreds of officials who are nominated by the president and subject to Senate confirmation. These tend to be departmental undersecretaries, deputy secretaries, and assistant secretaries. All serve at the president's pleasure and can be replaced without cause. Venturing further out, the president nominates scores of officials at the senior ranks of independent agencies outside the cabinet. Presumably, the presidential exception regarding propaganda ends somewhere beyond those officials, certainly for civil servants who hold an office indefinitely and can only be ousted for cause. These are the faceless bureaucrats that Congress wants to keep out of the propaganda business.

The third exception to the taboo against government propaganda relates to war. Given a declaration of war by Congress, it becomes the declared purpose of the country to successfully fight a war. This includes mobilizing the populace in support of such a national effort. That, in turn, may necessitate persuasive communication, not just information. The World War I Committee on Public Information (CPI) and World War II Office of War Information (OWI) epitomized that exception.[15] But, even within the context of a congressional declaration of war, both agencies were still very controversial with Congress, which even in wartime was leery of executive branch propaganda.

Things get much more complicated in the twilight between peace and war. So, at issue is not only what's OK and what's not, but also *who* does it. Depending on who is doing the what, does that make something otherwise OK not OK? Or vice versa? A case in point occurred in the run-up to the US invasion of Iraq in 2003. President George W. Bush's administration conducted an extensive public relations effort to convince Congress and the public that an invasion of Iraq was justified due to the regime's (alleged) pursuit of weapons of mass destruction and its (equally alleged) cooperation with the Al Qaeda terrorist network. In the critical postmortems of that PR campaign, critics charged that the administration had exaggerated information it liked, suppressed information (confidential or otherwise) it did not, and, in general, manipulated the news media to give a distorted view of reality, enough to obtain Congress's approval for the use of force.[16] For those critical voices (and there are, of course, defenders of the president's actions), this PR campaign was Exhibit A in what was wrong with the expansion of government's ability to control information, especially using propaganda techniques that had little to no relation to the truth. Did the president's leadership role of the executive branch include the power to prevent government agencies from releasing information with which the administration did not agree? And, if given such information controls, were civil servants obliged to acquiesce to them?

As is often the case with historical exemplars, they can confuse as much as illuminate. One could argue that as the constitutional chief executive, President Bush would be assumed to speak for and lead the executive branch. Separately, as an independent elected official, a president would be assumed to be able to say whatever he (or she) wants and to advocate in favor of any preferred position on a public policy issue. In this case, the propaganda campaign in favor of invading Iraq was that of a president, not of the bureaucracy and certainly not that of an individual agency. Still, the kernel of this example helps focus on the subject of this study, an unusual and tightly packed historical period when one practitioner of government PR occupied the precarious and controversial political space between the general prohibition on propaganda and the three exceptions to it, namely widely held values, presidential communication, and war emergencies.

Robert Horton's Career as Exemplar of Controversies over Government PR

History has accorded Horton and DOI a modicum of attention.[17] This book is an effort to restate the narrative without Catton's melodrama and with documents by archival and original sources. In particular, it examines two themes. First, based on the preceding discussion, how did the generally accepted template of government PR play out before and during World War II? Is it possible, using a fine-grained examination of the detailed practices of PR categories and subcategories, to distinguish information from propaganda, facts from persuasion? Is it possible to differentiate government PR when it qualified under one of the three propaganda exemptions as opposed to any of the others? The second theme relates to the organizational structure of government PR. Generally, the conventional model is for each agency to have its own PR shop. This gives the agency control over its own public voice. Any other structure, especially one that denies an agency control over its external communications, is both unusual and a threat to an agency's autonomy.[18]

The professional career of Robert W. Horton in government PR provides a focal point for examining these two themes. From 1938 to 1946, he headed the public relations offices of several federal agencies including the Maritime

Commission, Office of Price Administration, Interior Department, and War Shipping Administration. In particular, Horton was the only person who headed the Division of Information of the national defense production effort during its entire existence (1940–42). Regarding the first theme, Horton's career spanned the spectrum of government PR work in nonwar, wartime, and postwar periods. Generally, he operated within the context of the normative definition of acceptable PR in the public sector, which permitted dissemination of information and frowned on advocacy. Yet his roles also touched on the acceptable exceptions to propaganda, namely, widely held values, presidential communication, and war. Therefore, his work can be a historical lens for greater understanding of the practice of government PR, whether under what could be considered normal conditions or abnormal ones. Simply put: What did he do and how did he do it?

The second focus is on the power structure of government PR. Horton did not like the "one-agency, one-PR-office" template. He preferred the opposite. When he headed DOI, he forcefully advocated for a centralized PR office that served about a dozen line agencies, loosely federated within the President's Office for Emergency Management. He continually had to protect and defend this structure against the inherent desires of his clients for their own PR office. Examining the successes and failures of this unusual centralized approach to PR provides a glimpse into what could have been: namely, an entirely different structure to federal PR services than what is now the norm. How did it go? Did it operate well, by servicing each agency's PR needs while integrating all their external communications into a more coherent and coordinated whole? Perhaps there were some economies of scale, with this structure able to provide each client-agency with highly specialized PR services they couldn't otherwise afford on their own? Was Horton able to impose some degree of communication discipline on fractious and competing agencies? Given the inherent centrifugal dynamic for bureaucracies to seek autonomy, was Horton's structure powerful enough to countervail it? Or was Horton's centripetal effort something of a mirage, with each line agency really controlling its own PR, even though conducted by staff who were technically within Horton's shop?

Audiences

This inquiry will likely interest audiences in three areas: communication, history, and government. It is published as part of the Media and Public Affairs series of Louisiana State University Press, the goal of which is to examine the interactions in democracy between the news media, the citizenry, and public officials. Reflecting the focus of the series, the book concerns issues related to the academic disciplines of journalism, mass communication, public relations, and public affairs. For example, public relations history is emerging as a distinct field of inquiry.[19] In the humanities, the volume seeks to be of value to historians with interests in American history, World War II, the FDR presidency, the twentieth century, and management history. Finally, in social science, it could be of interest to political science and public administration, especially those interested in the subfields of the executive branch, presidency, political communication, bureaucratic politics, and American political development. This is a case study of the operations of the US national government at a time of the evolution of big government, what eventually led to the contemporary federal leviathan.

Given that earlier volumes in the series focus more on political side of the public sector than on the bureaucracy, this book's relevance to the series probably deserves some elaboration. First, the book partly focuses on the nearly invisible line in American government separating politics and administration. In some respects, Horton was heading a standard-issue government agency staffed largely by civil servants appointed through the procedures of the Civil Service Commission. On the other hand, Horton viewed himself as part of the president's official family, to the point of conducting several press briefings at the White House on behalf of President Roosevelt. Was Horton a politician, a bureaucrat, or both? Can politics be separated from public administration or not? Should they be separable?

Second, there is an ongoing argument in the academic literature about whether public administration and business administration are essentially the same or whether their different sectorial placements make them qualitatively different. (Disclosure: I am in the latter camp.) Wallace Sayre quipped that business and public administration were "fundamentally alike in all unimportant respects."[20] Certainly, government's obligation to be accountable to the citizenry is an example of an important difference between public and business administration. Carl Friedrich argued as early as 1932 that a vigorous public relations program was central to the democratic responsibility of public administrators.[21] Businesses do not have the same duties of accountability and transparency that government has.[22] As an in-depth examination of the practice of government PR, the book contributes to an understanding of the differences between government and business PR, thereby demonstrating one of the major differences between public and business administration.

Third, communication is an important aspect of government operations in general. However, often it is not studied as prominently as other major elements of management, such as human relations (HR), budgeting, and planning.[23] The book could help facilitate a more textured understanding of public relations as an important component of the totality of public administration. Also, the conventional structure of American public administration is to attach staff services (such as budgeting, HR, and PR) to each vertical silo or stovepipe. Horton's unprecedented model of providing a staff service *horizontally,* crossing silo boundaries, was quite unusual. For specialists in organizational design, this provides an alternate model that challenges organizational orthodoxy and could be an option in future reorganizations entailing the provision of all manner of administrative and staff services.

Finally, two nomenclature clarifications: The Division of Information was usually referred to by its full name, occasionally by the shorter "Information Division."[24] The most widely used acronym for the agency, which will be used here, was DOI. But there were several other variations including D. of I. or D of I,[25] DIOEM,[26] DoI,[27] OEM/DI,[28] and ID (for Information Division).[29] Regarding Horton's name, his byline as a reporter appeared as "Robert W. Horton," and that was the construction he mostly used in government. However, sometimes he was referred to, or referred to himself, as "Robert Wyman Horton."[30] In another variation, he listed himself as "R. W. Horton."[31] Despite these variations, "Robert W. Horton" was the most common.

PART I

GOVERNMENT PR IN PEACETIME

CHAPTER 1

GOVERNMENT PR FOR WIDELY HELD VALUES

Horton at the Maritime Commission, 1938–1940

Like most public relations officers in the federal government during Franklin Roosevelt's presidency, Robert Horton was a former reporter. That earlier career contributed to his understanding of the role of the press in democracy, journalism's influence on public opinion, and the central role of public information officers in facilitating reporters' efforts to cover the federal government. Therefore, a study of Horton's career in government PR needs to begin with a sketch of his previous work in journalism, both as a print reporter and radio commentator.

Prelude: Mr. Horton Goes to Washington, 1929–1938

Born in Vermont in 1902, Horton worked for the *Springfield (MA) Republican,* the Associated Press news service in Boston, and the *New York Herald Tribune.* In early 1929, he moved to Washington, DC, and held several positions with the Scripps-Howard news corporation, including as the capital correspondent for its *New York World-Telegram,* telegraph editor for the *Washington (DC) Daily News,* and national feature writer for the Scripps-Howard news syndicate.[1]

The Scripps newspapers had begun as champions of "the common people" with a left-of-center and populist tilt.[2] Activist and crusading reporters like Horton felt ideologically comfortable working for the chain.[3] However, the company paid below-average salaries. To earn additional income, Horton often freelanced. These pieces tended to be nonpartisan commentary and analysis. In 1930, he wrote an article for the *Nation's Business,* and in 1934–35, the "Washington Letter" feature in *Canadian Forum.*[4] A few years later, in 1937, he did live radio commentary and analysis.[5] The radio gigs gave him a higher profile than most of his peers, making him a relatively well-known Washington reporter. Some other of his non-Scripps writings were more openly politically liberal. In 1935, he wrote a searing piece in the *Nation* about the racism of law enforcement and criminal justice in Mississippi. He recounted a trial of three African American men who were tortured to confess to a murder they had not committed.[6]

When founder E. W. Scripps retired, his successor, Roy Howard, gradually shifted the chain's editorial position to the right. The change crystallized around FDR's 1937 court-packing proposal, which Howard opposed. This, in turn, made many of its liberal staff increasingly uncomfortable with their employer, Horton and his boss, *Daily News* editor Lowell Mellett, included. Horton considered Mellett "the best editor I ever knew; . . . absolutely honest, scrupulous, and if he thought a story was true he would run it no matter what it might cost the paper in advertisers or circulation."[7] Feeling a need to act on his principles, in late 1937, Mellett resigned. A few months later Roosevelt appointed him to head the National Emergency Council, especially to revitalize its information activities. (In 1939, FDR renamed it the Office of Government Reports.)

From the beginning of his presidency, Roosevelt had consistently expanded the public information activities of the federal government, in both the "alphabet" agencies of the New Deal as well as the traditional departments and agencies.[8] Many working reporters were hired for those new positions. In that respect, Mellett's appointment was merely de rigueur. However, it was different from the past practice in two ways. First, Mellett was the public relations director for a central *presidential* agency, not out in the boondocks of the sprawling executive branch.[9] Second, Mellett had an unofficial role to recruit and hire more reporters for public relations positions and then serve as the informal leader of this network of PIOs.[10] Four months after Mellett began working for FDR, the PR director for the US Maritime Commission resigned. Mellett offered the job to Horton. In August 1938, Horton became the chief of the Maritime Commission's Section of Information.[11]

The Mission of the US Maritime Commission: Implementing Widely Held Values

The Maritime Commission had been established in 1936 as the successor agency to the World War I–era US Shipping Board. Generally, its role was to promote construction and operation of US-flagged vessels, be available to supply the Navy's fleet, train the Merchant Marine Cadet Corps, and maintain the "Ghost Fleet" of World War I vessels in case they were ever needed.[12] In the introductory section of the Merchant Marine Act of 1936, Congress explicitly declared the underlying national policy of the act and role of the Maritime Commission (MC).[13] According to the new law, "It is hereby declared to be the policy of the United States to foster the development and encourage the maintenance of such a merchant marine."[14]

From a public relations perspective, the act was a legal and formal statement of the widely held values undergirding MC's activities. Therefore, external communications activities that promoted and advanced these purposes were, at least impliedly, fully acceptable, almost mandated. The declaration of policy provided a justification for persuasive and advocacy PR that helped advance these goals, explain them to the citizenry, and convince the citizenry of their rightness and appropriateness. This was propaganda by another name, except that it was permitted by the vague consensus of Washington politics.

Upon its creation, Roosevelt named Joseph P. Kennedy to chair the new commission.[15] Based on international developments in the mid-1930s, the commission quickly adopted a long-range plan of building fifty ships per year for ten years. Congress approved up to $350 million in new construction and subsidies to existing shipping companies. The commission's construction and operations activities frequently brought it into the middle of seemingly endless labor-management disputes, whether at shipyards, ports, or seamen unions. Congress, especially the senators and representatives from areas with ports or shipyards, had a deep interest and involvement in MC's policies and decisions.[16] Whether during peacetime, war, or somewhere in between, MC was in the middle of the action, an important agency involved in important public policy. For America in the time before jets and interstate highways, maritime shipping and railroads were *the* forms of transportation, whether internally or internationally.

This also meant that the press paid closer attention to MC's activities and controversies than to those of some other federal agencies, necessitating a robust public relations office to facilitate news coverage. To deal with the above-average press and public interest in the new agency, in spring 1937, shortly after being confirmed by the Senate, Kennedy hired former reporter Harry R. Stringer to serve as the commission's PR man.[17] However, Kennedy's MC tenure was brief. After about a year there, he resigned in early 1938 to become ambassador to Great Britain. Stringer then also left the MC to become a public relations consultant.[18] Stringer's resignation created the vacancy that Mellett asked Horton to fill.

Context of Horton's Service at the Maritime Commission

Horton intuitively understood that, politically, the Maritime Commission was pursuing a statutory policy goal that was widely shared. Its PR could therefore be somewhat more persuasion-oriented than other, more controversial, executive branch agencies. As long as he could justify a PR activity as fulfilling the explicit statutory purpose of the MC, he had significant leeway to promote the agency and its programs. Publicly, he could even be "doing a little special pleading."[19] Congress usually viewed that as verboten for federal agencies.[20]

The two years that Horton headed PR for the Maritime Commission (mid-1938 to mid-1940) were tumultuous in world affairs and domestic politics. As indicated in table 1, the world was teetering on a major war (the Munich Agreement), then Hitler and Stalin started World War II by invading Poland in September 1939. France and the United Kingdom did little militarily after declaring war in reaction. Then Hitler invaded France, with the Britain almost miraculously evacuating most of its soldiers from Dunkirk. President Roosevelt was maneuvering to help Britain and France, but not beyond what Congress (and isolationists) would permit and not to kill his option of being able to run for an unprecedented third term.

Government PR as Persuasion: Horton Promoting Widely Held Values

As a former reporter, Horton knew how to write and quickly. He and his staff prepared speeches for commissioners. The public talks by MC officials provide a window into the PR message that Horton was seeking to propagate. Those texts were also distributed as press releases under the aegis of Horton's office. So, Horton's voice and efforts at persuasion can be heard most clearly in these speeches. The metanarrative of his PR was the "intense need and the efforts necessary to meet it."[21] Some of the points made in the talks he drafted and released included focusing on the widely held values that MC was mandated to implement, including its continuation of a national historical legacy,[22] patriotism,[23] the high quality of American seamanship,[24] the implications of falling behind other nations,[25] and national pride.[26] He also ventured slightly into the arena of political advocacy with statements of the MC's need for public support[27] and, while it was spending large amounts of money, it was not wasting taxpayer funds.[28]

Horton's voice can also be heard through the persuasive communications embedded in the commission's official publications. Like most government PR offices, the MC issued publications for the lay audience. These were intended neither as news nor as retrospective public reporting. Rather, they had a more general aim of informing and persuading the public of the mission, purposes, and activities of the agency. They were designed for a generalist rather than expert reader and tended to include brief text and many

Table 1
Events when Horton headed PR at the Maritime Commission

TIME PERIOD	INTERNATIONAL	DOMESTIC
August–December 1938	Munich Agreement	Roosevelt's effort to purge incumbent congressional Democratic conservatives largely fails; Republicans gain in November elections.
1939	Germany invades (remaining portion of) Czechoslovakia; successfully demands the port of Memel from Lithuania; Italy invades Albania; Germany and the Soviet Union sign nonaggression treaty; Soviet Union defeats Japan in Mongolia; Germany invades western Poland; United Kingdom and France declare war on Germany, large force at the Maginot Line takes no offensive action; Soviet Union invades eastern Poland, then Finland.	FDR calls for repeal of arms embargo and neutrality laws; Congress approves selling arms on cash-and-carry basis; Congress approves presidential reorganization power (based on the 1937 report of the Brownlow Committee); FDR creates the Executive Office of the President; proclaims limited national emergency due to European war.
January–May 1940	Germany invades Norway and Denmark; Churchill becomes UK prime minister; Germany invades Holland, Belgium, France; Dunkirk evacuation.	FDR orders the Navy to keep its fleet in the Pacific indefinitely; requests congressional funding for 50,000 planes a year.

illustrations and photos. One such publication issued in 1940 was the sixty-two-page *America Builds Ships*. Its purpose was to present and explain MC's long-term ship construction program. This was justified as an imperative: "Why a building program? Different types of ships are needed for varied services required by American shippers and travelers."[29] While not intended as a news release, it was praised by a columnist in the *Los Angeles Times* (a newspaper serving a port city), praise that amounted to a bank shot by a PIO, whose publication got the benefit of further press coverage.[30]

A more formal publication—signified by being published by the Government Printing Office (GPO) instead of the agency itself—was *New Ships for the Merchant Marine*.[31] It, too, was aimed at a lay readership by providing clear and easy-to-read summaries of the different categories of ships that MC was then building. As with all the persuasive communications emanating from Horton, this one, too, focused on the need for a modern merchant marine and how the commission was fulfilling that need. Ship aficionados and hobbyists would have likely enjoyed the details provided in the booklet. Notwithstanding his career as a writer, Horton displayed his PR skills in understanding that a picture is worth a thousand words. The January 1940 revised version of a publication on the commission's personnel training programs contained fifteen pictures (in addition to the text) while its first version, published a year earlier, had only eight.[32]

Government PR as Persuasion: Presidential Communication and (Potential) War

While the major justification for persuasive PR from the Maritime Commission was based on the widely held values that it was implementing, Horton's PR also, but less emphatically, invoked the other two exemptions for propaganda: presidential communication and the potentialities of war. The second loophole in the ban on propaganda by federal agencies is a loosely defined exemption for the president to be able to communicate publicly. Since the Maritime Commission was part of the executive branch, some of its PR can be interpreted as an element of presidential communication, giving voice to the administration's perspective. This can be especially notable in reelection years. So, for example, references to FDR's activities and praise for his leadership in the commission's PR were quite explicit, such as "President Roosevelt recognized the disease which was destroying our shipping and informed Congress that a remedy should be applied promptly."[33] Horton even ventured to address the conservative political attack line that the New Deal amounted to socialism, having a commission official state in a speech: "Government ownership and operation [of shipping lines] is the last thing that I personally want to see but if we analyze the picture very carefully, I believe that we are going to find some government ownership and private operation necessary and in remote cases, perhaps government ownership and some form of government operation."[34] Horton was clearly identifying the work of the commission with the president, giving him public credit and generally praising the president's leadership.

Congress had included in the commission's founding statute a mission of being "capable of serving as a naval and military auxiliary in time of war or national emergency." Horton took full advantage of the war-related loophole for relatively aggressive persuasion-oriented PR for the commission. For example, a speech he drafted for the commission chairman stated that "the merchant fleet is the life line of the Navy" and that "every ship we build for our own account or in conjunction with private operators, is approved as to national defense features by the Navy Department."[35] In another speech by a commission official, Horton made the point that the merchant fleet "potentialities as naval auxiliaries make them *essential to our national defense* if our Navy is to function properly."[36] Horton was carefully trying to persuade the public that the current activities of the commission deserved full support because they might be needed *in case* of a war, not because the United States should be involved in the conflict already going on abroad.

A Comprehensive Government PR Program

Having delineated the justification for active and persuasion-oriented external communications, Horton gradually built up a comprehensive PR program. It covered the two most conventional, long-standing, and by now no longer controversial functions, press relations and public reporting.[37] But, he also extended his PR program to other venues and activities. In retrospect, Horton was developing a template for active government PR that he would later fine-tune at the Division of Information before and during US involvement in World War II.

Press Relations

The most traditional role of an agency PR director reflected the template of its earliest federal ancestor, the press secretary to the president. This was press relations, dealing with the media sometimes as the spokesman for the principal, sometimes as a behind-the-scenes facilitator, and sometimes as an encourager of coverage. Horton performed all three media relations roles and his professional experiences as a reporter served him well. Following the then-common norm that government PR men were to be heard, but not seen, Horton sometimes was the official, though unnamed, spokesman for the agency, even when being quoted.[38] Later in his tenure, he began to be mentioned by name.[39]

As a former reporter, Horton understood the centrality of press releases to facilitating newspaper coverage. He routinely released news on the work of the commission, such as major decisions, major contracts, and texts of speeches given by senior MC officials, whether in the capital, out of town, or on national radio. By February 1939, the press office had issued three hundred releases since its establishment.[40] As an indication of the fast pace of the work, sixty-seven releases were issued between mid-September 1938 and early February 1939, averaging more than three per week.[41]

Another way Horton showed his understanding of the needs of the working press was through the advance release of texts of speeches, with an embargo on reporting on the speeches until after they were delivered. For example, on Friday, February 3, 1939, he released the text of a speech to be delivered by commission chair Emory Land on Saturday, February 4, and embargoed until the Sunday-morning papers of February 5.[42] This permitted reporters to do their work on a weekday (Friday) and still have a new story for the big Sunday paper.

Besides press releases on stories of potential national interest to the Washington-based press corps, Horton also sometimes bypassed the national media by issuing releases tailored to specific media markets. For example, similar to the practice of the Army and Navy, he issued press releases to hometown newspapers on local boys graduating from MC training programs or being promoted.[43]

Public Reporting

In American government, public reporting, like press relations, was another well-established and largely noncontroversial PR activity. The tradition dated back to annual reports, which were a comprehensive summary of the past record of an agency. Besides accountability to the legislative branch and chief executive, the rationale for public reporting was that it contributed to an informed public in a democracy.[44] Significantly, Mellett's agency was renamed the Office of Government *Reports,* signaling the importance of executive branch reporting *to* the people (as well as from them).[45] Horton, too, understood that the main purpose of periodic reports was to engage in direct accountability to the public at large. For example, after FY1940 ended, Horton's unit issued a comprehensive report providing cumulative figures for MC's shipbuilding contracts in the most recent three years. This was not necessarily *news,* but the aggregate tabulations provided a much broader view of the agency's work than did the daily coverage by newspapers.[46] Sometimes reports were a news peg for press coverage, giving the report two bangs for the same buck.[47] Horton also used the reporting approach for some of the radio talks he drafted for commissioners. For example, MC chair Land began a radio talk in 1938 by saying his goal was "to make a brief report to the taxpayers on what the United States Maritime Commission has been doing and to give you as briefly as possible a little of what may be expected in the future."[48]

Movies

One of Horton's PR initiatives was film. He began by borrowing a film crew from another federal agency to shoot a cruise to southern ports sponsored by the Maritime Commission.[49] The footage of sunny southern ports could then be used for various film shorts and documentaries about the travel and tourism business and, specifically, the role that American ships could play in them. This was a promotional effort on behalf of the entire shipping industry, not just a plug for the work of the agency. In support of FDR's Good Neighbor policy toward Latin America (partly motivated by a desire to counter German activities there), the commission released a film documentary called *Good Neighbors.* It made multiple copies and placed them in its (domestic) regional offices for easy availability to civic and educational groups.[50] Another documentary was planned as "a full-length feature on American maritime history."[51]

Publications

Besides publications already mentioned regarding promotion of widely held values and public reporting, the commission also issued a variety of other publications. As a former reporter, Horton understood the need to be aware of the impact of news developments on the agency's work and, relatedly, its publications. One of the more official and industry-oriented publications that

MC issued in mid-1939 was a detailed listing and directory of *American Flag Services* to foreign ports. The information in the booklet had been updated through April 1, 1939. But, the fast pace of European war developments that summer and fall threatened to make the report obsolete before it was released. At the last minute, Horton made sure that a typed (as opposed to typeset) text would be inserted on the inside of the front cover that provided an update of the situation: "Passage of neutrality legislation in November, 1939, closed all ports in Great Britain, France, and Germany to American vessels. American ships were also barred from travel through danger zones which were to be proclaimed by the President."[52]

Exhibits

Two staff members in Horton's office were exhibit specialists.[53] They prepared both MC-oriented exhibits and those for use at more general federal events such as fairs, as well as travelling exhibits that were displayed in lobbies of major public buildings.

Campaigns

Horton served as the commission's representative on several executive branch–wide task forces to promote tourism and travel by Americans.[54] His selection was, in part, due to the marketing aspect of such federal efforts to promote tourism. This policy became especially topical with the beginning of the war in Europe causing some public fears about cruises, even though these were limited to coastal and Caribbean waters. Horton's participation in this campaign was a substantive and programmatic activity ("line," in the organizational parlance of the time), rather than merely that of ancillary staff support. His colleagues on these committees were not from the PR offices of their federal agencies. That MC's public relations director was the only PR man chosen to represent his agency can be interpreted as indicating the confidence that the commission had in him and his ability to handle line as well as staff responsibilities.

Administrative Sketch

The MC public information office was modest in size. In 1939, the annual payroll (excluding Horton's) was about twenty-one thousand dollars, with seven full-time staffers, all of whom had civil service status.[55] By the time he left in

1940, the number of full-time staffers had risen to ten.[56] Indicating some expansion of its technical capabilities, Horton's office was budgeted for twenty thousand dollars for buying new equipment in FY1941. While a modest sum, this increase was second only to the MC's Technical Division, which was at the center of the new shipbuilding effort.[57]

Notwithstanding its relatively small size, the Section of Information was a full-service public relations office, engaging in press relations (not just with newspapers, but also magazines and radio), speech writing, and public reporting, and producing publications, films, and exhibits.[58] During Horton's slightly less than two years at MC, his office was upgraded from a section to a division, and the unit's title became "Maritime Promotion and Information."[59] Both changes hint at expanded activities and a broader range of PR services.

Summary and Commentary

In May 1940, less than a month before he was to leave the commission, Horton's assessment from the inside looking out was that he had largely accomplished the goal of persuading the citizenry of the rightness of the commission's existence, work, and spending. An article submitted for publication in Chairman Land's name stated that "the support from the public has in general been excellent." Part of the credit, Land/Horton stated, should be attributed to media relations: "The program has been fully described by the newspaper and periodical press and editorially supported."[60] In at least one case, the view from the outside was also positive. Not all reporters made a successful transition to government PR work. Understandably, some were good at media relations, but public relations covered a broader gamut of activities such as outreach, publications, exhibits, and speech writing (and sometimes marketing). An indication that Horton became skilled in the non-press relations aspects of government PR was a characterization of him by a nationally syndicated columnist as a "shrewd publicist for the Maritime Commission."[61] Horton had done his job well, without stepping on any of the political mines that circumscribed public relations by federal agencies. He had reason to feel successful. Mellett thought so, too.

CHAPTER 2

GOVERNMENT PR WHEN THE PRESIDENT IS RUNNING FOR REELECTION

Horton at the National Defense Advisory Commission, June–November 1940

As PR director for the Maritime Commission, Horton had to learn quickly the do's and don'ts of government PR. It was not as though he had been thrown into the deep end of the pool, but professionally it was not the shallow end, either. The commission was engaging in major new spending, was significantly subsidizing shipbuilders and shipping lines, and, in some cases, outright owning and operating shipping enterprises. Still, with Congress's declaration of purpose in the 1936 Merchant Marine Act, Horton was engaging in persuasive information efforts for widely held values that were largely noncontroversial (at least politically). If someone wanted to criticize him for doing more than neutrally disseminating information, they could have tried to make the case, but the red line he might have been accused of crossing into advocacy was a dull, rather than bright, one. In any event, there were no major and sustained criticisms of his PR record at the MC from conservative and anti-FDR members of Congress or the press corps.

The next act would not be as easy. Spring of 1940 was a period of major developments, both internationally and politically (see table 2). The German invasion of western Europe proved enormously successful. Hitler now controlled France, Belgium, Holland, Denmark, and most of Norway. With France defeated, and Russia not a threat due to a nonaggression pact, Hitler could turn ferociously on Great Britain. Still reeling from the defeat of its expeditionary force in France, the near-miraculous evacuation from Dunkirk was hardly a victory. While it had saved military manpower, the matériel left behind had equipped an entire army. Whether for civilian or military needs, the United Kingdom depended greatly on ship-delivered supplies, but German submarines were sinking the ships faster than they could be replaced. The United States was legally neutral in the war, so England could depend only on its own stretched navy to protect convoys. Its fighter planes and pilots were in a similar situation, dueling it out against a larger Luftwaffe.

Yes, Churchill's indomitable personality and bottomless hostility to letting Germany win was a major factor in keeping the United Kingdom in the war. But, given the stunning fall of France, could Britain truly hold on alone, with only the Commonwealth countries aiding it? Would Churchill's government fall and be replaced by one willing to negotiate an end to the war with Hitler? In retrospect, these counterfactual scenarios may seem far-fetched. At the time, however, with the end of the story still unknown, these potentialities were real and realistic. Truly, the Allies (effectively only Great Britain and the Commonwealth, with France defeated) were on the brink of collapse, and the United Kingdom was nearly broke.

Roosevelt did not have much room to maneuver, internationally or politically. US public opinion was generally isolationist, and a majority in Congress opposed entering the war. Furthermore, it was a presidential election year, and an unusual one at that. Republicans thought they had an excellent chance of regaining the White House, perhaps as a result of voters' Roosevelt-fatigue, continued deficit spending, reaction to big government, and the party's deep roots in conservative and isolationist Main Street (although it had equally thick links to internationalist Wall Street). If Roosevelt dared to run for an unprecedented third term, that could well be the winning issue for a Republican victory. If Roosevelt did not run, then Republicans' chances were increased by the lack of an incumbent in the race. If Roosevelt tried to enter the war on Great Britain's side, that would provide another boost to an antiwar Republican candidate. Politically, things could not have looked better for them.

Roosevelt remained circumspect about any plans to run for reelection. He ostensibly encouraged a variety of candidates to seek the nomination, even appearing to indicate various degrees of public or private support for several of them. But he refused to say what he planned to do, keeping open the option of breaking with George Washington's model of a two-term limit for presidents. There was a strong link between international and political developments. If the world was at war (even if the United States was not a combatant), would there be a strong preference by the electorate to keep an experienced president at the helm, rather than a newcomer? Hence, international developments could have the effect of increasing the chances of FDR running for a third term. Yet, equally, perhaps international developments (a peace treaty between Germany and the United Kingdom, even the surrender of the United Kingdom) might lead to a global shift from war to peace, obviating the need to keep Roosevelt in office. No one knew how developments outside the United States might affect internal American politics.

Organizing for National Defense, 1939–1940

In terms of reacting to developments abroad over the last year, Roosevelt had taken some actions, but none that were irrevocable politically regarding the key issue of his position on war or peace for the United States. Germany's invasion of Poland on September 1, 1939, triggered FDR to use the new reorganization powers recently delegated him by Congress to begin the operations of the new Executive Office of the President (EOP). Within days after the invasion, he met with Louis Brownlow, chair of the eponymous committee that had recommended a reorganization of the executive branch in 1937. They talked about implementing the committee's recommendations, specifically activating EOP and what agencies should be in it. They also talked about the implications of Hitler's invasion of Poland, which, in turn, had trig-

Table 2
Events when Horton headed PR at the National Defense Advisory Commission

TIME PERIOD	INTERNATIONAL	DOMESTIC
June–November 5, 1940	France surrenders; United Kingdom withdraws from Narvik; Norway surrenders; United Kingdom sinks Vichy French fleet off North Africa; Soviet Union invades Estonia, Latvia, and Lithuania; Romania cedes Bessarabia to Soviet Union after war ultimatum; Battle of Britain; Germany, Italy, and Japan sign Tripartite Pact; Italy invades Egypt from Libya; Japanese begin occupation of Indochina.	United States sells United Kingdom "obsolete" military supplies; United States and United Kingdom trade 50 old destroyers for bases; United States grants financial aid to China to resist Japan; Congress approves for defense $1 billion in taxes and $5 billion in spending; Congress approves peacetime draft; Republicans nominate Wendell Willkie; FDR reelected to third term.

gered French and British declarations of war against Germany. A major war was clearly under way. FDR and Brownlow discussed the organization of the executive branch that might be needed to deal with the new world situation. They agreed that EOP should include an organizational contingency if necessitated by international developments.[1]

A week after the invasion, Roosevelt signed Executive Order 8248.[2] It placed five agencies in the new EOP, the most important of which was the Bureau of the Budget (BOB), previously in the Treasury Department. (EOP also included Lowell Mellett's agency, now rechristened the Office of Government Reports.) Brownlow included in the Executive Order a sentence on the option for a sixth EOP agency. It stated that EOP would also include, "in the event of a national emergency, or threat of a national emergency, such office for emergency management as the President shall determine." The use of lowercase was intentional. Brownlow later wrote that it "was so disguised in small print, with no capital letters, that it occasioned no remark in the press or in the general discussions" of the executive order. Then, in Brownlow's colorful characterization, "that little rabbit went right back in the hat."[3]

During the winter of 1939–40, Roosevelt was walking the most difficult political tightrope of his career. Economically, he was still trying to reverse the effects of the Great Depression with emergency and relief spending programs. Electorally, he was keeping the option open to run for an unprecedented third term, all the while publicly implying he was not. Internationally, he was sympathetic to the Western democracies and hostile to antidemocrats Hitler, Mussolini, and, at least impliedly, Stalin (then party to a nonaggression pact with Hitler). (This was also awkward given that the so-called "Republic of China," no democracy it, was then in the process of being conquered gradually by Japan.) FDR was hemmed legally in by the US Neutrality Act and by an arms embargo on *all* nations engaged in war. The isolationist mood of the country and Congress was dominant, and there was only so much he could do that would be viable politically. The most difficult of these dilemmas was whether he could run for a third term as an opponent of war while siding openly with the democracies struggling to survive in a war.

A policy termed "National Defense" became, temporarily, the magic wand. A variation on it was "Hemispheric Defense," relating to enforcing the Monroe Doctrine. That long-standing policy of the United States opposed any intervention by European powers in Central and South America, a position that isolationists supported. Another phrase related to making the

United States "impregnable" to attacks.[4] This faintly echoed and partially co-opted the "Fortress America" term used by antiwar groups. Even isolationists could not oppose efforts to strengthen American defenses as a way to keep the country safe, including: a larger and modern two-fleet Navy (eventually three); a well-equipped Army; more airplanes; shoreline defenses; defending the approaches to the Panama Canal; protecting America's great harbors of New York, Philadelphia, Boston, San Francisco, and Pearl Harbor; using the latest developments in munitions and ordnance; tanks that could match anything which could be thrown against the United States by any enemy; a trained and equipped National Guard that could be federalized as needed; and so on. Just about everybody understood the double game that Roosevelt was playing, but he played it so well that even his opponents could not credibly prevent it from occurring. Who could possibly be against defending the country with the greatest vigilance possible at a time that full-scale wars were occurring in Europe and Asia, literally on the oceans that formed the coastlines of the United States? It was against this backdrop that events played out and Roosevelt maneuvered.

There was another important detail, but one more in the nature of "inside baseball": Who was in charge of this national defense buildup? The Constitution had created a legislative branch that was primus inter pares. While American civic textbooks talked of three equal branches of government checking and balancing each other, the operational reality was that regardless of the power issue at hand, Congress was always the last stop.[5] It could make laws without presidential approval by overriding vetoes, pass laws to overcome constitutional issues found by the Supreme Court, initiate constitutional amendments, impeach presidents and judges, fund or not fund the executive and judicial branches, and attach any conditions it desired to federal spending. The era of so-called "congressional government," with weak presidents as somewhat glorified clerks, had dominated nineteenth-century American politics (except in the cases of Lincoln and then, at the turn of the century, Theodore Roosevelt). Eventually the size and function of government became something of a partisan divide, with Republicans for small government and Democrats for more activist government. The juxtaposition of two relatively recent presidents before FDR, Democrat Woodrow Wilson (1913–21) versus Republican Calvin Coolidge (1923–29) reflected those two competing ideological philosophies.

No matter his preference for so-called "big government," FDR was as hemmed in by Congress's powers as his predecessors had been. Yes, he was very successful with Congress in his first term, but by his second term it seemed that "normalcy" was returning. Not only did he lose the court-packing fight, but generally the conservative coalition in Congress, consisting of minority Republicans and Democratic conservatives, was beginning to coalesce and flex its muscles.[6] His efforts in the 1938 election cycle to purge conservative congressional Democrats by denying them renomination had largely flopped. Now his intended victims were eager for revenge and Republicans were glad to help them.

In the context of managing the national defense buildup, Roosevelt wanted maximum flexibility and the greatest possible personal control over federal actions. He did not want Congress creating statutory agencies, boards, and councils. He wanted to create them and be able to change them at the stroke of a pen. Nor did he like neat and clean organization charts. Just the opposite. He made sure that all big decisions ended up on his desk (if he *wanted* to intervene) by giving out overlapping, even confusingly duplicative, assignments. He wanted all senior public administrators to be accountable solely to him. No confirmation by Congress, no fixed terms, no protections from presidential "interference," no mandated reports to or appearances before Congress. This would be a *presidential* national defense effort. Famously, when one very high, but ambiguously ranked, defense production official (who came from the business sector) asked FDR who his boss was, Roosevelt replied sprightly, "Well, I guess I am!"[7]

As the situation in Europe worsened, FDR was firm in his desire to control federal activities that events might dictate. All the while, he was (secretly) running for reelection, or at least keeping that option open. On April 9, 1940, Hitler invaded and conquered Denmark and Norway. Then, on May 10, he attacked western Europe. The blitzkrieg was on. Holland and Belgium were buckling, the Maginot Line was being circumvented, and France was not prepared for such an eventuality. Roosevelt needed to act, while still appearing to be against the United States getting involved in the war.

Moving fast to co-opt any congressional statutory handcuffs, he decided there was a need to create a more formal, but still solely presidential, infrastructure to oversee the significant expansion of national defense preparedness and military production. In a series of closely tied actions, on May 16 he asked Congress for an additional $500 million for national defense (a few weeks later increased to $1 billion). With Congress preoccupied with that, he turned to management issues. From his service as assistant secretary of the Navy in World War I (then called the Great War), he recalled a congressional act in 1916 establishing a cabinet-level Council of National Defense. After the war ended, Congress had never repealed it. He decided to mobilize the council for a token existence and use it as the legal fig leaf to cover creating an advisory commission to the council. The advisory commission would be accountable to him and exist purely by presidential action. On May 25, 1940, he signed an administrative order (*not* an executive order) activating the Office for Emergency Management (OEM) within EOP, the contingency provided for in his 1939 executive order creating EOP.[8] The main purpose of OEM was to house what came to be known as the National Defense Advisory Commission (NDAC). Roosevelt blithely announced this at a press conference on May 28, *not* in a message to Congress. He most definitely was not asking Congress to do anything or to approve anything regarding this organizational structure. Brownlow chuckled in his memoir that "the magician pulled the rabbits out of the hat for keeps" by creating two entities, one of which had been hidden in the September 1939 executive order creating EOP, and neither of which was under congressional control.[9]

There would be no head or chairman of the Advisory Commission.[10] Instead, it would have seven members, each of whom would "coordinate" specific sectors of the political economy. The president would appoint the seven. Each would be accountable to him and serve at his pleasure. As an advisory body, the commission would not automatically have any coercive or compulsory powers. Lacking a chairman, when NDAC members could not agree on a common approach, the disagreement would by necessity rise to the president. Finally, while most of the other entities in the EOP were headed by *someone* (Bureau of the Budget and Office of Government Reports *directors,* etc.), OEM would not have a director, staff director, executive director, or the like. NDAC would have only a secretary who provided (ostensibly ministerial) secretariat duties and acted as channel of communication to the White House. William H. McReynolds, a White House staff member, was designated by Roosevelt as having *liaison* responsibilities between NDAC and the president, but that was about it. This fluid, obscure, opaque, confusing, duplicative, and hazy structure reflected Roosevelt's managerial style not only in the substantive details of the structure, but also because it was a wholly presidential concoction, with no legal constraints, limitations, or parameters imposed by Congress.

Organizing for National Defense PR, May–June 1940

The commissioners FDR appointed included Republican business pooh-bahs William Knudsen (CEO of General Motors), Edward Stettinius (U.S. Steel's chairman of the board), and Donald Nelson (executive vice president of Sears, Roebuck). The commission quickly convened to begin its work, meeting for the first time on May 30, 1940. As a joint body, it would need a public information office. McReynolds demurred from assuming any role relating to public relations, deferring to Mellett. Mellett knew just the man: Bob Horton.[11] Horton agreed and immediately began organizing the PR office for the nascent commission (while on leave from MC, but still on its payroll). The commission formally appointed him on June 3 and quickly announced the appointment in the second press release it issued, which Horton, of course, had written. It was only two sentences long, the first stating Horton's title, director of public relations, and the second, his qualifications as federal PIO and former reporter.[12]

Business was brisk from the start. Gosnell described what press relations looked like early on: "A typical scene in these days was a crowd of reporters milling around Mr. Horton's desk seeking to get a word in between telephone calls."[13] Within a few weeks of starting, Horton said reporters were already complaining that the PR office's phone numbers were constantly busy and they could not get through to him. He urgently asked for more lines, both for the nascent press desk as well as a direct line to him. Not wanting to raise the level of grumbling by reporters any higher (which they could quickly turn into a news story), he carefully asked that the phone work be done quickly, over a weekend.[14]

Horton was creating a public relations operation from scratch. That gave him the luxury of establishing an organizational culture with values that reflected his own preferences. Also, he was somewhat autonomous. He worked for the commission as a whole, but as a provider of a central management service, he was not accountable to any individual commissioner, unlike his peers in charge of various substantive areas of military production: raw materials, manufacturing, agriculture, labor, transportation, and so on. McReynolds, the White House aide also serving as NDAC's secretary, declined to consider himself as Horton's superior or supervisor. So Horton did not have a boss in the conventional sense of the term in the federal bureaucracy, short of the president formally but indirectly, or Mellett very informally, more collegially.[15]

Press Relations and Public Reporting before Roosevelt Declared for Reelection, June–July 1940

Horton was now the PR man for an agency that was within the president's executive office, that is, his official family. And this president was considering running for reelection. In this overheated partisan and political atmosphere, everything that Horton did would be scrutinized carefully by FDR's political opponents for any hint of the president politicizing national defense to benefit his own reelection campaign. Horton needed to be seen as speaking on behalf of the president's national preparedness effort while avoiding anything that could be seen as propagandizing for FDR's potential reelection. This would be much more difficult than engaging in propaganda for widely held values such as the merchant marine. What FDR was doing, in this deeply intertwined political and wartime effort, was anything but promoting a widely shared value. This was government public relations about a controversial topic and so closely tied to a president that, rather than reflecting the communication efforts of a neutral civil service, probably pushed past the normal boundaries and taboos of public administration PR into political advocacy.

Horton quickly settled on a PR doctrine for his office that could be defended as necessary information, but not labeled as political propaganda. He would be a reporter who was inside government, rather than outside it. He would collect as much information as possible on NDAC's activities and then release that information in a stream of press releases. Whatever the media decided to pick up, fine. Whatever they opted not to cover, fine, too. But that was *their* decision, not his. He would give them more than they needed, always careful to present factual and informative summaries of NDAC activities. No adjectives, no hyperbole, no characterizations. Similarly, for the specialized press (such as trade associations) he would be glad to *reply* to specific media inquiries, but he would not try to flood them with all manner of releases for which they hadn't asked and in which they weren't interested.[16] He would stay within the red line banning propaganda. If the neutral information he was providing the press contributed to an informed citizenry that interpreted the information as favoring the stewardship of the president, fine. But no one could accuse him of overtly propagandizing for the president's reelection or in any way politicizing the defense production buildup for Roosevelt's benefit. Writing after the war, his admirer (and subordinate) Bruce Catton waxed lyrical about Horton's emerging philosophy of government PR:

"This fixed idea was quite simple. It was a conviction that the sole job of the mouthpiece for a government agency was to tell the people the plain, unvarnished truth about the things that agency was doing. . . . [B]eneath the reporter's ingrained impatience with double talk, and the government man's awareness of the ineffectiveness of the cover-up—there was a sturdy, old-fashioned Vermont belief in democracy taken straight; a conviction that in the end the people have enough sense and enough decency to come up with the right answers if they are just given all of the facts."[17] The commissioners were not an easy sell for this approach. This was partly due to a comment that the president had made in his first meeting with them. He said that he did not want them to hold press conferences or give public speeches. Apparently, given the policy and political delicacies of a major national defense effort in an election year, Roosevelt wanted to control and be the source of news about such developments. The last thing he needed was a furor created by public comment from politically naïve businessmen (Republicans to boot) who were new to government. Such a scenario was easy to imagine. But the president quickly gained confidence in the political maturity of the commissioners and in Horton's tight oversight of public relations. As a result, he promptly contradicted his own verbal directive by asking the commission to hold a press conference on its progress.[18] With that, Roosevelt's original ban on press conferences and public speaking evaporated.

At some early meetings (which were always closed to the public and media), Horton had to push for *some* openness to press coverage, but he got push-back, too. One of the early decisions related to doing business mostly through negotiated contracts instead of competitive bidding. After adopting the policy, none of the commissioners thought of releasing that publicly. Horton had to raise the issue. Grudgingly, they agreed to consider a draft press release he would prepare, but they noted that it would need to "be approved in writing by each member of the Commission before it is released."[19] That was at the June 28 meeting. Horton submitted a draft at the July 3 meeting, and it was discussed at the July 10 meeting.[20] The commissioners asked for a redraft "incorporating all of the suggestions of the members of the Commission," and that it then be circulated "to each member of the Commission for his approval." Once that was completed, the draft should be sent to the White House press secretary, who would be asked to clear it with the president personally.[21] By the time the commissioners were preparing for their own meeting with the president in mid-July, they still had not released anything.

This would not do. For an advocate of what, in the next century, came to be called transparency, this was a recipe for a press relations disaster. By the July 12 meeting, Horton laid down the law. From now on "each Commissioner would be notified," not consulted, "when press conferences were to be held," and "copies of all press notices were being sent to the different offices" upon release.[22] No advance approvals of every piece of paper by every commissioner. Horton would be the judge of what information would be released and when. By July 17, the tone had changed. The commissioners were on a steep learning curve about media relations. By now there was general consensus that press conferences should be held from time to time, frequently enough "so that the public may know of the progress being made by the Commission as a whole."[23]

In early August, when discussing whether to send reports to Congress, the commissioners agreed that there was nothing in particular to give to Congress because it would be "the same as was being given out from day to day by the Commission in the form of press releases because *the Commission considered that the public was entitled to have all of the information available* with respect to the Advisory Commission."[24] Horton had largely won, but not totally. The commission had a relapse in early September. Horton had just mailed a series of feature-style articles to newspaper and weeklies on the production effort (discussed later in this chapter). The commissioners felt Horton should have cleared with each of them the contents of the column describing their own division's work.[25]

Besides news relations, Horton's philosophy of the role of government PR also included the corollary tradition of public reporting. As NDAC's PR director, Horton directed a planful approach to reporting, one that was not dependent on reactive and spot news coverage. Certainly, the concept of direct public reporting can be criticized as covert advocacy propaganda by an agency or even by a president. However, it is hard to argue that any publicly funded entity should *not* routinely inform the public of its stewardship of public funds and efforts to fulfill its mission. The rubric of public reporting provided a central thematic model for most of Horton's PR at NDAC. The initial impetus for a comprehensive public reporting campaign came up early, when the commission was only in its second month of existence. Commissioner Leon Henderson, who was in charge of the Pricing Division (and a New Deal ideologue), brought it up in a memo he circulated to the other commissioners at the July 12, 1940, meeting. He noted the importance of communicating to the public that the commission's work was making a difference in actual production of defense matériel. He called this "a public relations job of first order." Significantly, he stated that "the country is likely to judge the Defense Commission as to whether *by October or November of this year* there are definite signs of increase."[26] The timing was suspicious, by aiming for the public reporting effort just before the presidential election.

Whatever Henderson's motivation, such reporting activities were fully justified in the context of nonpartisan and nonpolitical public administration. In the discussion at the commission meeting of Henderson's suggestion, Horton agreed, saying that "this is the time for the Commissioners to state, in the nature of *simple progress reports*, what they have accomplished thus far."[27] Horton's description of such an effort captured the principles of public reporting by focusing on bypassing routine press coverage with content that is more summative and comprehensive, the need for utilizing news outlets other than daily newspapers, and the need for tangible and illustrative examples: It "can not be confined to the newspapers and will primarily have to be done through the newsreels, radio, etc., that it has taken time to work out such a [PR] program but that it was expected that full cooperation of the different news media would be had. He [Horton] added that one form which such publicity would take will be to have accredited newsreel and radio men visit the plants where the actual work is under way and have descriptions of such work broadcast and shown in the newsreels."[28]

Horton got to work. He had started with a desk and two secretaries.[29] In less than a week after the commission's decision to engage in public reporting, one of the commissioners released a four-page document on his unit's work titled "Progress Report," and Horton then helped prepare and coalesce a report summarizing the work of all seven commission silos.[30] With Horton six weeks into the job, on July 16, President Roosevelt released that report during one of his routine biweekly press conferences. (Only a few hours later, at the Democratic National Convention in Chicago, it would become clear for the first time publicly that he was willing to run for a third term.) Perhaps in seriousness, perhaps playfully, perhaps both, at the press conference, Roosevelt read verbatim from the seven sections at great length, interposing his comments and observations. His reading of the report covered more than eight transcript pages.[31] Assuming a political motivation, the release of the report permitted FDR's renomination to be presented in the context of a national defense emergency, with him focusing on national needs, not electoral ones. It also helped frame the election as one occurring in a warlike situation (even though the United States was not a combatant) and implying that it would be a bad idea to change presidents in the midst of such events. Still, as a method of public reporting, having a president read long portions of an agency's report at a press conference is about as good a platform as a public administrator could ask for. The next day, the political news from Chicago was presented side by side with the president's report on national defense production. AP moved the entire text of the report to its members.[32]

Government PR as Persuasion: Horton's Involvement in Presidential Press Relations, July–November 1940

Even before Roosevelt became a declared candidate for reelection, the political coalition opposing him (whether for reelection or for entering the war) was on a hair trigger regarding presidential propaganda. With Horton in office less than a month, the *Washington Post* (then loosely siding with the coalition) reported that the president had on his desk plans for "a Government agency for publicity designed to 'sell' national defense to the country." One of the scenarios to implement this plan, according to the paper, would be that Horton, the "young" chief of PR for NDAC, would have his portfolio expanded "to become a full publicity bureau covering all phases of educating the country on defense."[33] The report was false (both Horton and Mellett were quoted as denying it unequivocally), but it clearly was a political shot across the bow. No "selling" of the president's national defense activities, especially not in this election year.

With Roosevelt finally revealing that he would, indeed, run for reelection and accepting the renomination by the Democratic National convention, the context of Horton's PR work changed instantly and significantly. Now, Horton was engaging in public relations as the senior PIO for an agency within the Executive Office of the *President*. He was a public administrator trying to conduct the kind of generally noncontroversial public relations programs that civil servants are expected to conduct, and, simultaneously, he was a political appointee within the administration of a president who was now an active political candidate. All that on top of the very controversial activity in which his agency was engaging: preparing for a war that was opposed by many Americans. In the overheated and hothouse partisan atmosphere of Washington in that period, every step Horton took had the potential to trigger a political landmine.

On July 30, at one of his routine press conferences (if "routine" is the word to apply to a president running for a third term in the midst of a war), Roosevelt's major news announcement was an agreement between NDAC and paper pulp producers to prevent price increases and avoid product shortages. The president began by saying, "I have a story here that Bob Horton will have more in detail in case you want it." After reading from the NDAC statement, he concluded: "I don't think I have got anything else. You can get copies from Bob Horton."[34] Horton was on hand, and, at the end of the press conference, he handed out copies of the NDAC statement to any interested reporter. Most were not. Eye-glazing industrial agreements paled in comparison to a president running for a third term.[35] While Roosevelt had a tendency to assume quick familiarity with everyone he met (except Army Chief of Staff George Marshall), his reference to Horton as "Bob" suggested that he knew him, at least casually, as did most reporters.[36] And Horton was comfortable engaging in press relations from the White House.[37]

Another turn by Horton at the White House was much more controversial. In late July, a banner headline in the Sunday *Chicago Tribune* blared across the entire width of the front page, "Reveal Muddle in Air Plan."[38] The article alleged that notwithstanding all the happy talk emanating from Roosevelt and NDAC, the rearmament program was being bungled, no contracts for combat aircraft had even been *signed,* and that at this pace FDR's declared goal of producing fifty thousand planes would not be reached until 1945. While the *Tribune* was one of the most virulent anti-Roosevelt papers in the country, the article was detailed and documented. At the end of the week, conservative syndicated columnist David Lawrence chimed in, stating, "The National Defense program is bogged down."[39] This was political dynamite. If left unanswered, it would be picked up by the Washington press corps and become the new conventional wisdom and potentially defeat FDR's reelection.

On August 2 (three days after the pulp paper session), Roosevelt had another routine press conference. Again, he refused to say anything political or comment on much of anything else for that matter. In fact, he began the press conference saying, "I do not think I have got any news today." But a few minutes later, he said that contrary to several articles in the last few days, contracting for production of military matériel was going well. In fact, some airplanes would be delivered "as early as October."[40] He complained that those newspaper articles were wholly inaccurate and factually wrong. However, Roosevelt refused to provide a point-by-point rebuttal of the articles. Rather he would leave that for the reporters to take up, after the press conference, with his press secretary, Stephen Early. With that, he adjourned the session.

Early was waiting in the Cabinet Room with Horton. Horton gave a detailed briefing on the status of airplane production as well as a more general overview of armament manufacturing.[41] He said that $80 million worth of airplane production contracts had been "cleared" by the commission, but not yet signed, largely due to a soon-to-be-resolved controversy in Congress about an excess profits tax. But, he said that plane manufacturers were "generally" going ahead and producing the airplanes, merely that the delivery would be held up until the tax issue was resolved and the contracts formally signed. He also related that most of the airplanes being produced were for training purposes, rather than fighters or bombers, reflecting the current early stage of the national defense buildup effort. Based on NDAC's statistics, work was proceeding on $1.8 billion of orders (including, apparently, unsigned contracts). He said that based on current plans, the US military would have twenty-five thousand airplanes by mid-1942. Also, he announced that a company producing tanks was doubling its production pace from the current 2½–3 per day within five months.[42] It was *very* confusing. Still, he accomplished the goal of knocking down the *Tribune* story and preventing it from going viral and becoming the "A" topic for the Washington press pack. For example, two days after the Horton briefing, the *San Antonio (TX) Express* editorialized about the situation (including quoting Horton), but blaming it largely on Congress for not resolving the tax issues, not on candidate Roosevelt.[43] For the time being, political and PR crisis averted.

Ever attuned to the press pack, Horton subtly changed the commission's reporting format to highlight airplane production. The same day as his press briefing at the White House, he released a routine summary of recent contracts cleared by NDAC. The category of aircraft production contracts was on the last page of the seven-page release. A week later, the next update placed aircraft first.[44]

The subject would not go away. When the seven commissioners made a joint radio appearance on August 8, the fourth question from an interviewer was about airplane contracts.[45] The story in the next day's *New York Times* on the joint interview led with that subject.[46] In midmonth, an editorial in the *Los Angeles Times* (a Republican newspaper) mocked Roosevelt's claim that everything was "going awfully well" and referred to the figures Horton had used at the White House briefing.[47] Horton made sure that in the next few weeks his office would issue several seemingly routine press releases on NDAC's approval of arms contracts, with a special focus on airplanes.[48] They had the desired effect. Headlines that month included "$11,335,631 Order for Planes Given," "Army Indicated Ready to Place Remaining Orders for 4,000 Planes," and "2,800 Planes under Contract."[49]

This highly politicized situation almost guaranteed that Roosevelt's opponents in the congressional conservative coalition would try to make the most of it (and help the campaign of Republican nominee Wendell Willkie). On Saturday, August 24, 1940, in time for the Sunday newspapers, Senator Harry Byrd (D-VA) asserted that only 343 *combat* planes had been ordered in the preceding one hundred days, in contrast to the thousands claimed by NDAC. He said he was "disturbed and astonished" by this low number. Congress should investigate, perhaps create a permanent committee to oversee the national defense production effort. Whether for political or managerial reasons, this was the last thing Roosevelt wanted. The editors of the *New York Times* placed coverage of Byrd's statement on the front page of the Sunday paper, signaling their assessment of the significance of the issue.[50]

The administration went into high gear to suffocate the Byrd charges. First, on Monday morning, August 26, Horton delivered to the White House a new untitled report by NDAC on airplane contract statistics, one that tried to harmonize the confusing information with authoritative data. It was largely based on data from the Treasury Department, which was the disburser of all funds for signed federal contracts.[51] John H. Biggers, the acting head of NDAC's production division, was listed as its author, or at least as the person from whom it officially came.[52] Early quickly convened what the *Times* called a "special press conference" at the White House.[53] He told the reporters he wanted a session in reaction to coverage that "you probably have seen in the newspapers over the weekend." He wanted to counter that coverage with information "which gives you an up-to-date picture of the entire question of planes, contracts, deliveries, orders and what have you." However, waving some sheets densely printed with figures, he said: "You can see [it] is in statistical form. We do not have [it] in narrative form." Early then turned the briefing over to Horton. Without handing out copies of the report itself, Horton summarized the important data contained in it. As far as he was concerned, they confirmed what he had said earlier in the month. He answered questions from the reporters who were seeking to make sense of the confusing back-and-forth arguments of the last few weeks.[54] Horton's interpretation of the statistics was essentially a veiled attack on Byrd and Congress, the former for providing misleading statistics, and the latter for supposedly still sitting on an appropriations bill that would fund, among other things, more contracts for planes.[55] Early had scheduled Horton's press briefing in time to make the deadlines for Monday's afternoon newspapers.[56] The news cycle for the next twenty-four hours was dominated by a running debate between Horton and Byrd. Dueling headlines, tilted by a newspaper's general editorial stance, captured the exchanges: "Byrd Refutes New Deal Claim on Plane Orders" versus "Defense Board Puts Blame for Plane Delay on Congress."[57]

The next day, Tuesday, August 27, Roosevelt held a press conference in the Oval Office to address the issue. The *Washington Post* described it as "an unusually long press conference which kept 200 reporters scribbling notes for 40 minutes."[58] Deftly, FDR refused to be drawn into a fight with Byrd (or anyone else, such as Willkie). No good (politically) could come of it. Trying to stay above the fray, he blandly said that the argument was "largely a question of terminology," that is, signed contracts versus cleared contracts versus formal "letters of intent" to sign a contract. Without criticizing Byrd personally, Roosevelt pointed out that Byrd had, presumably with some deliberate intent, focused only on *combat* planes (when the early needs of the military were for trainers) and on contracts signed in the last one hundred days, versus contracts from before then or that were at present committed, but not executed. Showing a mastery of details, he referred to and quoted from the NDAC report on which Horton had briefed White House reporters the day before. In conclusion, he said, Byrd's "actual figures were correct and the implication was dead wrong."[59] That zinger was worded carefully, in that the president made a very quotable and easy-to-understand point, but neither attacked Byrd personally nor explicitly questioned Byrd's motivation. It was a front-page story nationally. Separately, to give the administration's claims a sense of bipartisanship, Republican Frank Knox, secretary of the Navy, also talked to reporters that day and "bolstered the President's optimistic figure with statistics" of his own.[60]

If Byrd had been hoping to draw the president into a one-on-one fight, he failed. Roosevelt's mastery of political communication permitted him to float above the fray, both politically and administratively. Now, if Byrd wanted to slug it out in follow-up stories, he had to deal with Horton, not Roosevelt. Byrd was left arguing with an opponent much farther down the food chain from the president, stuck with a lower-tier bureaucrat largely unknown to the public at large, a lousy *publicity man,* no less. Still, Byrd tried to keep the issue alive for a few more news cycles. For example, he telegrammed Horton, asking for a copy of the report or the transcript of Horton's White House news briefing. Horton disingenuously claimed he could not comply with Byrd's request because "No written statement was given to the press by me on Aug. 26. I answered questions orally."[61] The topic quickly faded from the front pages.[62] Not taking any chances, up to the election, Horton issued a steady stream of press releases on airplane contracts approved by the commission, a dozen between September 16 and November 2.[63] Rather pointedly, in one of them, after the boilerplate language giving the specifics of the new contract, he added a summary listing of "Total airplane awards to date."[64] The commission also announced that it had decided to appoint a man from the aviation industry to head a new division to oversee aircraft ordering and production.[65] Horton was smothering the press with news about aircraft production.[66]

In the end, Roosevelt had largely outmaneuvered Byrd and succeeded in muffling the argument. Still, Byrd had drawn some blood. First, he attracted some editorial comments from newspapers around the country that were willing to accept the basic credibility of his charges. In editorials that pointedly mentioned Horton, the papers were not willing to take sides, such as saying that FDR and Horton were factually right and that Byrd was wrong. Instead, they took a seemingly balanced perspective, which by default gave Byrd's accusations legitimacy.[67] Second, Byrd succeeded in planting the basis for what would become the metanarrative of a long-running conservative attack on Roosevelt's conduct of the war, that there was a production "mess" and that Roosevelt was mismanaging the military buildup effort. This line of criticism permitted conservatives to say disingenuously that no one was disagreeing with the president in terms of the *goal* of a strong national defense (and, after Pearl Harbor, victory), but that they were merely questioning the president's competence and efficiency in pursuing that goal.

During that campaign season, Horton was the heavy for one more attack on the administration that had the potential of becoming a scandal. Nationally syndicated columnists Drew Pearson and Robert Allen claimed that high-level nepotism was occurring within the president's official family. They wrote that White House assistant William McReynolds, who was concurrently serving as NDAC secretary, had arranged for his daughter to be hired by NDAC's personnel office. They insinuated that she was performing under par, because congressmen were complaining they could not get her to respond to their inquiries about pending job applications of constituents. They also focused on the fact that her salary was secret, implying she was paid more than she deserved. Horton was one of the fall guys in the story. He refused to release her salary to the columnists.[68] That meant the columnists were dead-ended and could not do much more to keep the story alive.

Government PR as Persuasion:
Public Reporting during the Presidential Campaign, July–November 1940

Besides press relations, would the president's political candidacy also affect Horton's public reporting program? After all, Horton was more than a run-of-the-mill federal PIO engaging in routine reporting to the public on his agency's record. He served at will rather than holding a permanent classified civil service position. (*Whose* will was unclear.) He was conducting public reporting for a presidential agency, not a bureaucracy out in the boondocks of the executive branch. The reporting was about a national defense effort that was controversial in its implicit prowar (or at least pro–United Kingdom) tilt. These competing, overlapping, and, in some cases, mutually exclusive roles drew his reporting efforts inexorably into the political vortex.

As discussed earlier, in mid-July (shortly before the president announced his intention to run), Commissioner Henderson had made a motion at a commission meeting that NDAC conduct an extensive public reporting campaign to show the public the results of its work by October and November. Horton implemented the motion by engaging in a comprehensive and ostensibly nonpolitical public reporting effort. Some reporting could be packaged in a way that it might engender spot news coverage by daily newspapers. So, for example, using as a news peg the milestone of the commission's three-month birthday in late August, Horton released a progress report summarizing what it had accomplished so far. The Associated Press moved it as a news story on its national wire.[69] But, knowing that public reporting was largely incompatible with the imperatives of daily coverage and spot news, he focused on providing such reporting more directly to the public at large (that is, bypassing spot news coverage by newspapers) via radio, other print publications, and newsreels.

Horton worked aggressively to arrange for the NDAC commissioners to report regularly on their work over the radio, especially about the contracts "cleared" by the commission. Radio stations, as Republicans ceaselessly pointed out, were regulated by a federal agency, the Federal Communications Commission (FCC). It had been established by law in 1934, a year after Roosevelt took office. The commission comprised seven members, all of whom were nominated by the president and subject to Senate confirmation. The president also had the unilateral power to designate which of the seven commissioners would serve as chairman. The FCC awarded licenses to corporations to use a specific radio frequency that did not interfere with other frequencies. The license was (theoretically) limited to three to five years. Losing a license was the same as having one's business shut down with almost no vestigial value (besides any real estate). It was the equivalent of a corporate death sentence. The license was *everything.* The law required licensees to engage in the activities that were in the "public convenience, interest, or necessity." Every renewal required a station to document that its operations met this standard. If the commission were to rule that it had not, the license would not be renewed. No wonder Republicans felt radio stations were exceptionally vulnerable to requests from federal agencies in general, and the president in particular, to carry certain programs sponsored by the government.

Horton moved quickly to schedule some commission reports on the radio. The first was a half-hour program on August 8. All seven commissioners were scheduled to be present to answer questions from a panel of four reporters from all the radio networks.[70] Showing his awareness of the needs of journalists, a few hours after the broadcast (that is, in the same news cycle), Horton released a transcript of the program to assist other reporters seeking to use it for news stories.[71] Indeed, the *New York Times* covered the broadcast as a news event.[72] But Horton wanted to provide regularly scheduled reports, not occasional ones. By late summer, the commission approved Horton's plan for radio-based public reporting. The goal was to have a regularly scheduled fifteen-minute weekly program in which one or more commissioners "will *report* plans and progress in the Defense program to the country."[73] These programs would be offered free to all the radio networks, and the commission would not buy commercial time to broadcast them. Horton shrewdly scheduled eight programs for the fall, beginning on September 19 and with all but the last one taking place before the election.[74] The last one was set for two days *after* the November election. By doing that, Horton could innocently explain that the schedule of the broadcasts was not politically motivated—otherwise, why would one have been scheduled after the election? He did the same for written progress reports and compilations, continuing to issue them after the election.[75]

Hewing closely to the conventional and noncontroversial template of public reporting, a ten-minute radio address by William Knudsen on October 10, 1940, framed the purpose of his speech with the opening phrase: "In *reporting* to you the results of the past months' work," quickly followed by the spin of the underlying message, "I am happy to say that some progress has been made."[76] To maximize both his control over and the professionalism of these regular weekly reports, Horton contracted with the radio studio of the Interior Department to tape, edit, and copy this first series of radio reports, which he titled *Building for Defense*.[77] Planning ahead, he also anticipated following up on that series with two more radio series, one on the Army and the other on the Navy, also to be produced by Interior.[78] Besides those that were aired live, Horton also arranged to make three hundred copies of the radio reports and provided them free to radio stations requesting them.[79]

Horton organized a similar effort for the print media, separate from the spot news releases coming from his office to Washington-based reporters. They covered the same three rubrics as the radio series had. Horton mailed them directly to the editors of all dailies, semi-weeklies, and weeklies. They were structured as feature-style stories that were preformatted and ready for publication as is (sometimes called mats). Many included graphic sketches depicting how a particular weapons system would work. Horton understood that many understaffed publications welcomed feature material, especially on topics relevant to their readership. Official reports, written in journalistic style, format, and length on national preparedness fit the bill. In late July, he sent to the editors of these publications a ten-part series on NDAC's work, with a focus on what the Army needed. Each column had an embargo date a half week apart. If a paper published all ten articles, the series would extend from August 5 to September 7. In his cover memo, he stated: "Numerous requests have indicated the need for an authoritative series of articles on our national defense program. In response, the National Defense Advisory Commission has prepared this series outlining our needs and the way in which they will be met. It is hoped that this material will prove informative. It may be used, of course, as presented here or in such other form as editors may find desirable. Please observe the release dates on each article."[80]

Before the expiration of the Army series, Horton sent the editors a six-part series on the Navy and its production needs. The release dates began on September 9 and ended on September 28. Finally, partially overlapping with the Navy series, in September he mailed a seven-part series on NDAC in general, but with no embargo dates for the individual columns after September 3. His cover memo gave a slightly different rationale for this series compared to the Army and Navy ones: "Press conferences here have brought many questions on the problems of 'Building for Defense' and on the speed with which our defense program is being carried forward. To give press and public a background, the National Defense Advisory Commission has prepared this series."[81]

Some newspapers welcomed the material. Between September 10 and 21, the *Huntington (PA) Daily News* published five of the columns, three on its editorial page and two partly as fillers on the classified ads page.[82] The *Oakland (CA) Tribune* ran three between September 4 and 26, all on news pages.[83] The *Portsmouth (NH) Herald* published at least one column in August.[84] In all cases, the features were identified as part "of a Series Prepared by the National Defense Advisory Commission." Columnist Paul Mallon sharply criticized what Horton was doing: "Mr. Horton actually wrote under his own signature suggested articles for newspapers, which were printed at government expense and sent to newspapers throughout the country, in a form so they could be published without changing a word, as if an impartial reporter had written the account. Not even the most zealous of government propagandists had seen fit to try this hoary but generally ineffective publicity device before."[85]

Newsreels were another major venue for reporting to the citizenry. Before the emergence of over-the-air television in the late 1940s and early 1950s, movie attendance was at an all-time high. Among a population of about 150 million people, 90 million went to the movies at least once a week, not to see a particular release but rather as a weekly habit regardless of what was playing.[86] If most newspaper publishers were Republican and used their properties to advance their political agenda, then newsreels (and radio) were the media that could bypass these hostile gatekeepers and reach the mass public directly. On July 26, the week after Roosevelt came out of the political closet, Horton received via Mellett a plan from Arch Mercey, formerly with the US Film Service and now with OGR, calling for a systematic effort to create newsreel reports on the defense production effort. In the context of routine public reporting in public administration, the purpose of the series would be to provide basic information about NDAC (now two months old), such as "why it was formed, what its objectives are and what it is doing." Politics was not far from the surface. His proposed timing was similar to Henderson's, suggesting that "this reel series would begin about the middle of August and extend for eight weeks," which would take it to the middle of October.[87] Over the next few months, Horton and Mercey continued refining their plans for a systematic newsreel program.[88] While the archival record is spotty, some newsreels on national defense production made it to the screen before the election.[89] For example, a newsreel shown in early August depicted "an airplane factory, and a young man applying camouflage to a plane" and others as encouraging applying for jobs at factories producing armaments.[90] Several newsreels showed the president on supposedly nonpolitical "inspection tours" of plants manufacturing national defense matériel, prompting complaints from Republicans.[91] According to industry statistics, 18 percent of newsreel clips in 1940 covered some aspect of national defense.[92]

The timing of much of Horton's PR work in the fall of 1940 seemed to be invisibly linked to the political calendar. Echoing the "good news" theme of the radio reports, Horton issued a press release four days before the election that began with the phrase, "With the majority of primary contracts under the defense program already awarded."[93] Commissioner Henderson's regularly scheduled radio update report was broadcast on November 3, two days before the election. He stated explicitly that some of his comments were in response to "the excitement of electioneering." He said that progress had been "vast" and tried to counter political criticisms that NDAC's record compared unfavorably to the same effort in 1917.[94]

Was such reporting through radio, print, and newsreels merely factual information for the benefit of an informed public in a democracy, or also something(s) else? A relatively overt advocacy campaign in favor of national defense readiness? Perhaps even laying the groundwork for supporting involvement in the war? Political propaganda to help a president win reelection? They were all that, simultaneously. For example, in content, all the articles in the three series mailed to editors were factual and descriptive. However, the underlying premise of the text was that such military preparedness was justified given the international situation. So, they were advocatory, too. Similarly the timing of this public reporting campaign was both justifiable and questionable. That these were important developments and of great significance at any time would be an accurate characterization. Yet, the public reporting campaign was occurring as Roosevelt was running for an unprecedented third term and running in a nonpolitical way, as the commander in chief protecting the republic in a time of war abroad and conducting "inspection tours" of defense production plants.

An Alternative to the Orthodoxy of Staff Services: Horton's Centralized Structure for Government PR

Horton's philosophy of government PR included not only his guiding principles for dealing with the press, but also organizational structure. He believed in centralization. At the time, the norm was for each federal department and agency to have its own small public information shop. In part, this was a politically shrewd way to organize because it kept units small and low-profile. A large centralized PR office for the entire executive branch would have been a juicy target for legislators opposing such information dissemination activities —exactly what happened to Mellett's OGR. But, the main explanation for this decentralization was the bureaucratic imperative for autonomy. Being able to control the agency's own public voice was a vital element of the larger goal of struggling to survive and to expand its autonomy.[95] This decentralization also meant that most federal agency PR was—whether overtly or covertly—self-serving to the agency's own interests.

Now, with the establishment of NDAC, Horton was attached to a kind of superagency that was seeking to coordinate all production decisions of the entire executive branch. Also, as an entity within the Executive Office of the President, NDAC was a presidential agency, this giving it—at least impliedly—some jurisdiction over all federal agencies and departments. Horton liked this potential for a unified federal voice and sought to operationalize it. Simultaneously, but separately, centralization was a beneficial activity during the president's reelection campaign, as it could be a device to control unwanted or harmful publicity and, generally, to keep a political lid on federal PR to prevent embarrassments to the president.

Horton's initial centralization focus was to ensure that none of NDAC's divisions, which operated somewhat autonomously, would have the staffing or authority to issue press releases without going through Horton's office. As his staff increased, he gradually assigned press release writers to work exclusively with "their" division. This was a way to increase the expertise of the writers and improve the quality of information contained in the releases. It also assured that everything would be released from a central office and that

Horton would be fully informed of relevant activities throughout the commission's domain. The PR officers may be assigned to a particular division, but they worked for *him*.

As a result of the midsummer brouhaha over airplane production contracts, behind the scenes Horton tried to reduce the confusion about nomenclature, such as regarding NDAC "clearing" a contract versus the military signing one. On August 12, he wrote the secretaries of war and the Navy suggesting a way to resolve the confusion so that there would be "a unified, coordinated public announcement" of all contracts. He proposed a standard wording for releases that would eliminate the ambiguity: "The following contracts have been cleared by the National Defense Advisory Commission and awarded by the War/Navy Department."[96] As the most autonomous of all federal agencies, the Army and Navy were the most resistant to any outside control. However, as long as Horton did not try to tamper with their internal decision making and schedules about contracts, no harm could come of coordinating the announcements. That would help reduce the chances of future repeats of the near-fiasco in the summer about airplane numbers. By the end of the month, when Navy Secretary Knox announced a major contract for airplane engines, he explicitly stated that the contract (and impliedly, the *announcement* of the contract) was "cleared through the National Defense Commission, under present procedure in the defense program."[97] This approach would reduce (political) confusion about the progress of the production effort.

Still, the military was prickly to deal with. In early October (a month before the election), the Army abruptly announced that it would provide no further information on airplane production and delivery (under already-signed contracts). The reason was to prevent giving potential military enemies a sense of the timetable of the future buildup of the Army air force. Based on the rationale for the Army's new secrecy policy, Horton had little choice but to accept it. He gamely tried to provide reporters with some rough statistics, based on his own sources, on the "present monthly rate" of plane deliveries, including those provided to Great Britain.[98] But such figures were quite ephemeral, given that US production was ramping up and, therefore, the *rate* was increasing quickly.

In early September, Horton initiated another effort to centralize and control executive branch PR. He sent a memo to the information officers of all federal agencies requesting that any radio-based activities "pertaining to national defense" be coordinated in advance with his office. The scope of his request was quite wide, including "using or planning to use broadcasting facilities, either network or local stations, for programs or announcements." The rationale for the directive, he wrote, was "to avoid duplication of effort by the Federal agencies and the burdensome and conflicting demands made upon the radio stations." To give more weight to his request, Horton was working in league with the industry group, the National Association of Broadcasters. So, seemingly, his memo reflected the endorsement of all radio stations.[99] Implicitly, Horton was asserting his authority to impose such a policy on all executive branch agencies. The scope of his memo "pertaining" to national defense was so broad as to encompass just about any activity of a federal agency, including such nonobvious ones as agriculture, education, or New Deal–related relief programs.

Within a few weeks, Horton's radio memo was severely criticized in two syndicated columns. Pearson and Allen's "Washington Merry-Go-Round" column noted that the recipients of the memo were "furious" about it and that Horton had "no authority to issue such an order." In any event, they wrote, "none of the agencies has any intention of complying."[100] Paul Mallon, a conservative commentator, wrote a scathing broadside attacking all of Horton's centralization efforts, including the radio coordination memo. Calling it "the Goebbels system of National Defense Commission publicity," Mellon referred to Horton as "Herr Horton," suggesting that Horton's centralization efforts were as bad as those of Nazi Germany. Mallon described Horton not only as a "bottleneck" who was trying to control other federal agencies, but also as having "gagged" and "hermetically sealed" the NDAC commissioners from public and press contact.[101]

But the criticism of Horton's centralization efforts did not reflect the unanimous view of the press corps. Some reporters wanted *more*, arguing that Horton was not centralizing *enough*. The same month as the critical columns, Warren Francis, the *Los Angeles Times'* Washington correspondent, complained about "conflicting publicity, contradictory advice and misinformation." He praised Horton as "a competent, experienced former reporter," but lamented that Horton's work "often is short-circuited" by other agencies "declaring they are vital to the preparedness drive, without consulting the Defense Commission." Therefore, he urged creating a "centralized public relations unit" covering the entire national defense effort.[102] Horton could not have agreed more. Also in September 1940, after the controversy over airplane production statistics had settled down, columnists Joseph Alsop and Robert Kintner still thought well of Horton's work, writing that he "has done an excellent job and the commission is well satisfied." They thought it was a good idea that he was well connected to the White House, helping assure that the administration stood behind his public statements.[103]

A Broad Approach to Government PR

Earlier sections of this chapter detailed the major PR outputs of Horton's office, including news releases, press conferences, public reporting, radio programs, movie newsreels, and ready-to-use feature articles for weeklies and other publications. The Division of Information also worked on a few other public relations products, including public speaking, photo stills, and movie shorts.

Speeches

It will be recalled from the discussion on the period before Roosevelt declared for reelection (June–July 1940) that he had instructed the commissioners at their first meeting with him not to hold press conferences or give public talks. The ban on press conferences had evaporated quickly when Roosevelt subsequently requested that the commission hold a press conference on its progress. In late August, the commissioners discussed whether the ban on public speaking was still in effect. Forgetting Roosevelt's instruction, one of them had already accepted an invitation and then, remembering the president's directive, wondered to his fellow commissioners if he should cancel it. Commission Secretary William McReynolds, who was simultaneously an administrative assistant to the president, gave a clear signal. He said that he "did not see how anything but good could come from" the commissioner going ahead with the promised speech. One could practically hear the sigh of relief in the room. If the president's assistant said it was OK—notwithstanding Roosevelt's original verbal instructions—then it must be OK.[104]

But the commission wanted to proceed in a centralized and coordinated way, not let each member decide such things willy-nilly. They agreed that "there should be worked out some coordinated plan, that this should be a responsibility of Mr. Horton, and that all invitations received by the commissioners to speak should be referred to Mr. Horton." A few minutes later the question came up regarding public speaking by *staff* of the commission, not the commissioners themselves. (In this case, it was about W. Averill Harriman, who worked in Stettinius's office.) The commission approved such an appearance, just as long as the "speech would be *prepared* by Mr. Horton."[105] Clearly, Horton had the confidence of the commissioners, and they were more than glad to include explicitly in his domain the control of public appearances. After that, the floodgates opened. Commission minutes repeatedly included notifications of invitations received and accepted.[106] Besides controlling this aspect of agency public relations, Horton also occasionally gave public talks himself.[107]

Photos

In the fall of 1940, Horton began creating a comprehensive photo collection of national defense activities. This library of stills would be available for use in NDAC publications, but mostly was intended for use by magazines and newspapers seeking stock photos for feature articles. For example, in September, he asked the admiral heading the Navy's Bureau of Yards and Docks for any "dramatic views" of shipyards and especially close-ups of men working to be used publicly. Hinting at a specific use he had in mind for the latter category, he wrote, "We particularly want pictures which will illustrate the general activity and the types of jobs for which men are needed."[108] This reflected NDAC's efforts at manpower recruitment, training, and housing in areas of shortages. The next month, the division hired a freelance photographer (based in New York City) to shoot pictures of several military production facilities, including the Army's arsenals in Watertown, Massachusetts, and Frankfort, Kentucky, and the Washington (DC) Navy Yard Torpedo Station.[109]

Movies

It will be recalled that as part of Horton's public reporting effort during the election season, he had worked with newsreel companies to obtain ongoing coverage of progress in the defense program as part of their weekly newsreels. He also sought to encourage Hollywood studios to produce, on their own, shorts on defense subjects. Shorts (sometimes called short subjects or trailers) were a standard component of the weekly entertainment package offered by movie houses, which included a feature, a serial, a B movie, a newsreel, and several shorts.[110] There were standard categories for shorts, including brief historical vignettes, documentaries, travelogues (especially concerning exotic places and people), nature, and humor. Hollywood, largely internationalist in orientation and Democratic in its politics, was willing to help.[111] For example, in August, Horton corresponded with MGM regarding topics for shorts.[112]

Earlier that summer, Horton hired Leo Rosten to be his (and Mellett's) liaison with the movie industry in Los Angeles.[113] Rosten helped facilitate production of several items, including a two-reeler to be shown before the election.[114] Generally, Rosten was actively involved in generating story ideas (whether for shorts or for other Hollywood projects), obtaining background information from Horton's Washington staff on the defense effort to share with the studios, and engaging temporary help for some projects.[115] According to industry statistics, shorts on national defense produced by the Hollywood studios were shown regularly in nine thousand theaters in 1940.[116]

In the fall, Horton began exploring having his division *produce* shorts and documentaries, instead of relying on Hollywood's cooperation.[117] For example, he engaged a film production specialist from another federal agency for a week to shoot footage for a documentary about the Tennessee Valley Authority (TVA).[118] He also began advertising the upcoming availability of a thirteen-minute color short on merchant ship construction as part of the national defense buildup.[119] However, the election season was not a good time to inaugurate potentially controversial public relations products. Horton was making early arrangements that would remain in-house and confidential for the time being. He was being careful that these government-made movies would not be released until after the election (see chapter 3 for the release of those movies).

Administrative Sketch

From the start, Horton was struggling with a niggling problem of legality, or, at least, legitimacy. Yes, the commission had appointed him as director of public relations, but did the commission have the legal authority to engage in public relations? This is no mere pedantry. The General Accounting Office (GAO, a legislative branch agency) could disallow expenditure of funds appropriated by Congress if the federal agency did not have legal authority to engage in a particular activity. It could even issue a finding that an agency's expenditure was illegal, occasionally insisting on a claw-back of the money. To prevent this from happening, Horton was forced to go back to the only legal authority the commission had, which was as an advisory body (invented by FDR) to the statutory Council of National Defense, created by Congress during World War I. He strung together four phrases from that 1916 law to give some putative legality to what he was doing: "It shall be the duty (of the Commission) . . . to supervise and direct . . . the giving of information to producers and manufacturers as to the class of supplies needed . . . and the creation of relations which will render possible in time of need, the immediate concentration and utilization of the resources of the nation."[120] It was a stretch, especially because that wording had not been used as the basis for any PR activities of the council in World War I. (CPI functioned wholly separately from the council and under the authority of its own presidential executive order.) Even Horton knew it. He could not even keep a straight face when describing it as his unit's legal basis in an interview with a BOB staffer.[121]

Horton had a freewheeling management style. According to that BOB historian: "Staff meetings were held frequently in order to give and receive advice, but a more familiar sight within the Division was to see the Director or Assistant Director engaged in informal conversation with a knot of his top policy men. Horton and Straus always maintained an open-door policy for their staff also, and many major decisions were made without the frills and fuss of agenda and long conference tables. Frequently, the major decisions were made after a group of staff dropped in for an evening chat."[122]

Staffing

Horton was starting from scratch when NDAC appointed him in early June. In a neat bureaucratic maneuver, he was able to staff up quickly with support personnel who had experience with government public relations. Congress had refused to fund the US Film Service (first in OGR, then in the Office of Education) for FY1941. That meant it would go out of existence on the last day of FY1940 (June 30, 1940), but was funded until then. Arch Mercey, the head of that film unit, and Horton knew each other through Mellett. Given that the Film Service was winding down (and its staff about to lose their jobs), Mercey and Horton arranged for four Film Service staffers to work for Horton during their last month on the Film Service's payroll (and then shift to Horton's payroll on July 1, the first day of FY1941). By doing that, he picked up four administrative staffers to be the core of the secretarial support for his new agency. By midmonth, he had also hired the first professional staff member, Chester Crowell, with the title of assistant director of public relations.[123]

Horton continued staffing up quickly, focusing on hiring reporters because they could write fast and succinctly, understood what information would be helpful in a press release and what would not, and generally understood journalists' technical and professional needs. By mid-July, he had eleven staff members, about half paid from the budgets of other agencies (just as he was initially still paid by MC).[124] A month later he had fifteen staffers,[125] and by late October, twenty-six.[126] Horton had gone from one (himself) to twenty-six in about one hundred days. Of the twenty-six, about half were communication professionals whose titles included cameraman, newsreel specialist, photo editor (a woman), and information specialist. Rosten, Horton's liaison in Hollywood, had the title of expert consultant. The other half of the staff were administrative support, mostly stenographers and clerk-typists, reflecting the large amount of written material that was being produced and the need for quick preparation of transcripts of important events (such as the text of a radio interview).

Horton had a casual attitude about paperwork and was sometimes chastised by the HR professionals in the NDAC secretary's office for incomplete recordkeeping and submissions. In early July, he received a complaint about not having all the right employment forms in yet for his staff: "May I impress upon you the necessity for having the Civil Service forms" filled out so that staff could be paid, he was told with some exasperation.[127] NDAC's central secretariat office had to remind him to designate a timekeeper for purposes of filling out timesheets, the basis for payroll payments.[128] Two weeks later, Horton had to sign a new form on the same subject.[129] The pot finally boiled over in late October, when NDAC Assistant Secretary Sidney Sherwood sent Horton a stern letter complaining that "because many individuals have been put to work without prior clearance of the Personnel Office, the records in that Office are necessarily incomplete. In order that requests of this nature may not recur, we definitely ask that no person be assigned to work in *any capacity whatsoever* in any part of your Division without formal clearance with the Office of Personnel."[130]

Nomenclature

When he was first appointed, Horton's title was director of public relations and his administrative unit was called the Public Relations Division. However, the term "public relations" was unpopular in the federal government, partly due to general congressional hostility to that activity in public administration (including a legal ban on employment of "publicity experts" adopted in 1913).[131] It also had faint aura of deceptiveness, manipulation, and propaganda. The less controversial and more neutral title was "information," à la Horton's eventual MC title. He preferred that terminology for his NDAC unit, but initially did not feel he had the standing or automatic support to petition the commission to make the formal change. Plus, if the general topic came up at a commission meeting, who knew what unintended consequences could occur? For the time being, as a cautious bureaucrat, he opted to let sleeping dogs lie.

Behind the scenes, Horton was gradually trying to create a fait accompli. The *US Government Manual* issued in July 1940 listed him as NDAC's director of information. Given that the *Manual* was published by Mellett's OGR, it is likely that the "mistake" reflected Mellett and Horton's preferences.[132] In another permutation, later that month OGR released a mimeographed directory of defense offices listing Horton as director of public relations and information.[133] In late July, when he mailed to editors a package of feature stories (described earlier in the section on public reporting), he signed it "Director of Information."[134] Horton began using the title in all his official correspondence in early August.[135] In a speech on August 1, one of the commissioners referred to him as the director of information, as did the appended NDAC organization chart.[136] But, NDAC's official *Handbook*, issued in September 1940, seemed still confused on the subject. Horton was variously listed as the director of information, public relations, and public information on three different pages.[137]

Eventually, all official documents fell in line with practice, but without any official commission action—reflecting Horton not having any direct supervisor and the commission as a whole not exercising that function either. The commission's minutes for August 28 identified him for the first time as director of information, and the inaugural issue of NDAC's new weekly magazine referred to his unit as the Division of Information.[138] Finally, on September 20, in a coup de grâce, Horton felt comfortable peremptorily notifying NDAC Assistant Secretary Sherwood (who was something of Horton's bureaucratic nemesis, having complained repeatedly about Horton's incomplete paperwork) "that the name of this division has been changed from Public Relations to Information."[139] The use of passive tense obscured that Horton had been the one who changed it.

Summary and Commentary

The size, scope, and outputs of Horton's NDAC work were that of a major PR bureau. However, most of the techniques would be considered relatively mainstream for government PR activities. For example, he issued 230 press releases between the founding of NDAC in June 1940 and Election Day. While that is a very high output (several a day), issuing handouts was a conventional and uncontroversial PR activity. Similarly, a significant part of Horton's work focused on public reporting. The subject matter on which he was reporting was controversial politically, but reporting was not. Releasing summary reports through less traditional outlets such as radio appearances, newsreels, public talks, press conferences, and news releases was an extension of public reporting and still within the general political consensus about government PR. Most of Horton's other PR activities were similarly traditional, such as maintaining a library of photo stills.

If any of Horton's outputs were somewhat new, it was how extensively he was involved in radio and Hollywood. For example, the production of film documentaries about federal programs and projects was quite controversial from the perspective of the conservative coalition. But, by 1940, radio and film as news and entertainment media had become so central to American daily life that Horton's use of it was more of an extension of the existing pattern for government PR. Complaints from reporters, columnists, and editorial writers about Horton's PR work was part of a larger professional concern about the potential of government publicists slanting the news and denying reporters direct access to sources and high-ranking officials. So, the negative comments about Horton's coordination and centralization efforts need to be interpreted in this professional (and political) context. His work, and their complaints, were relatively de rigueur and, in that respect, unexceptional.

The events of the summer and fall of 1940 starkly showed the near-impossibility of conducting government public relations based on the bland consensus of solely providing noncontroversial and neutral information. Just about everything Horton did was controversial to *someone*. The imperative to separate supposedly neutral facts from advocacy communication collapsed in practice. As far as Horton was concerned, *all* he was doing was releasing information. But, to conservatives, isolationists, and FDR's enemies, *everything* Horton was doing was propaganda. In the more modern term, they felt he was spinning. Even the most innocuous press release on a decision by NDAC was subtly promoting the *premise* that the United States was facing a national defense emergency and that organizational, financial, and production decisions were necessary to protect the nation. Lots of people disagreed with the assumption underlying Horton's PR work. To them, these "facts-only" public relations activities were pro-war or, at least, pro-buildup of a large and more permanent military establishment.

American political culture generally granted government public relations three exemptions from the ban on persuasive and controversial PR: for widely held values, presidential communication, and war. When Horton headed the PR office for the Maritime Commission, he was clearly engaging in persuasive communication efforts as well as releasing neutral information. However, as established by the statute creating the Maritime Commission and the general attitude of the Washington establishment, the advocacy work he was doing was for relatively widely held and noncontroversial goals. This was not the case for his NDAC PR. The national defense work of the commission did not occur in the context of widely held values—just the opposite. It was operating in a context of major controversy over its raison d'être. That meant any PR activity that smacked of persuasion violated the norms that political culture imposed on government information work.

During the summer of 1940, just about everything Horton did was related to the second exemption, regarding presidential communication. In August, he was practically operating out of the White House. So, in that regard, with Horton acting as a temporary spokesman for the chief executive, his advocacy communications about NDAC's successes fell within the presidential exemption for government PR and were, theoretically, OK. The problem was that this presidential work was occurring in an election year, with the incumbent finally revealing that he was a candidate for reelection and, unprecedentedly, for a third term. This context meant that Horton's presidential PR work was political, partisan, and related to influencing election results. He thoroughly violated the etiquette of public relations in public administration of being noncontroversial, apolitical, and nonpartisan. But Horton did not view himself as a civil servant holding a classified position and who was obliged to be apolitical under the Hatch Act. On the contrary, he was appointed (at least indirectly) by the president, served (at least indirectly) at FDR's pleasure, and was therefore part of the administration. His job was to show that the president's policy agenda was successful. However, this raises a different issue. Is it possible or a normative imperative to separate government PR as conducted by a neutral civil servant from that of a member of the president's official family, down to such subcabinet officials as an assistant secretary for public affairs? Generally, the field of public administration has found it nearly impossible to separate either politics from administration or policy from administration. Still, this hardly seems to legitimize disseminating highly politicized government information.

What to make of Horton's bit part in President's Roosevelt's campaign for a third term? There is no doubt that he was compromised (however willingly) by Roosevelt's reelection effort. Horton's statements and maneuverings were those of a political operative. His behavior contradicted Catton's hagiographic image of him as a flinty, apolitical, and full-disclosure truth-teller with a consequences-be-damned attitude. In a crunch, Horton cared about the impact of the information he controlled. He opted to protect FDR politically and help the president's reelection campaign. He did that most clearly when he rebuffed Senator Byrd's request for either a copy of his statement at the August 26 White House press briefing or for the NDAC report from which he had quoted. Horton was quite blatantly putting the political needs of a president to whom he was loyal above his operating principle that government PR should engage in maximal release of information. In general, Horton's behavior regarding airplane production statistics showed he was willing to be the (political) heavy and take as much heat as possible off the president. This seriously reduced his credibility with some reporters, subordinating any straight-arrow image to the president's political needs. One (conservative and relatively hostile) columnist claimed that a few weeks after Horton had stated something on the record, he blatantly denied having said it. In reaction, five or six reporters supposedly circulated a signed affidavit that they had been present at the earlier event and that he indeed had said what he was now denying.[140] He was losing the trust of at least some reporters.

The third generally accepted exemption from the ban on persuasive communication in government PR relates to wartime and like national emergencies. However, Horton's work in mid-1940 would not qualify. While Roosevelt said repeatedly that the country was facing an important and urgent situation and even though a war was raging in Europe and Asia, the United States was not at war. Legally, constitutionally, and politically, the war abroad did not give Horton the automatic right to conduct propaganda. So, in some respects, Horton's information work at NDAC in the summer and fall of 1940 conformed to the accepted conventions of government public relations, including extensive release of information, proactive dissemination efforts to reach the citizenry, and qualifying for the presidential exception to the ban on persuasive communication. However, he became so closely identified with the president's political needs that Horton's commitment to facts and neutral information could reasonably be questioned. Catton got it wrong.

PART II

GOVERNMENT PR IN THE TWILIGHT BETWEEN PEACE AND WAR

CHAPTER 3

HORTON AT THE OFFICE OF PRODUCTION MANAGEMENT

November 1940–February 1941

Everything changed with Roosevelt reelected. The omnipresent political fears, the cautious trimming of the sails, the efforts to keep a lid on bad news, and all other similar considerations could now be relaxed a bit—but not a lot. The United States was still a noncombatant in a war, public opinion was still against any military involvement, and Roosevelt had seemingly promised in his reelection campaign that he would not send American boys to die in a foreign war.[1]

The entire thirteen-month period from the election to Pearl Harbor was an awkward and complicated one. It was a twilight for the United States, somewhere between peace and war, if that were possible. A world war was occurring in Europe, Asia, and Africa. The United States was legally neutral and a noncombatant nation. Yet, it was inching toward a state of quasi-belligerency short of a formal declaration of war. On the other side, Spain's Franco was similarly trying to thread the needle carefully. In 1940, Spain declared that it was shifting from neutrality to "nonbelligerence," by which it meant that it was siding with the Axis powers, but not yet formally in a state of war or in combat.[2] Roosevelt was increasingly explicit that Hitler was the enemy, both in terms of Hitler's threat to democracy as a form of government and his desire for hegemony not just in Europe, but globally. FDR was more and more openly seeking to support the United Kingdom, which at this point was the only major power waging war on Germany. This was a period of evolving toward belligerency, not jumping into it in one fell swoop, even though the conventional historical telling makes Pearl Harbor seem that way. Given the complicated and fluid situation (see table 3), Horton would be conducting

Table 3
Events when Horton headed PR for the Office of Production Management

TIME PERIOD	INTERNATIONAL	DOMESTIC
November 6, 1940–February 1941	London Blitz; Germany bombs Coventry; Japan signs peace treaty with Nanking government; Rommel takes command in North Africa; Churchill to United States: "Give us the tools and we will finish the job"; Germany sinks 215,000 tons of supplies on British ships in two days.	FDR tightens limits on exports to Japan; calls on United States to be "Arsenal of Democracy"; urges military support for countries with "Four Freedoms"; inaugurated for third term; asks Congress for $350 million for 200 new merchant ships; Navy organizes new Atlantic Fleet.

government PR in an ill-defined environment in which the rules of normalcy could not easily be applied. He was in nearly uncharted territory.

As discussed in the previous chapter, Roosevelt had a well-developed and nuanced management philosophy for the exercise of presidential power. He liked to improvise, respond to new developments, and, above all, to be the decider in chief. Once the election was over (and he returned from a post-election cruise), FDR felt a need to tinker with the NDAC structure he had created in May. At a December 20 press conference, he explained his rationale for a reorganization because "about a month ago [in November] it became apparent that we were coming to the end of the study period, and had learned thereby of certain needs," which now required a more action-oriented procurement structure.[3] The press conference took place right after his weekly meeting with NDAC. Roosevelt announced he had decided to supersede NDAC (confusingly, without abolishing it) with an Office of Production Management (OPM).[4] OPM would be an entity within the Office for Emergency Management (OEM), itself an agency in the Executive Office of the President (EOP). In management terms, this somewhat consolidated the independently functioning silos of NDAC into a more integrated organization. It also added a somewhat more centralized and overhead manager, with FDR giving William Knudsen the title of OPM director general, compared to the chairless commission (but promptly undermining that by naming labor leader Sidney Hillman as a kind of co–director general).[5]

Not coincidentally, a few days earlier, Senator Byrd had criticized the lack of satisfactory information on progress in the armament buildup and called for a special Senate committee to investigate.[6] The same day of the president's announcement, a Republican House leader said the defense program was "bogged down" and in "utter confusion." He called for a House investigation.[7] Roosevelt's political ear was finely attuned. He deflated and co-opted the potential mounting criticism through unilateral action.

It took a few weeks for the legal paperwork to catch up to Roosevelt's decision making. On January 7, 1941, he first signed an administrative order revising the OEM/NDAC structure and then, separately, an executive order establishing OPM within OEM.[8] Just two days after that, Horton's well-oiled machine quickly and smoothly began including the OPM terminology in its press releases.[9] For DOI itself, the external reorganization affected its operations and size little, if at all. The only change was in terms of the boxes on the larger organization chart. But, still, it was confusing and unclear. Some continued referring to DOI as within NDAC, while others described it as a unit within OPM.[10] FDR did not mind messy and unclear delegations of power. Horton did not much care either, just as long as he maintained his autonomy and there was no change in the centralized approach to the public relations for the defense production buildup.

Planning and Evolving

As soon as the election was over, Horton began working on a policy and planning document to guide the division into the next calendar year. His general assumption was that the United States would not be in a state of war in the foreseeable future. Rather, it would continue to focus on enhancing national defense without joining the war. Horton's first concern was that "with the election over[,] a lot of legitimate criticism withheld for political reasons will be out in the open."[11] These political reasons varied from Democrats and other FDR supporters who wanted him to win reelection to Republicans who held back on certain virulent attacks for fear of looking unpatriotic. Horton enumerated a long list of potential negative headline items relating to the production buildup, including rising prices, new draftees complaining in letters home, and accusations against NDAC for carelessness in awarding and enforcing contracts. His second concern related to his fears that the defense buildup would negate the social progress accomplished by the New Deal. In this regard, Horton was foreseeing what became a major fault line in Washington during World War II, between dollar-a-year businessmen seeking to help win the war while protecting their long-term economic interests versus New Dealers who wanted the war effort to be consonant with New Deal principles. Horton identified several political and policy issues on which he hoped the postelection administration would draw the lines. They included "that labor and the people must not lose the gains of the last few years," and "that we will not sell out to the military."[12] Shifting to matters more directly related to the information program he headed, Horton worried that the production information program "is top-heavy with guns, tanks, and planes, and not enough of what the hell we are going to protect in the way of democracy."[13] This, too, foretold a major issue that would arise later in the war, namely if this was a war to save democracy, then how could the United States justify aiding two nondemocratic allies, the Soviet Union and China?

Horton had a broad vision of expanding the work of the division to accomplish its goals, including the need for projects that would involve the individual citizen, programs to highlight productive workers and plants, more transparency in commission decision making, and a high-profile effort to locate and prosecute violators of defense contracts. Finally, part of his focus was on more tangible aspects of DOI's organization, including the need to expand staffing to accomplish the tasks assigned it. He assumed an eventual increase in staffing, but did not expect this expansion to "be complete for many months to come."[14] In general, he liked the way the centralization approach was working. DOI staffers were assigned to "cover" individual component agencies of the defense effort and develop expertise about those activities. They would work with centralized staff to issue press releases about developments in their agencies and to answer questions put by reporters.

Press Relations

As before the election, press relations continued to be the central thrust of the daily work of the Division of Information. It maintained a central and busy newsroom. From the day after the election to mid-January 1941, DOI issued 114 press releases, resulting in at least one release per day, sometimes two, seven days a week.[15] There were no slow news days for the production effort. It was, using twenty-first-century parlance, 24/7/365.

DOI staff were careful to designate some releases for afternoon papers so that morning papers did not have a permanent news advantage over their competitors.[16] Responding to the needs of reporters, an internal document discussed pacing the flow of releases so that important news was not issued too close to deadlines or in time to make only the late editions of the papers. The author pointed out that on Saturday afternoon, February 8, 1941, "four or five good stories made only the final sports editions of eastern and middle western papers."[17] This reduced press coverage of important decisions and announcements.

DOI was also diligent about submitting early releases of texts of major speeches to be given by senior officials, with an embargo until delivery. This gave reporters the convenience of writing their stories on a more leisurely basis in advance.[18] Another method of facilitating coverage was for DOI staffers (often former reporters) to attend press conferences by production officials and then release an accurate and verified summary of the statements made by the official at the press conference. This helped assure accuracy and prevent misquotations of important details.[19] DOI also issued some press releases that were essentially summary and feature stories that were not tied to any hard-news developments. Some of these feature-style releases were timed for the high-circulation and bigger Sunday papers.[20]

Public Reporting

Horton continued engaging in public reporting on a methodical and systematic basis through as many media as possible, including newspapers, radio, newsreels, and publications. This continuation of his preelection activities helped confirm retroactively that his focus on reporting during the election season was neither a fluke nor solely a campaign tactic. In a budget-planning document for FY1942, prepared in early December 1940, Horton articulated a justification for public reporting that is nearly a classic definition of its underlying public administration rationale: "The Commission has advised that it must depend on an informed public for cooperation to succeed in its work. To be successful in a democracy—in fact, to work at all—the nation must understand the aims, activities, and accomplishments of the Commission, in order that we may have a coordinated defense program."[21]

Some of the reporting was in the form of summaries and tabulations issued as press releases. For example, a release in November 1940 provided "an analysis of the $2 billion defense construction program," and a January 1941 release provided a compilation of all signed production contracts on a state-by-state basis.[22] The latter was well suited to tailored coverage by local newspapers rather than merely an aggregate national story. Another venue for reporting was a major radio address by a senior official. On November 28, 1940, the production effort's director of research and statistics gave a detailed summary on the radio of results upon the six-month anniversary of its start.[23] Similarly, in early January, Morris Cooke, a consultant to the production effort, reported (again on the radio) on the new initiative to subcontract portions of major defense contracts to small businesses.[24] Horton's press office issued the transcripts of those two speeches as print press releases to further extend media coverage of those reports.

During the postelection period, DOI experimented with a new form of public reporting on the radio. Instead of relying exclusively on talking heads and statistics, it produced a series called *Defense in Action*. This was an attempt to present in concrete terms and dramatize the production effort's record of accomplishment. The theme of the first broadcast in mid-December 1940 was aircraft manufacturing (a touchy subject during the election campaign). The broadcast included live remote segments from a steel mill in Chicago, a tooling company in Cleveland, an engine plant in Hartford, Connecticut, and an aircraft assembly line in California. It concluded with a segment from an Army bomber taking off from New York and flying over the city.[25] This sequence was an effort to track the production of an airplane from start to finish, raw materials to flight. Sensitive to the potentially controversial issue of labor versus management, the speakers at each location were carefully selected to represent both workers and executives. As far as DOI was concerned, the new formula for radio reporting worked successfully, and the division followed up with additional broadcasts.

DOI continued seeking coverage in newsreels. No longer crowded out by election campaigns (or accusations that coverage of the production buildup was covert pro-Roosevelt advertising), the proportion of defense- and DOI-related stories in newsreels increased discernibly. A postelection newsreel by Paramount, a DOI manager told Horton, contained "four or five stories bearing on defense. Two of these were subjects bulletined [*sic*] by this office."[26] Similar increases in coverage were occurring with other newsreel production companies. DOI was actively submitting story ideas. A letter to newsreel editors on November 20 proposed stories on industrial production and apprentice training. All the details for coverage, such as locations, contact persons, and background information, were worked out in advance and provided the editors. DOI wanted to make it as easy as possible for newsreel companies to cover these "stories." Division staff were also working on potential new visual stories. One was to depict the "ghost town" production effort, which involved locating vacant factories and other installations that could be brought back to life for the armament effort. Other potential stories that November included defense highways, consumer protection, Forest Service research on new ways to use wood (at its lab in Madison, Wisconsin), and US Marine Commission ship construction.[27] In general, during the winter of 1940–41, DOI tried to assert its role as the coordinator of all newsreel coverage of defense activities. For the newsreel companies, DOI would be the one-stop liaison office for all requests from the companies. For federal agencies with defense stories worth covering, DOI would be the central coordinator of these potential stories.[28]

The six-month anniversary of the commission's work provided a news peg for another venue for public reporting. In late December, DOI released a summary of arms production activities in pamphlet form. This was a new output for Horton's PR, with the advantage that a publication could be circulated more widely to citizens and had more longevity than a radio broadcast or newsreel. A brochure was a form of retail and direct reporting, rather than indirect and wholesale reporting through the media. The sixteen-page pamphlet was divided into two parts. The first described what the commission was (just before being superseded by OPM), its goals, and how it was structured to implement its mission. The second half of the brochure summarized the contents of NDAC's actions in its half-year life. That part included details on the major contracts and activities in which the commission engaged.[29] While the report was upbeat and positive, it nonetheless was a form of generalized democratic accountability.

Government PR as Persuasion: Widely Held Values, Presidential Communication, and War

One of the notable postelection changes occurring in this transitional period was the first faint flickering of a different tone, a shift from PR that was purely informational to a tilt toward persuasion. This would be the beginning of Horton's effort to come to terms with agency PR that he could declare was not propaganda, but that explicitly involved convincing the audience of a certain value or the correctness of an activity. Still, he was quite hemmed in. The importance of national defense may have been a widely held value, but Roosevelt's evolving and aggressive effort to define it beyond defending the shores from a foreign invasion was not. Certainly, the United States was not in a war, so that exception to the no-propaganda rule of government PR could not be invoked.

One of the earliest manifestations of a new, but slight, persuasion-oriented tone to DOI PR came into view in a late-December radio talk by a consultant to the production effort. His theme was that "if the English-speaking peoples retain their control of the sea, they will retain control of the raw materials necessary to *win* the war."[30] This was an exhortation of the audience that the United States should consider itself in the same category as the United Kingdom and Commonwealth countries, which were in a state of war with Germany and Italy; that the United States needed to participate with them in controlling the seas; that the United States needed to work with them to control raw materials; and that the goal of such action by the United States was to join and win the war. These statements went far beyond the stated policy of the United States in December 1940, far beyond Roosevelt's public statements, and very far ahead of public opinion. Horton, who could explain away that DOI was merely reporting factually what the speaker had said, was nonetheless inching toward a PR program that was ahead of policy and public opinion. Another example of persuasion-oriented PR came from an observer unconnected to DOI. A Harvard researcher wrote a short article on recent developments in radio for *Public Opinion Quarterly.* She described the increase in radio activities. In some, the production effort had "taken to the air to *report* its activities in a series of talks," a noncontroversial public reporting activity. But other series were intended "to *sell* Americanism."[31]

These were two postelection examples of PR that sought to persuade the citizenry of the rightness of a certain activity. The coming year of 1941 would more strongly demonstrate this. It would require Horton to square efforts at persuasive communication with the round hole of "just-the-facts" information activities, which he had posited as DOI's central operating principle. (See the section on posters below regarding persuasive messages for factory workers.)

During this postelection period, Horton also continued to have a direct relationship with the White House regarding press matters, considering himself part of the president's communications team. At the January 3, 1941, meeting of the (soon to be superseded) commission, he said that "the White House" had contacted him. There had been three leaks recently "purportedly coming from Commission sources concerning matters which should be held in confidence until some formal statement is made on them." One of the leaks was extremely sensitive politically because it dealt with confidential matters discussed during the commission's December 20 meeting with the president about reorganizing the defense effort.[32] Commission Secretary (and White House aide) William McReynolds picked up on Horton's comments at the commission meeting and "warned" the commissioners about leaks.[33] The power structure was upside down during this brief imbroglio: Horton represented the White House, McReynolds accepted Horton's directive by telling off the commissioners, and the commissioners were at the bottom of the political heap. It offers an example of the fluid way Roosevelt liked to exercise presidential power. It also provides an example of Horton trying to control PR so that it reflected the president's desires.[34]

Horton's Centralized Structure for Government PR

Horton fervently protected the centralization of all public relations activities of the far-flung, but loosely affiliated entities within NDAC and then OPM. It was a constant battle to negate the inherent autonomy imperative of bureaucracies. For example, he was concerned that the individual silos were beginning to print and distribute brochures and pamphlets to the public without his involvement. For Horton, centralizing the release of printed materials was as important as centralizing press releases. He had a broad view of what government PR encompassed, and it included much more than press relations and public reporting. Showing some skills at bureaucratic in-fighting, he succeeded in having the NDAC's secretariat issue a memo to all entities in January 1941 that the duplicating unit (part of the secretariat's central administrative services office) would accept duplicating jobs "only after such requests have been approved by the Division of Information."[35] This policy would give him the total control he felt he needed to implement his mission.

That same month, Horton complained to the commissioners at a commission meeting of a staffer who spoke at a conference and then gave the news he was announcing in his speech to one newspaper in Detroit. Eventually, AP put it on its national wire, but only as minor news. Other newspapers that ran it, buried it.[36] Horton complained that this muffed a major "opportunity of getting badly needed publicity for a program as significant as this farming out of orders to smaller industries." Commissioners needed to understand that newspapers did not like to report a story after another one had already broken it. That was the rationale for DOI simultaneously releasing information to all reporters in Washington. Everybody got the story at the same time and broke it at the same time. He "emphasized the importance of handling such matters through the authorized channels in Washington."[37] The rarity of subsequent recurrences indicated how relatively successful Horton was in imposing news discipline throughout the rapidly expanding empire of the production effort.

The most intense bureaucratic wrangle over power to control external communications related to the weekly publication *Defense*. It had been launched in late August 1940 by the newly created Division of State and Local Cooperation. The purpose of that division was to muster the participation and involvement with the production buildup by state and local governments and, in turn, the citizenry. This reflected the precedent of World War I, with state and local defense councils helping with the war effort. Similar to the production effort's consumer affairs office, the bulk of the work of the Division of State and Local Cooperation involved disseminating information and encouraging active participation in the national defense effort's far-flung work. Given the importance of information outreach to that division's success, it began publishing a glossy weekly magazine called *Defense*. The magazine was free, but its circulation was limited to members and staff of state and local defense councils. A typical issue, eight pages and in color, contained text on the division's suggestions of activities for state and local councils, examples of what some of their counterparts throughout the country were doing, news summaries on NDAC, and other Washington developments that might affect them. Graphics and photos were liberally used as a way of increasing the appeal to readers.[38]

Given that *Defense* was a venue for disseminating information, Horton thought it belonged in DOI. But his interest was more than a petty bureaucratic turf battle. He felt that the magazine was something of a wasted, or at least misdirected, effort. Rather than sending it only to members of the state and local defense councils, he envisioned giving the publication a much broader readership, including opinion leaders, editors of weeklies, special-interest journals, libraries, and other attentive audiences. They would be, to use the modern term, force multipliers, as the information they received would likely be passed on to ever-larger audiences of which they were at the nexus. He also thought the magazine was unnecessarily fluffy in content and in production values. Glossy paper and the color printing were not worth the cost and potential criticism, he felt.

The annual budget-planning cycle taking place in December 1940 (for FY1942) was an appropriate time to raise these questions about the future of the magazine. On December 19 (the day before Roosevelt announced creation of OPM), NDAC Secretary (and White House assistant) William McReynolds raised the subject with Frank Bane, director of the Division of State and Local Cooperation. Bane quickly responded with a formal letter stating that his plans for the future of the magazine were to continue the status quo, except perhaps increasing the size of each issue. If anyone wanted to receive *Defense* who was not on a state or local council, they could subscribe for a fee.[39]

A few weeks later, Horton replied, similarly in a letter. He summarized his criticism of the current orientation of the contents, its mailing list, and its having "too luxurious a format." He envisioned a more spare publication (on newsprint, black-and-white) with double the pages per issue. It would contain information on all the activities of the production effort, not just those of the Division of State and Local Cooperation. In part, he made the argument based on the premise of public reporting. A magazine with a broader circulation "is necessary for enlightened and intelligent understanding of the development and progress of the defense effort." He also argued that a bigger circulation, which included weeklies and semi-weeklies, would increase the coverage because those outlets were not served by national wire services and other general sources of news originating in Washington. Finally, he shrewdly argued that his takeover of *Defense* would not be a zero-sum decision. Instead, it would be (using modern terminology) win-win, because each issue of DOI's magazine would always include news from the Division of State and Local Cooperation intended for the current readership. So, his takeover would be an add-on, permitting a dual-purpose magazine.[40]

The showdown took place at NDAC's January 3, 1941, meeting. Bane and Horton both made their pitches to the commissioners (who had already received both of their letters). There was "considerable discussion" between the commissioners, a few siding with each division director. Eventually, they reached a consensus, giving *Defense* to DOI, but with "the specific understanding that an amount of space agreed upon in advance will be reserved for the Division of State and Local Cooperation" and giving that division full control over the content of its section of *Defense*.[41] Hardly a compromise, it was a major and clean win for Horton.[42] Now he would have a national venue for widely disseminating information on all of the defense production activities. Also, it would be another way to bypass the Washington press corps and directly reach editors (of other than daily newspapers) and opinion leaders at the grassroots level. Horton transformed *Defense* into the "publication of record" for the entire defense effort, even adding a semi-annual index to permit locating relevant stories on specific subjects.[43]

Incidents such as these demonstrated Horton's forcefulness and intraorganizational talents. But they also gave him, on the outside, the image of a bureaucratic player. In February, columnists Drew Pearson and Robert Allen criticized Horton as "a red-tape past master."[44] In the context of him imposing PR discipline on a large government agency, it was an accurate characterization.[45] Horton's advocacy of the centralization of defense news led to *Newsweek* publishing a rumor supposedly attributed to Lowell Mellett that Horton was about to be given power over all defense-related news, including the War Department and US Army. Only the Navy would be excluded, at least in the first phase of the centralization, *Newsweek* reported.[46] Horton would have loved that happening, but nothing came of it.

A Broad Approach to Government PR

DOI's central foci on the two traditional PR activities of news relations and public reporting covered multiple media venues, including (as discussed above) spot news press releases, feature-oriented press releases, radio appearances, radio programs, newsreels, and brochures. But DOI also significantly enhanced some of the other PR product lines in which it had engaged before the election, including photo stills and movies.

For example, the division significantly expanded its capability to deal with direct inquiries from the public at large, whether in person, by phone, or through the mail. Horton reported that DOI was receiving about three hundred visitors and phone calls per day with requests for information.[47] While no archival statistics could be located on the volume of mail, an internal document referred to handling "large quantities of general informational correspondence replying to inquiries by mail."[48] DOI also operated a small clipping service of daily newspapers so that all senior officials would receive, by midday, a digest of relevant press coverage in that morning's papers.[49] The operation of public inquiry and press digest units by DOI is somewhat surprising, given that Mellett's OGR had such offices, which were intended to serve the entire civilian side of the executive branch.[50] Further, Mellett and Horton ostensibly still had a good relationship, with Mellett functioning somewhat as Horton's mentor and informal presidential supervisor. It could be that Horton rationalized that this was not duplicative because OGR handled general inquiries and DOI limited itself more specifically to those relating to the defense production effort (which was, arguably, closely tied to the military departments, definitely outside Mellett's jurisdiction). Later, during the first six months of 1942, both claimed quite insistently in public that there was no significant overlap or duplication in federal civilian information services between their two agencies. However, at least regarding public inquiries and press clipping, their claims do not appear to have been wholly accurate.[51]

Photos

DOI continued trying to build a comprehensive library of still photos of the national defense effort to depict developments visually for use by publications. It hired a private photographer, Alfred Palmer, to photograph and submit negatives of Army arsenals that were producing ordnance, the Navy Yard in New York, and several midwestern factories. DOI's instructions to him were to provide long shots, medium shots, and close-ups. Palmer had a tendency to take mostly close-ups, which were welcomed by scientific magazines and trade papers, but newswires preferred photos that captured a more encompassing view of a locale. In terms of usage of its collection, the manager overseeing the operation reported, "Business is good, and continues to increase with a big play from trade papers as well as the photo syndicates."[52] To increase the quality of the collection and maximize usage, DOI hired a new full-time staffer to run that office.

By early 1941, the office had grown to the point of needing a formal title and delimitation of its responsibilities. Following Horton's ambition of serving as a superunit over all federal information activities relating to the national defense buildup, the document stated that one of the roles of the office was to "Coordinate the Defense Picture activities of the Government," that is, the entire executive branch.[53] This was an ambitious power grab, and another DOI official noted that if the intent was a single centralized file of negatives, that would be "a real threat to the bureaucratic identity of all government picture agencies." On the other hand, the problem with a more modest mandate of focusing solely on OPM activities was that it did not do much directly. Rather, it cleared contracts signed by the line departments, coordinated multiagency efforts, and the like. "It is hard as hell to conceive of a picture of CO-

ORDINATION. It is hard to photograph," he dryly commented.[54] Through the winter of 1940–41, the stills operation continued muddling through without formally trying to pursue either the broad or narrow definition of its role.

Movies

Besides increased coverage in newsreels after the election as a form of press relations and public reporting (discussed above), Horton used the winter of 1940–41 to expand significantly DOI's involvement in motion pictures. He more formally organized a Motion Picture Section within DOI and named Leo Rosten as its chief.[55] As during the campaign, Rosten continued feeding ideas for shorts on national defense to be produced by the studios.[56] For example, one of the potential studio projects involved filming William Knudsen doing a short standup at the beginning and end of the documentary. Studio executives knew that Knudsen spoke with a soft Scandinavian lilt, and wondered if his voice was a good fit for movies (which tended to advantage men with deep voices and clear enunciation). Horton arranged to send Rosten a demo recording with Knudsen's voice. Another studio wondered about filming a short in nearby Death Valley. It was not only a photogenic and dramatic backdrop, but also relatively accessible to Hollywood given the rather clunky and lumbering technical needs of shooting on location. Horton checked for a national defense angle, but only came up with Borax being mined there for industrial uses. That was not dramatic enough for the medium. The studio was disappointed, apparently hoping for large-scale Army maneuvers there, which would tie in with headlines about desert warfare then under way in North Africa.[57]

As mentioned briefly in the preceding chapter, the expansion of the defense production effort led Horton to seek an alternative route in case Hollywood did not want to produce a short he thought was needed or if the angle the studio wanted did not satisfy him. Horton was glad for anything he and Rosten could get for free from the movie industry. But being utterly dependent on the goodwill and voluntary cooperation of these companies was inadvisable. In the winter of 1940–41, he took major steps to escape Hollywood's exclusive control over what reached the screen. Horton wanted DOI to make its own films. His new film unit would produce shorts from start to finish. He also made sure that exhibitors (who were downstream from producers and sometimes in separate corporations) would accept documentaries that were made by the government.[58]

Government film production had been a very controversial activity during the New Deal. FDR liked the government films, and the conservative coalition in Congress did not. That is what had led to the defunding of the US Film Service at the end of FY1940. Horton felt he was in a somewhat different situation politically and bureaucratically. National defense was a more acceptable subject than, say, movies about a new role for the federal government in the dust bowl. Also, funding for DOI came from a general congressional appropriation that was subject to the exclusive discretionary control of the president, as long as it was for national defense. Congress would not be as willing to meddle in the subdivision of these national defense funds as it was in funds for the US Film Service.

TVA was the first documentary from Horton's office and was released in late 1940. Arch Mercey (of OGR) was the producer. Like government films themselves, the Tennessee Valley Authority was another topic of controversy between the administration and conservatives, with the former approving of publicly generated (and cheaper) electrical power versus power produced by private corporations. While the twenty-minute film had a special emphasis on the relevance of TVA to national defense, it mostly was a straightforward depiction of the multiple purposes of TVA's dam system, not just for power generation but also to reduce flooding and expand the navigability of the rivers.[59] A committee of pedagogues specializing in the use of film judged that the technical quality of *TVA* was "excellent" and the editing handled "skillfully." However, the committee noted that in some places the "commentary and picture are not correlated."[60]

In early February, DOI released a second documentary relating to TVA. This ten-minute short was called *Power for Defense* and more explicitly made the case that building more TVA dams was necessary for the electrical needs of the defense production effort, in particular aluminum.[61] Aluminum was a strategic material that was energy-intensive to manufacture. That is why Alcoa had located many of its plants near major sources of electrical production, in this case, dam sites.[62] Before the release of the new short, exhibitors representing ten thousand movie houses had already agreed to show it, meaning it would reach an estimated audience of 65–70 million people.[63] In late March, Horton reported that *Power for Defense* had "the largest distribution any film has had."[64] The same pedagogic committee that reviewed *TVA* judged *Power for Defense*'s content as "admirably selected to give great unity and dramatic intensity," but so condensed and news-oriented that it would be a good fit for a current events class, but not for a more in-depth class on the subject matter in general.[65]

These movies represented a major qualitative leap for DOI's film activities. The division was institutionalizing the capability to produce its own shorts and documentaries. But this step also reduced the differentiation between information and persuasion. Both films were factual in that they presented what TVA actually did. In that respect, they could even be categorized as a form of popular reporting. However, the subtext of each was the necessity and justification for TVA's existence and activities. Especially with *Power for Defense,* the unstated argument was that the national defense emergency trumped domestic ideological differences over government-produced electricity. Conservatives fumed that FDR was exploiting the cover of national defense to do what Congress otherwise might not have permitted him to do, namely build more TVA dams. The documentary presented a seemingly convincing case that it was a good thing for US national security to expand TVA. This was persuasion by another name, even propaganda in at least one respect, intended to convince the audience of the rightness of a certain governmental action.

The expanding library of video products also led DOI into a new medium: television. While TV gained popularity in the postwar era, it was in existence and functioning before World War II. In late November 1940, Robert Collyer, who headed DOI video efforts, reported to Horton that he had received inquiries from NBC's TV program director seeking to broadcast just about any film stock that DOI could furnish, such as *Power for Defense* and *Men and Ships.*[66] Foreshadowing the 1950s debate about free TV versus the movies, Collyer wondered if the free broadcasting of *Power for Defense* on TV might reduce the willingness of movie exhibitors to show it. He concluded that it would not, that the "advance publicity" gained by TV broadcast would outweigh exhibitor qualms regarding exclusiveness. Collyer also reported on his inquiries to two other TV companies, CBS and DuMont. CBS was not yet on the air, but expressed interest in showing DOI material when the time came. DuMont was already on the air, but had not yet responded to Collyer's initial letter of inquiry.[67]

New PR Activity: Posters

Horton's expansive view of the scope of DOI's mission and brand, along with the intensification of the war abroad and the increase in the defense production effort, led DOI to start a new product line: posters. An origin of this initiative came from Morris Cooke, an industrial consultant to the production effort, who had suggested that DOI promote some competitions and awards in order to increase the morale (and subsequent productivity) of the workers in industrial plants.[68] This led to DOI considering worker morale as part of its portfolio. This was no stretch. In November, a Harvard professor specializing in government and communication emphasized that the morale of civilians working in the production effort was as important as the morale of the troops.[69] DOI began this new initiative by issuing a poster to help motivate the workforce in defense industries. The first poster was released in mid-January 1941. It had very little artwork and was mostly text, first some quotes from the president followed by some exhortations from OPM director general William Knudsen.[70] This first OPM poster for defense workers was such a novelty at the time that the *New York Times* reproduced it.[71] (Posters for the general public came later.)

Perhaps the unintended significance of this first poster was its explicit effort at persuasion, in this case of increased production. The copy included such appeals as, "Let's get squarely behind our President's appeal," "Let's work together building that 'GREAT ARSENAL OF DEMOCRACY' in record time," and "Let's go!"[72] Clearly, this new venue for communication and the underlying purpose of the message was to convince the audience of the rightness of an idea and then to influence the audience's subsequent behavior. This was far from DOI merely releasing neutral information. It was getting into the persuasion business, albeit in a narrow context.

Administrative Sketch

Budgeting

Horton's postelection policy and planning document segued to the annual budgeting exercise, his next management task. In the traditional routines of American government, winter months are dominated by the budgeting cycle. At the time, the federal government operated on a fiscal year basis, from July 1 to June 30, with fiscal years named by the year in which they ended. Hence, FY1942 would begin on July 1, 1941. In order to give Congress adequate time to review and pass annual appropriations bills, presidents usually submitted their annual budget proposals in January. Working further backward, that meant the Bureau of the Budget (BOB) prepared its budget proposals for presidential decision making at the turn of the year. The process generally began in November and December, when agencies prepared and submitted their budget requests to BOB. Hence, with the passing of the election, one of Horton's immediate duties was to prepare and submit DOI's budget proposal for FY1942. This presented Horton with an opportunity to crystallize his conceptualization of the division, its scope, and its activities in a postelection context. His general planning assumption for his proposed budget was based on a continuation of the status quo in terms of the division's responsibilities, NDAC/OPM's work, and the state of the world war. During the winter of 1940–41, Horton followed through on the themes contained in his FY1942 budget-planning documents (even though the beginning of the next fiscal year was more than a half year away). He sought to continue the work of the division from the preelection period, but more specifically to expand, enhance, and sharpen those PR activities.

Along with the rest of the national defense program, DOI had now existed for a half year. With no end or significant change in sight, Horton's division was gradually taking on the routine characteristics of the life of a federal agency, such as generating in-house paperwork prompted by the FY1942 budgeting cycle. While the documentation is sketchy, for the second half of FY1941, DOI's annualized budget was about $186,000.[73] But it was growing so fast that some budgeting and planning documents for FY1942 were practically out of date by mid-FY1941, sometimes even before they could be finalized.

Staffing

The postelection sense that the lid was off was most evident in DOI's payroll. The agency could expand much more robustly to fulfill its mission. Its growth was so significant that DOI offices had to be moved to a building with more space, along with some other growing national defense agencies.[74] Horton's empire was fast becoming one of the major players in the federal information establishment of the entire executive branch.

In a draft of a budget justification document prepared in early December 1940, Horton stated that the division was "at present seriously undermanned" and was meeting the duties assigned it only due to the cooperation of noninformation staff in the various subagencies of the defense effort.[75] This was quickly remedied, not even waiting until the next fiscal year. During this winter period, DOI mushroomed from about 28 positions in early December to about 170, a quantum leap in size and scope.[76] Horton continued poaching the Washington press corps, hiring two more "top-flight" reporters.[77]

A significant administrative detail relates to the official personnel status of DOI (and other defense production) staff. Were they temporary federal employees outside the civil service system or permanent employees in the classified civil service who were merely in a (presumably) temporary agency relating to the national defense emergency? FDR wanted the latter. To help settle the issue, in mid-1940 (before the election) he quietly signed Executive Order 8514, which bolstered the status of employees in the national defense effort. It declared that probationary federal employees working in permanent agencies could transfer to the defense agencies without losing their status or the time already served on probation.[78] This had the effect of eliminating a barrier to DOI successfully recruiting civil servants to transfer to DOI, even if they were on probationary status.[79] The subtext of the new policy was equally important. The defense agencies were becoming integral parts of the executive branch and the classified civil service. Roosevelt was tearing down bureaucratic obstacles that would diminish the talent pool for DOI and its sister agencies. In that sense, the executive order (and other related personnel policies) helped DOI become a "regular" part of the federal government, with all the attractions of the classified civil service. This not only increased the professionalism of the workforce, but also helped rebut potential political criticism that the division (or any other defense agency) was a patronage haven for political hacks and cronies who lacked the skills and talents needed to do their jobs. That line of attack was a relatively permanent criticism by the conservative coalition on Capitol Hill of many of the New Deal agencies, which were sometimes staffed by appointees outside the classified civil service.

The downside of the expansion of the jurisdiction of the US Civil Service Commission (CSC) to DOI was that there was now a significant amount of

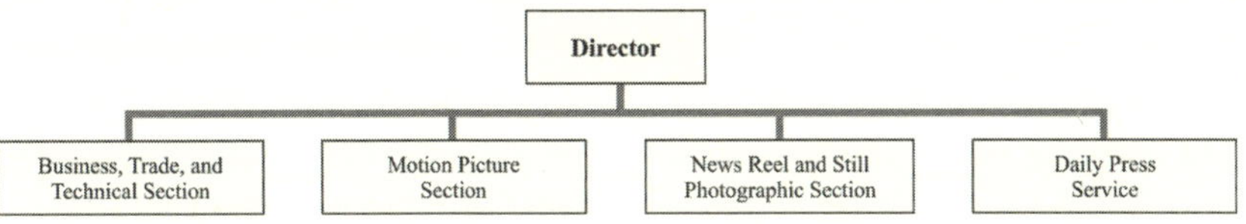

DOI Organization Chart, December 1940.

Attachment to memo from Mr. Olson to Miss Ruth Bledsoe, January 3, 1941. Folder: Personnel Recommendations, Box 9, Entry 576A, RG 208, National Archives II.

red tape involved in creating, recruiting, and hiring for these civil service positions. In particular, the need for a precise position description was required, because the salary range, professional category, and its place (called "grade") in that career track had to be approved. For example, the CSC maintained six grades in the stenographic and secretarial category: Junior Clerk-Stenographer, Assistant Clerk-Stenographer, Clerk-Stenographer, Senior Clerk-Stenographer, and the highest category (CAF-6 in CSC lingo) for "positions which involve duties and responsibilities very peculiar to the individual position."[80] Every secretarial position in DOI that Horton and his managers wanted to fill first had to be correctly categorized on this grade ladder and then approved by the CSC before any hiring (or transfer) could occur.

While position descriptions for secretarial responsibilities were well defined and easy to reuse, that was not necessarily the case for DOI's professional positions. Numerous PR jobs were nearly one of a kind, thus requiring writing a de novo position description practically every time. For example, for a photographic editor, the position description begins with it having "wide latitude for independent judgment," almost as an alibi for the inability to give the CSC the kind of precise and detailed information it routinely requested, especially when determining the grade within the larger category and career track.[81] For a former reporter to be the senior information specialist for the Defense Housing Coordinator, the description sought to peg the relative importance of the Housing Coordinator's standing compared to some other production divisions. It was "a program which is of less than the greatest importance from a public relations standpoint," but the position holder, nonetheless, "performs highly difficult and responsible informational and public relations work."[82]

Summary and Commentary

During the election campaign, Horton was figuratively walking on tiptoes, trying to help the president while minimizing unnecessary controversy emanating from DOI and NDAC. After the election, the lid was off. DOI now expanded rapidly. This was not only due to the postelection stage in the political calendar, but also reflected events abroad. As Germany advanced from triumph to triumph, the democratic front opposing it consisted of little more than the United Kingdom and its Commonwealth nations. As its fate was held by an ever-thinner thread, Roosevelt wanted to significantly increase defense production, partly to rearm the United States for national defense and partly for supplies that could be legally provided to Great Britain (with Roosevelt willing to stretch the definition of legality to its utmost).

Horton's PR activities during the winter of 1940–41 hewed in part to the definition of noncontroversial government public relations. He maximized release of information to the news media as part of the traditional role of government PR vis-à-vis the press. Horton also continued with a broadly defined public reporting activity, justified as a necessary aspect of democratic governance. He inaugurated some newer activities, too, such as more publications for public distribution, obtaining control over duplication services and *Defense* magazine, expansion of the photo stills library, in-house production of film shorts, and expanding DOI's capability to respond to increases in walk-in, phone, and mailed public inquiries.

As described in the introduction, there were three relatively common exceptions to the "just-the-facts" limits on government PR: widely held values, presidential communication, and wartime. In this twilight period of neither peace nor war, Horton was close to crossing some of the red lines defining government public relations. If he actually scaled any of the political fences hemming in government PR, it was probably the exception dealing with promoting widely held values. On a few occasions, he permitted DOI's PR to shift from ostensible information sharing to persuasion-oriented communication on subjects about which beliefs were not universally shared. There was no public consensus about the war overseas and the role of the United States. During the winter of 1940–41, a few of DOI's products appeared to be telling the American people what was needed of them and to garner their support. The underlying purpose of some of the speeches, radio programs, movie shorts, and posters was to justify activities that were not consensus values. These included the common link of the English-speaking peoples, radio series that were essentially *selling* Americanism, the positive value of the TVA (conveyed through the equally controversial venue of government-produced films), and a poster to boost the morale of war matériel workers in order to increase productivity.

All these were explicitly or implicitly exhortations, persuasive communication regarding the nonshared values of the public. Horton was promoting several defense-related causes, but these were not widely held opinions within the body politic at the time. Ever so gingerly, with caution and care, he was trying to *persuade* the public that the United States should do whatever was necessary to protect democracies from fascism. History vindicated Horton, as he was on the winning side. But the precedent for crossing one of the red lines circumscribing government public relations would remain, in principle, controversial.

Regarding the presidential exception to restrictions on government PR, during this period Horton retreated from being publicly identified as a de facto presidential spokesman. He was less closely identified with the president than he had been during the campaign. But he continued to work with the White House to assure that OPM PR would reflect the president's thinking. Concerning the wartime exception to providing neutral government information, Horton was careful that DOI's PR would not convey a warmongering or overtly war-supporting position. Yes, he was discussing the need for a strong national and hemispheric defense, but that was an acceptable stance, even hard for isolationists to argue with. He was not explicitly trying to mobilize public opinion to support going to war.

CHAPTER 4

AN OVERVIEW OF HORTON'S AUTONOMOUS DIVISION OF INFORMATION

March–December 1941

The "rules" of government public relations (as described in the introduction) were pretty clear in their application for times of peace and times of war. Only neutral information in peacetime, some persuasive communications permitted in wartime or comparable national emergencies. But things got difficult when it was neither, or, perhaps more precisely, both. A world war was raging; the United States was legally neutral, definitely not in a constitutional state of war, but something of an active noncombatant favoring one side. For that reason, Horton's work during this time was the most difficult and tricky (in both meanings of the word). The world war had begun on September 1, 1939, when Germany invaded Poland (and the Soviet Union followed later in the month). So, strictly speaking, Horton had been operating in this delicate environment during the second half of his time at the Maritime Commission, although the agency was somewhat distanced from the center of the action. Then, his work at NDAC in 1940 was dominated by Roosevelt's political career, first his coyness as to whether he would run for an unprecedented third term and then the campaign itself. Therefore, there is greater clarity regarding the complex public environment for practicing government PR in the period after the November 1940 election until Pearl Harbor in early December 1941. Given the significance of this thirteen-month stretch, this narrative divided the period into two. The first portion covered the postelection winter of 1940–41, when DOI became affiliated with the Office of Production Management (see chap. 3). This chapter and the next cover the second part, from March to December 1941, when DOI was more formally an independent agency within the Office for Emergency Management (OEM). During this period, there was an onrush of major developments in the war situation (even though the United States was still, formally, at peace), which in turn affected domestic developments (see table 4). Horton was again tiptoeing through a political minefield, trying to stretch DOI's persuasion-oriented work to the limits without triggering major backlash from FDR's isolationist and conservative opponents. In particular, he needed to keep a close eye on Capitol Hill and the media, stakeholders who were preternaturally opposed to government PR, whether in war, peace, or anything in between.

President Roosevelt Establishes DOI as an Independent Agency within OEM

From the beginning of his presidency, Roosevelt was attuned to the importance of public relations. Not just public relations by him and the White House press secretary, but by the federal government at large. In a 1939 radio interview hosted by Lowell Mellett, he explained his rationale: "It seems to me important that before the people pass on the size of, or the question of

Table 4
Events when Horton headed the Division of Information (before Pearl Harbor)

TIME PERIOD	INTERNATIONAL	DOMESTIC
March–December 6, 1941	Rommel attacks in North Africa; Germany invades Yugoslavia, then Greece, then Soviet Union; United Kingdom retreats from Crete; Japan and Soviet Union sign neutrality treaty; Churchill and FDR meet off Newfoundland, declare Atlantic Charter; German submarines attack US Navy destroyers *Greer, Kearny,* and *Reuben James;* Japan masses troops in Indochina; British counteroffensive in North Africa.	FDR signs Lend-Lease bill; declares unlimited state of national emergency; Congress approves request for $7 billion in military credit to United Kingdom for Lend-Lease; United States seizes Axis ships in US harbors; extends its naval protection to Greenland; occupies Iceland as forward base for shipping; extends aid to Soviet Union; freezes Japanese assets in United States; cuts off oil shipments to Japan; Congress renews draft by one-vote margin; permits arming of US merchant vessels; FDR permits Navy to "shoot on sight" German submarines in Atlantic; United States occupies Dutch Guiana.

continuing, these functions [that is, new government programs] *they should have an opportunity to obtain some factual information about them.* The people, through Congress, have the right, at any time, to end any individual function, to increase it, or to add new functions. That is why knowledge of what Government does today is of such great importance."[1] For FDR, robust public relations in public administration was an inherent part of democracy, accountability, and decision making. Simultaneously, it was also, of course, very beneficial politically.

Public relations continued to be on Roosevelt's mind a few months later when he strategized with Louis Brownlow on organizing a national defense production buildup (see chap. 2). During those conversations, he told Brownlow that one of the reasons he opposed the Army and Navy's plan for an all-powerful economic czar was that it would strip him of such a broad swath of executive powers that he would not only be ceding control over the economy, but "even the public relations of the White House."[2] This explicit desire by the president to control both national defense preparedness and the public relations for it culminated in the early spring of 1941.

During the late winter and early spring of 1941, President Roosevelt was actively involved in another aspect of government public relations, notwithstanding the important developments in the war. He wanted to institutionalize Mellett's public relations agency, the Office of Government Reports (OGR).[3] Ever since establishing OGR as one of the five original EOP agencies in September 1939, Roosevelt had sought to further "regularize" its existence by seeking to shift its funding (beginning with FY1942) from episodic emergency relief appropriation bills to the annual appropriations process, which in this specific case was the Independent Offices Appropriation bill. When Roosevelt failed to accomplish that indirectly—because OGR had no *statutory* basis—he realized that the only way to keep OGR alive and make it permanent was by obtaining congressional authorization for funding the agency through the regular lawmaking process. At his request, the chairmen of the House and Senate standing committees that had general jurisdiction over OGR introduced bills to do that on February 16, 1941. On February 26, after a public hearing, a House committee recommended the bill on a party-line vote. The conservative coalition tried its best the kill the bill at every step of the way, sometimes depicting it as a propaganda bill, sometimes contradictorily as a censorship bill.[4] The president's struggle to pass the bill through Congress was no run-of-the-mill controversy. The *New York Times* reported that the intensity of the fight over the OGR bill was comparable to the fight over the just-passed Lend-Lease bill.[5] The comparison of the OGR bill to the historic Lend-Lease legislative battle conveys the depth and intensity of Roosevelt's push for it and the conservative coalition's efforts to kill it. Overcoming immense political odds, the bill passed and Roosevelt signed it on June 9, 1941.

The FY1942 budgeting cycle for OGR drew similar presidential attention to DOI, its legality, and its authorization to spend congressionally appropriated funds. Budget-wise, DOI was a slightly different case from OGR. OGR had been funded up to then by occasional emergency relief bills. During the defense buildup, Congress passed several major national defense appropriations bills. Some of these bills assigned to the president full discretion to allocate those funds for specific activities and purposes. DOI received its funding under an overall sum that the president allocated from these national defense appropriations, initially for the general operation of NDAC.[6]

As discussed in chapter 2, the ongoing legality of DOI's operations continued to be somewhat tenuous. Nothing formal or official had occurred since the commission hired Horton as director of public relations on June 3, 1940. Everything that happened after that was Horton's own doing: the creation of the *Division* of Public Relations, the change of his title to director of information and the division's to Division of Information, and his assertions of the power to coordinate the radio PR of all federal agencies involved in national defense. All along, to justify the authority of what he did at NDAC, Horton had strung together several phrases in the original 1916 legislation creating the Council of National Defense, an entity that was wholly separate legally from FDR's *Advisory Commission* to that council.

The same month when FDR was fighting in Congress to get OGR legally sanctioned, he tried his best—within his presidential powers—to do something similar for DOI. On February 28, 1941, he sent a formal letter to OEM liaison officer William McReynolds informing him of the funding he was allocating to OEM from his discretionary national defense funds for the last four months of FY1941.[7] In the last paragraph of the letter, seemingly one last minor detail, Roosevelt stated: "I further authorize you to establish a Division of Information in the Office for Emergency Management and, within budgetary limitations, to appoint such personnel as is necessary for its operation. This Division, under your direction and supervision, shall provide central informational services to the several agencies in the Office for Emergency Management."[8]

Several important details were embedded in this short two-sentence paragraph.[9] First, DOI would now be a freestanding agency within OEM. It would not be a subdivision of the new OPM or the fading NDAC. Rather, it would be their organizational *equivalent*. This meant that Horton was not subordinate to the heads of any of the other existing (and future) silos in OEM. Second, while McReynolds was to direct and supervise OEM, he was not the *director* of OEM, whereas a director's position existed in some of OEM's sister agencies in EOP, such as BOB and OGR.[10] McReynolds was merely the OEM liaison officer. That meant his hierarchical powers over Horton were diminished compared to, for example, senior BOB managers who reported to the budget director. Third, McReynolds was being instructed by the president to establish DOI. This was not a mere suggestion of a possible course of action, but an explicit directive. Finally, the reference to "budgetary limitations" related to an earlier part of the letter where the president allocated to OEM units, including DOI, specific budget funding for the remainder of the fiscal year. DOI's budget was not McReynolds's to decide.

With that official letter, the president untethered DOI and Horton from any control by other agencies or senior officers in OEM other than, arguably, McReynolds. Roosevelt was re-creating it as an independent agency, a *presidential* information service relating to all aspects of the arms production effort. DOI was FDR's creation, for the specific purpose of conducting PR for the mobilization of the economy for defense.[11]

The DOI section of the letter was also important for what it did not say. Roosevelt would not be pursuing a statutory authorization for DOI as he was in the midst of struggling to accomplish that very week for OGR. The presidential letter, and its close link to a congressional appropriation delegating to the president full discretion to spend as he directed for national defense purposes, was as strong a legal footing for DOI as Roosevelt could accomplish. The president was also implicitly acknowledging the major legislative hurdles that he was facing at that time with the OGR bill. Even if the OGR bill passed (as it did), it was unlikely that political lightning could strike twice for presidential public relations. Playing out such a scenario further, if Roosevelt hypothetically had asked for a DOI authorizing statute and lost, then the legitimacy of its continued administrative existence could be challenged as violating Congress's decision not to approve it.

Following up on Roosevelt letter, on March 5, McReynolds sent Horton a brief memo.[12] First, "I hereby designate you" to be director of the Division of

Information in OEM. The choice of verbs is probably significant. McReynolds was not *appointing* Horton. That would have implied that Horton had held no related office before, that this was a de novo personnel action. McReynolds was merely re*designating* Horton for a duty that in the status quo ante Horton was already doing. Second, McReynolds stated that Horton would operate "under my direction and supervision," replicating the phraseology used in the president's letter. However, this was largely a de jure statement. When he had been NDAC's secretary, McReynolds had declined to supervise Horton. This would not change now. So, on a de facto basis, Horton was unsupervised. At most, Mellett was vaguely his informal mentor and contact person at the White House (as was Press Secretary Stephen Early). According to Catton, Horton now "worked for the President" and was answerable to no one in the hierarchy besides Roosevelt personally.[13]

The last step in the process was to release the news publicly. As a former journalist and PR official who advocated for maximal release of information, Horton knew that Roosevelt's decisions in his February 28 letter and McReynolds's implementation of them needed to be made public. But the strengthening of DOI's status could be very controversial if noticed by Roosevelt's opponents. So, Horton did everything he could to bury the news. He issued the release on Friday, March 14, 1941.[14] Friday was typically considered a relatively slow news day in Washington. Horton also designated the release for the afternoon and evening papers, which even then were beginning to become somewhat secondary to morning newspapers in importance, impact, and readership. Finally, he buried the news about DOI in a much longer and boring release about reorganization of the divisional structure of OEM, an eye-glazing subject to most reporters. The news went virtually unnoticed.[15] Only columnist Paul Mallon commented on it critically. He was amazed that the senior officials in OPM "do not even control their own publicity men."[16]

Roosevelt's maneuvers to give DOI as strong a legal status as he could (short of OGR-style authorization legislation or a CPI-style executive order) worked. In June 1941, a House Appropriations subcommittee was considering an omnibus deficiency funding bill that included, among many other subjects and agencies, funding of OEM's units for FY1942. Horton was called to testify on the DOI budget, in the same routine way that heads of other OEM silos did, such as Nelson Rockefeller testifying on his agency dealing with Latin American relations. During Horton's appearance, while some of the subcommittee members were relatively hostile to all government PR, none challenged DOI's legal standing or its ability to receive and spend funds appropriated to the president for his discretionary spending on the national defense emergency.[17] Roosevelt's handling of it had been pitch-perfect.

While FDR continued tinkering with the defense (and then war) structure for the rest of the emergency period, his February 1941 decision set a relatively permanent structure for the information apparatus of the production buildup. That status quo lasted until June 1942. This was a relatively long time based on Roosevelt's nearly constant tinkering with the structure of the (nonmilitary) defense and war effort, changes that were sometimes prompted by new realities, Washington politics, or all matter of other factors he was juggling.

Press Relations

Roosevelt's declaration of freedom for DOI was significant in terms of bureaucratic politics, power, and autonomy. However, in day-to-day terms, the president's letter didn't trigger any major qualitative change in Horton's and DOI's work. In a sense, Roosevelt's action was merely bringing legalities to catch up to reality. The absence of major structural change in standard operating procedures was evident in the most visible of DOI's PR work, press relations.

The big change was in quantity. DOI began issuing a flood of news. It had so many press releases that its press room was open twenty-four hours a day, seven days a week. A rough statistical comparison is stark. When Roosevelt established OPM in January 1941, Horton discontinued his series of NDAC press releases that were in the PR series (for "press release"). The last was PR-351 on January 15, 1941, roughly two per weekday since PR-1 in June 1940.[18] DOI then started a new series, "PM" (for production management).[19] From then until Pearl Harbor (about eleven months later), DOI issued 1,727 press releases in that series.[20] In April 1941, a DOI staffer calculated that the rate was an average of six per day, each one about four pages long.[21] In an average month in 1941, DOI distributed 4 million mimeograph pages of news.[22] To reduce costs and conserve materials, it began mimeographing all press releases on both sides of a sheet of paper.[23] A reporter described the DOI press room: "Its press room is a motion picture man's dream of frantic reporters, littered tables, shouted orders, ringing telephones. While showers of press releases pour down at all hours, announcing new orders and decisions, all of them fateful to some town, company or industry. Great personages are buttonholed for an interview while they stalk past the door to the board room. Often the reporters are summoned in for conferences with the top men."[24]

DOI tried to its best accommodate the needs of the press. But Horton's effort to create a well-oiled press release machine did not always function as planned. For example, DOI always wanted to release—on an embargoed basis—speeches by senior officials at least one day in advance. That would give reporters time to review its contents, decide whether to cover it, and, if so, to have adequate time to write an accurate and comprehensive article. It didn't always happen that way.[25] Other commonly recurring staff headaches included "Releases failing to make deadlines" and "Why in the hell can't we coordinate releases?"[26]

Horton could not always accommodate the press. For example, the reporters grumbled that they weren't getting enough access to the major decision makers and weren't permitted exclusive interviews. Horton was unapologetic. This was not feasible, given the number of reporters clamoring for such venues. Instead, he tried to schedule regular press briefings by the senior policy makers.[27]

Despite his best efforts to serve the press, reporters sometimes reverted to criticizing Horton. One particularly sharp comment described him as "cowardly" for not using his organizational independence to pry more information from OPM agencies. Given that he was not anybody's subordinate, he should be able to stand up to the senior policy makers in OPM, go toe-to-toe with them and have "more latitude in determining what's to be put out, what's to be soft-pedaled, instead of having to respect the wishes of OPM's assorted brass-hats."[28] Privately, Horton would have agreed with the sentiment and the goal, but even as the head of an independent OEM agency, he was able to push senior bureaucrats around just so much.

The central press office released information of the activities of eight units within OPM. While this was done on a centralized basis, DOI press staffers were assigned to each of the silos so they could develop expertise in the work of that unit. DOI provided reporters with the names and phone numbers of each of those staffers so that reporters could contact them directly with queries or for follow-up information.[29] However, Horton was careful to prevent reporters from luring a staffer assigned to one silo into contradicting a counterpart in another or from asking to go off the record to get inside information. To the disgust of reporters who liked to function that way, he directed that a phone call from a reporter to a DOI staffer who was detailed to an individual agency "is taken down in shorthand by a stenographer and transcribed for the OPM's permanent files."[30]

Assigning staff to individual OEM agencies always carried the risk that DOI's staff would "go native" and become advocates for "their" agency. At one point in 1941, a member of the central staff was concerned that too many press releases contained "cant," by which he meant releases that were too sympathetic to the perspective of their silo and "fail to realize their role—to keep the public fully and accurately informed."[31]

Horton cultivated an organizational culture with firm and explicitly stated values regarding press relations. In an internal document not intended for public consumption or to look good to reporters, he wrote: "It is the policy of the Division to move all information to the public through all media as fast as cleared. All announcements are statements of fact without comments, editorializing, opinion, or personality comment. . . . All news, good or bad, not a military secret, should be made available as early as possible."[32] This formal policy was distinctive, reflecting Horton's understanding of a reporter's perspective. He was essentially establishing transparency and freedom of information principles decades before those terms were invented. DOI official (and former reporter) Bruce Catton elaborated on Horton's operating principles in a speech to the Michigan Press Association. The DOI press service "is there to help the newspapers inform the public about the defense program. It is not there to cover up or to interpose a barrier between the public and the defense mechanism; it is not there to conceal mistakes or to impede the normal flow of information in any way. I can assure you that it does not so operate. It is designed to help you in your task of getting news about the defense program to the people."[33]

In 1941, the running battle inside the defense effort between pro-business dollar-a-year men and pro-labor New Dealers sometimes played out through competing DOI press releases. During this period, a Detroit advertising agency submitted to William Knudsen (the former GM CEO) a memo regarding who was getting more publicity in DOI releases: officials with business backgrounds or those who were pro-labor? The study concluded that DOI releases were heavily and deliberately slanted to highlight pro-labor messages and to understate the role of officials with business backgrounds. According to Catton, Knudsen showed it to Horton with some mirth and then theatrically threw it away.[34]

Horton was not exercised about public disagreements between silos. These sometimes reflected the business versus labor conflict, but just as often concerned nonideological disagreements on policy, priorities, and goals. Horton favored letting each silo release its position. He would not impose a gag on agency disagreements.[35] This happened, for example, regarding differences of opinion between two OEM agencies about potential shortages of silk for consumers. A magazine for the advertising and PR industry complained about such open and public disagreements between agencies. Yes, reporters liked conflict and DOI was chock full of ex-reporters who understood the business. But the journalistic approach to federal PR was the opposite of a "super-efficient propaganda machine," at least one that would stay on message and not confuse the consumers.[36] These kinds of open conflicts were leading to the impression of a mess in Washington. Horton was only nonplussed about airing disagreements if one side was plainly inaccurate about stated policy or perhaps even was reflecting an agenda other than OPM's. This happened in June 1941 when a senior official (who was formerly employed by electric companies) said in a speech that there was adequate supply of electricity to cover defense needs.[37] A DOI spokesman reacted quickly: "Four hours later, OPM issued a point blank repudiation" of the comments and asserted that there *was* a need to build additional power-generating facilities.[38] The official who gave the speech promptly quit.[39]

During this period, DOI began issuing a relatively novel permutation on newspaper releases: radio news releases. These were short segments on daily news developments, essentially converting the news into a (written) structure that fit the needs of radio. On June 9, George McMillan, who headed the daily press operations, pointed out to Assistant DOI Director Robert Straus that the division was overlooking radio news.[40] At the time, the national newswire services provided their radio subscribers with what was called a "radio wire." This consisted of daily news material that could be read on the air and was tailored for use by the news departments of radio stations. McMillan suggested creating a "Daily Defense Roundup" that the newswire services could include in their own radio wires.[41] This approach would focus on spot news, that is, the daily headlines on major developments. Indicating the fast pace that Horton set for all of DOI, this new product went from idea to reality in about three weeks, but with an add-on service.

Besides facilitating radio news coverage of daily news from Washington-based radio wires, DOI began offering directly to radio stations a (printed) daily radio news release mailing providing additional feature-style background information on headline stories.[42] This had the effect of cutting out the middle man and permitting DOI to work directly with radio news outlets around the country. By early July, DOI was routinely issuing radio news releases. An example related to a mailing to radio stations in the South urging residents to reduce their electricity consumption so that more could be dedicated to the production of aluminum. The distinctiveness of the radio release was that it was *not* written in the familiar formula of newspapers: a lead paragraph containing all the important who-what-when-where information, following by paragraphs of decreasing importance, so that a newspaper could cut off a story wherever it wished and the reader would still have the most important information. Instead, radio news releases were worded in a format that was friendly to the needs of the medium, particularly a format that told a story in a narrative style rather than the condensed telegraphic one that newspapers used.[43] By the middle of July, barely a month after McMillan suggested it, DOI had routinized radio news releases to the point that it needed a coordinator of radio news. It was already refining what it produced and to whom it mailed them. For example, it realized that radio commentators weren't interested in receiving the radio releases.[44]

DOI was also aware of the existence of significant foreign-language press and radio programming in the United States, with an audience often dominated by first- and second-generation immigrants. In part, reaching those populations simply called for translating and then distributing on a timely basis the general news announcements by OPM as well as feature material. In other cases, editorial materials could be prepared specifically for the immigrant audience due to particularized interests, rather than just translations of what was being distributed to English-language newspaper and radio audiences.

Immigrants often were disproportionately represented in some unskilled and blue-collar employment categories (due to below-average formal education and/or language barriers). This meant the foreign-language press was especially important to reach regarding labor issues. DOI's general concern about the morale of workers in production plants was especially salient for immigrants working there, partly due to lack of understanding, partly to discrimination. One memo noted: "Acute problems of discrimination in defense employment against foreign born or second generation workers, especially Italians, have been reported in a number of communities. These discriminations are widely heralded—in fact overplayed—in many of the foreign language papers and are grist in the mill of Axis agents."[45] DOI worked closely with OPM's Labor Division to reach the foreign-language press, especially about these sensitive labor-related issues.[46]

Public Reporting

DOI's public reporting expanded significantly in 1941. Quantitatively, there were more such reports. Qualitatively, Horton pressed for finding more ways to push summary information out the front door, seeking more venues to communicate what OEM was doing. At a meeting with publishers of technical and trade journals in midsummer, he plainly articulated the centrality of reporting to the defense program. Given the changes during 1941 in the US role vis-à-vis the war overseas (such as Lend-Lease) and the impact of these developments on the national defense production, he said that "the program cannot be a success if the public doesn't *understand* it."[47] DOI's comprehensive reporting activities in 1941 were aimed at reaching the public at large to explain what OEM was doing and why.

The first major reporting milestone after DOI became independent was the one-year anniversary of the defense effort in May. DOI organized a multimedia effort for this first annual report with the goal of the widest possible distribution to reach as many people as possible. It included a twenty-page booklet,[48] radio program,[49] press release,[50] and stills for feature stories.[51] Explicitly using reporting nomenclature, DOI conceived of these activities as "an annual report to the 130,000,000 shareholders of the cooperative called the United States of America."[52] Other print-oriented reports continued throughout the year including updated summaries of all major military contracts by state.[53] In itself, this was a form of reporting, but it sometimes generated local press coverage, too.[54]

Using a different approach to reporting, DOI continued sending out series of preformatted feature stories to newspapers and other print publications. A six-part series titled "War Against Waste" was distributed in mid-October with publication release dates for the last week of the month.[55] Another series, titled "Materials for Defense," was for November.[56] In a variation on this product, DOI also began providing a full-page preformatted layout combining text, art, and photos. For example, in mid-May, it distributed to publishers a spread on torpedo production. The spread included a heading, copy, and five photos depicting the manufacture of torpedoes. This was important, it stated, "to make more secure America's defense on the sea and to strengthen a fast-growing two-ocean Navy."[57]

DOI also invented a graphic way to depict the facts of the defense effort. Horton created a progress-report staff group with the mission of providing "an instantaneous visual picture, corrected weekly, of defense progress."[58] This had an in-house management and control role, but it was especially effective for public reporting purposes. Beginning in August, a box score headlined "Defense Progress" with a running summary of production statistics for the week became a permanent front-page feature in *Defense*.[59]

For radio reporting, DOI continued with its series *Defense in Action* (see chap. 3). This was an effort to make radio reporting more interesting and engaging to the audience by originating the broadcasts from actual locations of the defense effort. For example, the third broadcast of the series was aired on March 25 and had the theme of on-the-job training programs in the defense industries. It included remotes from New York, New Jersey, Ohio, Colorado, and California.[60] Additional reports in the series continued through the year.[61] An outside expert in the use of radio for pedagogic purposes praised DOI for making copies of its radio reports available to schools. The programs contained "up-to-date, accurate information concerning progress" in the defense effort. They were useful for teachers to use in class, he recommended.[62]

Besides the radio reporting series, DOI presented other radio broadcasts that were also explicitly presented as reports. They included Knudsen's "Defense Report" in September and Horton's "OEM Defense Report" in October.[63] In a slightly different format, Procter and Gamble donated some time on its radio "soaps" in early December "to aid the OEM in informing the public about the defense program."[64] The first program was broadcast on Friday, December 5, the last weekday before Pearl Harbor.

Horton also conceived of DOI's film shorts and newsreels as reporting. Specifically using the reporting terminology, he viewed films as a way to "give the public film progress *reports*."[65] So, for example, many DOI shorts began with the title card "The Office of Production Management presents a Defense *report* on film."[66] This was the cinematic equivalent of a print or radio report, but visually much more engaging. DOI also experimented with repackaging some of its documentaries into a multitopic reporting format. In December, it combined three shorts and rereleased them as a compilation package with the title *National Defense Review No. 1*. This was a different term, also suggesting the purpose of informing the public, but using a broader perspective than a single-topic short, a review of the bigger picture. Like the single-topic shorts, the card at the beginning of the film stated, "The Office of Production Management presents a Defense *report* on film."[67]

While DOI maintained this robust and multimedia public reporting program in 1941, the changes in the external environment had an effect on what such reporting encompassed and the tone of the reports. Even before Pearl Harbor and the declaration of war, reporting and persuasion were beginning to overlap. Gradually, any difference between neutral information, promoting public support, and morale for the national defense mobilization effort was getting fuzzier. In that respect, Pearl Harbor was *not* a bolt out of the blue for the defense production effort and affiliated information activities by DOI. The tone and orientation had already been changing throughout 1941.

Government PR as Persuasion: Widely Held Values, Presidential Communication, and War

The fluidity of events in 1941 before Pearl Harbor added ambiguity to the general prohibitions on persuasive communications in government PR. Certainly, the United States was not in an official state of war, and public opinion was still divided on a potential US role in a war. In 1940, most of the cover that Horton could muster for persuasive communications was based on actions and proclamations made by the president on his own. Constitutionally, Congress had the exclusive power to declare war or permit the use of force (as with the Tonkin Gulf Resolution regarding Vietnam or the invasion of Iraq in 2003). However, in mid-March 1941, Congress had passed the Lend-Lease Act.[68] This law was an overt determination of a national policy by the legislative branch to support the war operations by the United Kingdom and China (and later the Soviet Union) to the fullest extent possible with war matériel without a declaration of war. Congress was now in agreement with FDR on placing the United States on one side of the war. The United States was no longer neutral. It was doing whatever it could, short of becoming a combatant, to prop up those nations fighting the fascist coalition.

For Horton, Lend-Lease and other similar actions wholly reframed the impact of the conventional constraints on persuasive communication in government PR. Now, he could openly seek to influence public opinion on matters that had become settled in terms of national policy. As a result, during this pre–Pearl Harbor time in 1941, DOI engaged in efforts to mobilize public support for and cooperation with the production effort, to increase productivity and morale of workers in war plants, and generally to maintain civic morale at a time when tangible scarcities of certain consumer goods were beginning to occur.

In the spring of 1941, new vocabulary was being used in internal DOI planning documents. For example, a March plan for increasing subcontracting in defense production referred to the need "to *sell* it to the general public."[69] That month a draft of a summary of DOI's work and purposes included a list of three objectives for the division in 1941:

- The Nation *must* arm for defense.
- We *must* know what we are defending.
- The part played by each citizen *must* be made clear.[70]

DOI began viewing itself as having duties to bolster and increase "Civilian Morale" (as opposed to morale of just the workers at defense plants).[71] This was new territory. Another planning document explicitly stated that a divisional goal was "to *secure complete public support* of the national defense program and the national policy in time of emergency."[72] Using marketing terminology, one official sought to identify "specific 'defense products' which we wish to advertise and sell."[73]

As the year wore on and the news from abroad got worse, DOI's persuasive communication efforts became more explicit. In the summer, the heads of OPM were concerned about citizen "complacency" toward the defense program. They wanted to engender "greater appreciation" for the effort.[74] To that end, they asked for a comprehensive campaign to change public opinion. A week later they approved "a publicity campaign to rouse the public to the seriousness of the defense situation and to conduct a minuteman drive in industrial areas to help overcome lack of public support of the defense program."[75] It was up to DOI to design it.

Then, heading into the fall of 1941, an in-house assessment of upcoming PR problems regarding the expansion of defense production and beginnings of shortages of consumer goods was almost apocalyptic in tone. In a memo to Horton, several staffers wrote (in a somewhat journalistic telegraph style):

> The next 60 to 90 days will be most[ly] chaotic confusion. Control is shifting from industry to government. It is [a] period of instituting controls, of dislocations, of misunderstanding. Unless handled with great care, and complete

> understanding of [the] problem [it will] result in virtual distruction [*sic*] of controls and lawlessness, bootlegging, etc., calling for dictatorial policies, [and a] breakdown of [the] present system. Reports from our field information staff throughout the country indicate that conditions are already bad; [and] growing daily worse.[76]

They called for a massive PR campaign because, at heart, "*This is a morale problem.*"[77] As 1941 wore on, these themes dominated and undergirded most of DOI's PR work. The most audacious advocacy approach appeared in a mid-October planning document. It proposed that DOI organize itself around a new mission, called "The New Victory Program,"[78] a title suggesting that the United States was already at war.

Horton bared his teeth publicly with a pamphlet DOI issued in September. At first glance, *Guns Not Gadgets* purported to be informational, as stated on the back cover: "Every American has a place in National Defense. It is your right and your duty to know the facts, to know what your Government is doing and how you can help." However, the preface to the text was overt in its political attack on isolationist civic leaders and perhaps even members of Congress, essentially suggesting they were disloyal to the country:

> THIS NATION OF FREE MEN is engaged in an all-out effort to defend its freedom.
>
> Why?
>
> Because our security is threatened from without by guns, tanks, planes, and ships aimed at the heart of democracy.
>
> There are also those who would destroy it from within.
>
> Their scheme is to stimulate doubts deliberately as to the motives of the majority and the majority's democratically elected leaders.
>
> They try deliberately to confuse public thinking by false statements and insidious suggestion.
>
> They hope to prevent, or at least delay, prompt and decisive action for defense.
>
> They are doing a job for Hitler, who has said: "Mental confusion, contradiction of feeling, indecisiveness, panic; these are our weapons."
>
> If you have doubts about any phase of defense, ASK FOR FACTS![79]

This message was no one-time slip-up, disappearing back into the bureaucratic hole after one showing. The identical text was repeated in two other pamphlets that fall.[80] The premise of this persuasion-oriented message was that the United States was in a de facto wartime situation and that all patriotic citizens should support the defense mobilization. It was an audacious claim.

The timing is important here. These pamphlets were issued before Pearl Harbor, when the United States was not yet in a state of war. Nonetheless, to DOI it felt like a war. And, in late May, FDR had proclaimed an unlimited state of emergency (although the tangible meaning of the declaration seemed minor). So, these private and in-house characterizations that were oriented to designing PR programs to *convince* the citizenry of a particular value or goal seemed justified based on the circumstances. Still, these documents confirm that DOI was explicitly entering the persuasion side of the PR business. This was far different from sharing neutral information on government decisions.

It was one thing for Horton to express this hot political message publicly. After all, he considered himself as a presidential appointee serving at the pleasure of the president, a member of the administration, and with a rank comparable to that of a subcabinet official. But it was another thing altogether for an official DOI publication to level these aggressive attacks on isolationists. DOI employed two hundred civil servants, appointed by the Civil Service Commission to classified positions, with the duty to be faithful public servants in their work. *They* were the ones issuing this publication. Under Horton's supervision, these civil servants were writing, editing, formatting, publishing, disseminating, and advertising an overt political message. In retrospect, it is surprising that these statements did not trigger significant controversy and counterattacks from the conservative coalition on Capitol Hill. If ever Horton crossed a red line in the boundaries of acceptable government PR, this was it.

Another important indicator of the qualitative change in DOI's PR work during this period related to public salvage campaigns. In popular memory, these occurred after Pearl Harbor, *during* the war. In fact, the first campaign took place in July 1941 and involved collecting aluminum household items. A shortage of aluminum was looming, with its consequent implications for aircraft production and other war matériel. Conducted publicly under the auspices of OEM's new Office of Civilian Defense (OCD), DOI planned a multipronged campaign. Using all media venues as outlets, this was the first major national effort involving mobilizing widespread participation by the populace at large. Families were encouraged to donate items, hardware and other stores to receive them, and haulers to bring them to central collection centers.[81] Some were so eager for this first chance to help personally with the defense effort that they jumped the gun and began early.[82] There were public declarations of success,[83] although internal documents hinted at some disorganized, chaotic, and near-botched situations.[84] As an epilogue, DOI shrewdly released in November the documentary short *Pots to Planes* that depicted the transformation of the materials collected in July into aircraft.[85] This helped give credibility to later collection campaigns, implying that indeed there had been a need for—in this case—aluminum and that participation had had a tangible impact on the production effort.[86]

Was DOI becoming a propaganda agency when the nation was not at war? As with so much else regarding the norms of government PR, the answer is in the eye of the beholder. From Horton's perspective, he was not trying to impose any national goals or values on the populace. Rather, he was using persuasion to help implement formal national policy, in this case defense mobilization. True, these were not unanimously held values of the public at large, but his persuasion efforts were based on implementing the policy goals set by the national government, most approved by legislative branch, all by the executive. For example, in early December (before Pearl Harbor), Horton corresponded with Walt Disney about producing some shorts with Disney's cartoon characters. Trying to clarify what was propaganda and what was not, Horton assured Disney: "This is not to suggest 'propaganda movies,' but let me illustrate with a very small example. For instance, Donald Duck could, instead of going out for an evening of poker playing, go for an evening of training as an air raid warden—he certainly has the voice for it. In other words, the picture would then reflect more accurately what is going on in real life today."[87]

From Horton's perspective, such a cartoon was not propaganda even though it might be trying to persuade the public to do something. It could be argued that DOI's PR fit somewhat in the other two exceptions for government PR, namely that Horton was giving voice to the president's positions and this was at a time of such a major national emergency that it could almost be considered wartime. But the United States was not at war. It would strain credulity to claim that the third exception to the ban on government propaganda would really apply in this case.

Some felt Horton and DOI had crossed a line during this period. For example, in a speech Horton gave in Chicago in mid-June, his text was sprinkled liberally with the "must" construction. It was a pro-intervention speech, oriented to convincing the audience of the importance of preventing Hitler from defeating the United Kingdom. Hitler was a threat to free men everywhere, including the United States, Horton said.[88] An Ohio newspaper editorialized against Horton and his comments, denouncing them as "propaganda for war."[89]

Irrespective of any nuance in Horton's and DOI's public statements or other PR, the conservative coalition in Congress had a reflexive antipathy to Horton and DOI as part of its larger opposition to all government public relations programs, especially by Roosevelt (and, later, Truman).[90] The debate on the House floor in June 1941 over an omnibus appropriations bill for national defense, which included funding for DOI, provided the perfect platform.[91] Congressman Richard Wigglesworth (R-MA) criticized DOI as "a gigantic newspaper office set up in connection with an important agency of government here to manufacture news."[92] J. William Ditter (R-PA) denounced DOI as "probably the largest and most expensive information establishment in the Federal Government with the possible exception of the Department of Agriculture. . . . On this basis it is very difficult to see how this tremendous staff is required; and, in fact, Mr. Horton did not do very well [at the committee hearing] in attempting to justify the necessity for such a staff."[93] More generally, later that year, a Republican congressman criticized the operations of OPM and Lend-Lease, saying, "Despite our urgent needs in heavy equipment, millions of dollars are being squandered this year in government propaganda."[94]

Horton also had an implacable foe in the news media, which had a built-in professional antagonism to government press agents. Usually absent in straight news reporting, it was more evident in columns and editorials. In chronological order, here's how the period of March to November 1941 came across to news consumers. Columnist Paul Mallon criticized the "false impression" the public had of the authority of the leaders of the defense effort. Horton, he implied, was the puppeteer regarding all public statements and releases.[95] Drew Pearson and Robert Allen described "the maze of red tape in the defense agencies which hampers and confuses the average reporter and has the effect of censorship. The Office of Production Management, for instance, has some 30 different publicity agents."[96] In an editorial, an Ohio newspaper criticized Horton for being a partisan mouthpiece for the Democratic Party.[97] Columnist Peter Edson complained about Horton hiring "a staff of 20 ex-newspaper men turned press agents to ballyhood [*sic*] the show."[98] Without naming Horton, a magazine of the advertising industry criticized how poorly the news about potential consumer shortages was being handled by OPM and concluded that "censorship and propaganda are anybody's game in Washington."[99] An editorial writer complained to the DOI regional information officer about receiving "a publicity release of three or four thin mimeographed sheets enclosed in a monstrous envelope five times larger and more costly than necessary to hold it."[100] Columnist Frank Kent called DOI "the largest, the most elaborate and most expensive publicity bureau any Government has ever had. . . . It reeks with high-powered press agents."[101] James Reston of the *New York Times* described Horton as responsible for "the flood of copy that is now pouring into the newspaper, radio, and motion picture offices of the country."[102] An editorial in an Iowa newspaper complained about "too much government publicity" including from DOI.[103] A news story in the *Chicago Tribune* included DOI in its enumeration of the administration's "brigades of war ballyhoo."[104] Somewhat more neutrally, *Newsweek* described Horton as "probably the worst plunderer of capital reporters," and another news magazine described DOI as "responsible for the largest volume of defense releases."[105] A week before Pearl Harbor, a reporter wrote that DOI was the voice of the president, releasing to the public only "carefully formulated information for the domestic front."[106]

The hostility of the press corps to Horton came through in one of the humorous skits performed during the annual dinner of the White House Correspondents Association. Horton "was pictured in a scene ordering his police guard to shoot reporters on sight." While jesting, it reflected a tangible and shared negative attitude that reporters had toward PIOs in general and Horton in particular.[107] Even George Creel, head of CPI during World War I, got in the act.[108] He criticized DOI and several other government PR offices, absurdly claiming that "government press agents, as a matter of fact, already outnumber the nation's readers."[109] Sticking with the conventional wisdom of the news pack, the magazine that published Creel's article followed up with an editorial (the week before Pearl Harbor) denouncing the administration's PR for "mainly wasting paper and ink. . . . Why this gigantic and largely superfluous structure of peddlers of news that isn't, 'facts' that conflict, propaganda that hurts as much as it helps?"[110]

An article in *American Mercury* was specifically critical of DOI and Horton. It observed that "OPM publicity is frankly optimistic" and that "Horton feels that he must keep the agency's best foot forward publicly."[111] That particular criticism seems to have some validity, as it suggests that Horton was putting a positive spin on all news from OPM, even though he argued publicly and vociferously that he was merely releasing neutral information. For example, a draft (apparently for a potential publication) acknowledged, "We've learned a lot this past year," including through making mistakes.[112] Yet, going back over all of its releases and statements during that year, one is hard put to identify documentation of that learning curve. Yes, all released information was accurate, but none of it acknowledged mistakes. Perhaps this confirms the sheer intellectual impossibility of perfectly squaring government PR with neutral information. Sometimes they were compatible and overlapped, but this was neither automatic nor guaranteed. Horton's external communications, whether through press relations or public reporting, were consistent in focusing on accomplishments, not mistakes. If the partisan and ideological criticism from the right was that the national defense mobilization was a confused and wasteful mess lacking a clear strategic goal, then Horton felt it was his role to document the opposite. Fact or propaganda? Probably both.

Paradoxically, Horton also had his critics on the left, claiming the need for more aggressive PR. In midyear, Harvard professor (and anti-Nazi German émigré) Carl Friedrich wrote in the *Atlantic Monthly* of the "urgent necessity" for improving defense public relations because the current public impression was "that our defense effort is inept and inefficient."[113] He pointedly urged not creating another CPI, but instead developing stronger coordination of all agencies. To Horton's chagrin, Friedrich endorsed strengthening Mellett's OGR to do that, not DOI. A few months later, *Harper's* published an article that was more pointedly critical: "Our propaganda has failed. It has failed to accomplish the primary aim of any nation's propaganda, which is to provide a clear understanding both of the struggles of the nation and of the aims in view, and with a fervent desire to help achieve those aims."[114] At the same time, behind closed doors, Horton and Mellett were also fighting a rear-guard action against liberal voices within the administration who were similarly critical. For example, Interior Secretary Harold Ickes urged FDR to engage in much more aggressive informational activities to mobilize support for his interventionist foreign policy.[115] Roosevelt, who preternaturally preferred to finesse either-or decisions, was willing to try it both ways. If Mellett and Horton weren't doing something, that was fine. Maybe someone else could or would. If that alternate approach succeeded, great. If it failed, no serious harm done.

FDR's solution, not surprisingly, was to create a new agency. On May 20, 1941, he signed an executive order creating within OEM the Office of Civilian Defense (OCD) and named New York City mayor Fiorello LaGuardia as its chief.[116] According to the executive order, one of OCD's missions was to "promote activities designed to sustain the national morale."[117] At his press conference releasing the executive order, Roosevelt made a point of mentioning this goal.[118] By definition, a federal civilian defense agency would largely be an information dissemination activity, as first responders were typically part of local government. So, external communications about civil defense seemed closely tied to public relations for civilian morale in general. OCD was "a natural spot for a propaganda agency since a good part of its work was propagandistic in nature anyway," Catton wrote.[119] Indeed, in his first speech as OCD director, LaGuardia said that public opposition to the president's policies hurt the country and that everyone should rally behind the president.[120] However, while OCD went on to function about as expected regarding its substantive mission, as a persuasive communications agency, it was a flop.[121]

In a democracy, overt and successful governmental propagandizing of the populace was a near-impossibility, especially absent a state of war. During 1941 (pre–Pearl Harbor), Horton had probably pushed the envelope of persuasive communications about as far as could be accomplished under the constraining context and circumstances.

Horton's Centralized Structure for Government PR

Horton's model of being a centralized provider of PR services to all OEM agencies continued after DOI became an independent agency in February. It was now serving eleven entities within OEM, including such diverse policy areas as industrial production, housing, health and welfare, science R&D, labor-management mediation, price administration, supply and transportation, and—the latest addition—civilian defense.[122] A CIA historian would later interpret Horton's motivation for creating this centralized approach in face of a proliferation of new OEM agencies, including the precursor to the CIA, as seeking to "minimize agency and agency-head glorification."[123]

Horton was still on a roll bureaucratically. In January, he had successfully pushed for control over duplicating (see chap. 3). Now, he persuaded the new OEM liaison officer, Wayne Coy, to promulgate another policy extending Horton's centralized control to all printing. Before anything could go to the Government Printing Office (GPO), Horton would have to sign off on it.[124] This gave him control not only of content, but also of the public "look" of the agency, the power to impose a coherent and consistent presentation style of all OEM printed materials printed. Long before the marketing terminology existed, he was OEM's brand manager and logo cop, at least for its publications.

When Horton defended his budget at a hearing by a subcommittee of the House Appropriations Committee, he explained his philosophy of a centralized newsroom for multiple agencies. One member asked if that approach should be applied to other agencies. No, Horton said, but it was a good fit for OEM.[125] Actually, that's *exactly* what he thought. In drafts of two different position papers, Horton dreamed of coordinating *all* government PR relating to the emergency. He thought the model he had created for DOI serving OEM agencies could work for the entire national defense effort, not just for arms production. For a piece on DOI's mission that he drafted in late summer, he suggested that the president should direct larger swaths of the executive branch to coordinate their PR with and through DOI.[126] This would not be an executive order or a public statement, just a presidential letter to all agencies. In particular, Horton wanted these agencies to help disseminate to the public the various products that DOI was generating, including pamphlets, leaflets, clip sheets, and radio transcriptions. If all federal agencies distributed DOI materials in lieu of their own, then the same coherent and unified message on national mobilization would reach almost every household. Horton's dream list for expanding his turf to federal agencies that engaged in major information dissemination, included cabinet departments such as USDA, Commerce, Labor, and the Post Office; and independent agencies such as the Federal Security Agency (probably because it included the Office of Education) and CSC., Somewhat oddly, he also dreamed of controlling OGR, headed by his original patron, Lowell Mellett.[127] Horton was willing to bite the hand that (first) fed him.

In the fall, in a more formal document, Horton stated a goal that was broader than merely controlling distribution of publications: "There should be *one* Division of Information charged with top responsibility for all information relating to defense. The existing staffs of other agencies could and should be used for operating purposes; but there is nothing to be gained by duplication in planning, and much to be lost."[128] What did he mean by "planning" in this context? Later in the memo, he wrote about the need for "orderly channels through which all conflicting ideas and proposals *can be cleared* and discussed. . . . We ought to give the people a kind of defense 'framework' into which our day to day activities fall."[129] So, planning and clearing meant control. He would be in charge of *all* federal PR relating to defense, impliedly even the military. It is unclear how broadly this second document circulated. That it was mimeographed indicated a readership in, at least, two figures, perhaps even three. However, nothing ever came of it.

In midyear, Horton's PR centralization doctrine received an unexpected endorsement from Congress, specifically the House Appropriations Committee. The committee was handling the Second Deficiency Appropriations Bill for 1941. In its report on the bill to the full House, the committee stated: "A considerable sum can be saved by a closer coordination of the central administrative services of the Office for Emergency Management and some of the units, particularly, the administrative service of the Office of Production Management. Many of the units maintain *information services* and legal divisions and other small organization units which might be *centralized* to some extent with service for the entire Office for Emergency Management at less cost and with no loss in efficiency."[130]

Nothing happened. Instead of extending his centralization model as recommended by Congress, for the second half of 1941, Horton was fighting a rearguard action simply to maintain the status quo.[131] The two most troublesome were OCD and Housing. As already discussed, much of OCD's mission involved information dissemination and external communication. If so, then was OCD merely a hollow shell for DOI? That could not stand. Also, LaGuardia had an exuberant and hyperkinetic style along with limited time and attention, given his mayoral duties.[132] Throughout 1941, Horton sought to develop a stable PR relationship with OCD as existed with the other OEM agencies. But that standard operating procedure never seemed to work with OCD. There seemed to be no end to last-minute and special requests, inadequate advance notice, lack of planning, and lack of coordination.[133] For a poster on Bill of Rights Day, a DOI staffer complained that "there are, at present, entirely too many decisions yet to be made by the officials within the Office of Civilian Defense."[134] Another noted the many changes that OCD sought in the proofs and galleys of a publication. These were extremely expensive so late in any printing process. Why couldn't these changes have been made earlier?[135] A postmortem on Civilian Defense Week scathingly referred to OCD's "complete lack of organization," "lack of awareness" of important details, "no information," "incomplete, inaccurate and hopelessly disorganized" mailing lists, supplies "allocated entirely by guesswork, and incorrectly," and "lack of a central control."[136]

There were advantages and disadvantages to First Lady Eleanor Roosevelt serving as OCD's assistant director. As a public figure she could attract attention to the PR that DOI was doing for OCD and for the defense effort in general. For example, in her daily newspaper column, she referred to the upcoming DOI/OCD campaign to promote observance of Bill of Rights Day, intended to call attention to the rights Americans had and that Germans and occupied Europeans did not.[137] On another occasion, she appeared on a DOI radio program called *Keep 'em Rolling,* which focused on the importance of the defense production effort and civilian morale in general.[138]

Those efforts were counterbalanced by her numerous personal inquiries and requests for information, many more than made by any other assistant director of an OEM agency.[139] She was like a tireless do-gooder idea machine. Some requests made in her name came from her associates. One was a suggestion to begin shooting within two weeks "training films of dance classes for children which were to be set up in New York schools."[140] This ostensibly related to physical fitness, but seemed awfully far from the original purpose of healthy adults for military and production service. The men at DOI could do little but roll their eyes. If they were lucky, this was an idea that might be forgotten quickly. One didn't explicitly say no to the president's wife or those speaking on her behalf.

In the second half of 1941, DOI submitted to OCD multiple plans for comprehensive and systematic PR strategies, either for general or specific themes.[141] They were seemingly agreed to, but then never seemed to be acted on. Finally, in exasperation, Horton and DOI prepared a formal memorandum of agreement to be signed by the two agencies that explicitly enumerated the PR activities DOI would perform for OCD, and everything else that OCD would conduct on its own.[142] That didn't work either. It was like nailing Jell-O to the wall.

A problem with OEM's office of the Coordinator of Defense Housing was different. It was about control and power, and it went to the heart of Horton's centralization philosophy. Like most policy areas, federal involvement in housing was complicated and divided among several independent agencies.[143] As its title suggested, this agency's work was largely coordination. It had a few authentic powers relating to defense priorities, but not a lot. As a result, there were few times when there was a need for the Coordinator to issue press releases, only when he truly was making news.[144] This frustrated the incumbent, Charles Palmer. In November, he hired Howard Acton, then PR director of the Federal Home Loan Bank board, to be his special assistant.[145] Palmer wanted Acton to increase Palmer's news profile. Palmer promptly claimed that Acton would now oversee Dana Doten, DOI's PIO assigned to Palmer's office, and the small number of other DOI staffers working there. In a staff memo and press release, Palmer wrote that "Mr. Doten and his staff will continue their activities, *but under the direction of Mr. Acton.*[146] For Horton, this was a declaration of war, a true red line regarding DOI's role vis-à-vis OEM agencies. If Horton's monopoly over PR was broken by this little agency, that would set a precedent for all OEM agencies and destroy what he had built up.

A bureaucratic war was on. Horton's deputy, Robert Straus, told Palmer that Doten would be glad to follow PR advice that Acton gave Palmer and with which Palmer agreed, but Doten worked for Palmer, not Acton. Straus asked Palmer to withdraw the offending statement.[147] No dice. DOI flexed its muscles through its control of the weekly magazine *Defense.* DOI considered the magazine to be the journal of record for all news and decisions made by OEM agencies. Some reporters, librarians, and lawyers retained old copies and used *Defense* as a reference source. Because of that, DOI usually ran articles in *Defense* that repeated exactly what the original news announcements had stated. Not for Acton. The reprint of Palmer's announcement appointing Acton was a verbatim copy of the paragraph on Acton's qualifications, but deleted the claim in the original release of Acton's supposed new power over Doten.[148] It had been erased from official memory.

The conflict now escalated to the OEM liaison officer. Assistant Liaison Officer Sidney Sherwood tried to mediate the conflict and proposed a wording of the relationship that sided with neither and somehow papered over the disagreement. Ostensibly, Sherwood's proposal maintained "the accepted idea of a central Division of Information serving all defense agencies" within OEM, but gave Acton and Palmer some wiggle room.[149] Horton would have none of it. But, rather than push a confrontation, he wrote that it was not "a matter about which we should spend much time at the moment. Let's wait and see what develops."[150] As long as Acton wasn't bossing Horton's staff around, Horton would be satisfied. Horton apparently thought that Palmer wasn't long for the job, given some very public feuds he had unnecessarily already got himself into. Others might do to Palmer what Horton wished for.[151] Horton, again, was showing his ability to engage in bureaucratic politics. As long as he hadn't explicitly lost, he could bide his time.

While trying to protect the shrinkage of his empire regarding OCD and Housing, Horton was the beneficiary of a different bureaucratic war for which he was merely the bystander. The portfolio for consumer protection and information was held by the Consumer Division within the Office of Price Administration (OPA). There was a long-simmering fight between OPA director Leon Henderson and Consumer Division director Harriet Elliott over the latter's autonomy. She was seeking to upgrade the bureaucratic standing of her shop to be more independent, while Henderson was adamant that the consumer function should be within his purview. She lost and submitted her resignation on November 22.[152] Horton, for the time being, took over her division's Consumer Publications Section and, more broadly, was "for the next few months the public's source for data on economic controls."[153] This was a logical expansion of his turf, given that consumer affairs was akin to civil defense in that most of the work involved information dissemination and public education. Horton took it in stride.

A major threat to Horton's centralization policy began in late October, when Roosevelt created yet another agency that might provide the propaganda Mellett and Horton wouldn't. The Office of Facts and Figures (OFF) was "to facilitate the most coherent and comprehensive presentation to the Nation of the facts and figures of national defense." Furthermore, it should "facilitate a widespread and accurate understanding of the status and progress of the national defense effort."[154]

The motivation to create OFF was, in a sense, partly Horton's fault. Politicians and the media were scoring points about the so-called "mess" in Washington and "confusion" in the national defense effort. All along, Horton was comfortable if agencies expressed public disagreements. But politics doesn't rate that kind of honesty in public communications very highly. It *looked* bad. The criticism was getting traction partly because the implication was not only that the right hand didn't know what the left was doing, but they couldn't even agree on a common set of facts. That really made government look bad, as had happened with the seemingly contradictory data on airplane production in the summer of 1940 (see chap. 2). Even Horton had agreed with the importance of preventing that perception. FDR wanted to tamp down the accusation before things got worse in the fall of 1941. Now, a presidential agency that would be *the* source for authoritative information would contribute to the image not only of a coordinated national defense effort, but where there was only one set of facts with which everyone agreed.[155]

OFF posed a different kind of threat to Horton's centralization policy than did OCD. LaGuardia's agency had a PR mission that was somewhat boosterish: encouraging positive thinking, improving morale, increasing citizen participation in local organizations. That could exist side by side with DOI without necessarily competing. But OFF was a bird of a different feather. It was to deal with *facts*. Horton thought that was DOI's assignment and a negative reflection on Horton's reporter style and open approach.

Roosevelt appointed Archibald MacLeish, the Librarian of Congress and sometime behind-the-scenes speechwriter, to head OFF. By Washington standards, it was a relatively small agency and, therefore, dependent on the cooperation of the other PR units in the executive branch. Horton was decidedly unhappy, but knew he could not take on OFF overtly. Instead, he adopted a coldly formal and distant stance. For example, when MacLeish wrote an introductory letter and request for general information to Horton in early November, Horton waited for two and a half weeks before replying with an uninformative one-page response.[156] Seeking to prevent things from getting any worse, the next day MacLeish quickly thanked Horton for his reply, saying he "appreciate[d] very much the complete information you sent."[157] According to BOB's official history of the war, OFF's "authority was not fully recognized, however, by the Division of Information."[158] Nonetheless, MacLeish declined to fight with Horton, whether for lack of explicit authority or reflecting his personality.[159]

So far, so good.

CHAPTER 5

THE DIVISION OF INFORMATION'S PROGRAMS AND MANAGEMENT

March–December 1941

In 1941, during its existence as an independent agency within OEM, DOI was at its fullest flowering as a government PR department when the United States was *not* at war. The preceding chapter recounted the traditional government PR activities of press relations and public reporting, as well as some of DOI's persuasion-oriented activities. But DOI was more than that, with a scope comparable to a full-service PR, marketing, and advertising agency. It offered a full panoply of external communication product lines. This chapter presents the rest of the story, of how Horton pushed his agency to the limits of permissible PR when the country was formally at peace. Contrary to Catton's melodramatic telling, Horton wanted to *shape* public opinion, not just inform it. But there were political risks in doing so too overtly.

Speeches

Horton knew that speechmaking by senior OEM officials was an important method of communication, mostly for the indirect audience that would learn about the speech from newspaper, radio, and even newsreel coverage. In that sense, these speeches were an element of Horton's press relations strategy. In this pre-TV and pre–bowling alone era, many citizens were active in civic and religious groups.[1] That meant there was an almost bottomless demand for public speakers to address gatherings. At first, Horton tried to fill the need for local speakers by developing an exclusive relationship with the Junior Bar of the American Bar Association. The group already had in place a speakers' bureau on subjects related to the legal profession (such as the legal process, the judicial system, and the Constitution). It also provided speakers to discuss current affairs. Reflecting the culture of the legal profession, these talks relied on factual and dispassionate presentations. The Junior Bar's "Public Information Program" was well-organized, with volunteer state directors in all forty-eight states (plus DC and Puerto Rico) and, under them, at the beginning of 1941, more than three hundred volunteer speakers.[2]

For Horton, this group represented a blue-ribbon membership of educated and fact-oriented civic leaders located throughout the United States. They were perfect for Horton's approach to public information. In March 1941, DOI designated the Junior Bar as its official network for responding to local requests for public speakers on the national defense effort. By fall, Horton reported: "These gentlemen are serving entirely without compensation and with a minimum [of] administrative direction from this office. There are four hundred public information directors scattered throughout the country acting as field officers in this phase of our work. Their services have been highly satisfactory. . . . [T]he Junior Bar is working out so nicely."[3]

However, given international developments, even a speakers' bureau of (now) four hundred energetic young lawyers around the country wasn't enough to fill the demand. For highly specialized technical audiences, DOI began arranging for lower-level OPM officials, who were experts in those specific areas, as speakers. DOI then recruited officials of the Federal Reserve Bank regional districts (who were doubling as contacts for the effort to subcontract portions of large defense contracts to small businesses) as local speakers.[4] This added about thirty-six more speakers evenly distributed around the country. But that still wasn't enough. Next Horton suggested recruiting younger businessmen who were active in their local Junior Chamber of Commerce.[5] This provided him not only with another national network of highly motivated and responsible speakers, but also helped negate the ongoing hostility of some business audiences to FDR.

By late summer, an in-house memo indicated that the speakers from the Junior Bar and Junior Chamber of Commerce along with the in-house sources *still* weren't enough. DOI began contacting other groups to identify more volunteer speakers.[6] Each of DOI's regional information officers was given the assignment to develop a local speakers' program as a way of reaching more people in person, rather than through mass media.[7] This was an ongoing effort. For example, an update in late November noted that the regional PIOs were in the midst of "lining up a roster of field speakers."[8]

DOI's standard operating procedure for its speakers was to supply each sponsoring organization with background information and skeleton speeches."[9] This evolved into a more formal "speaker's kit," which summarized the major policies in effect, gave general background on the defense buildup, and provided up-to-date facts and recent changes in policy.[10] In November, DOI published a fourteen-page booklet for speakers. It covered the basic facts, history, and goals of the defense buildup. It was intended to be a useful source of information for the speakers addressing general, rather than technical, audiences.[11] Given the limited number of publications it issued (see below), publishing this one indicates both the large scope of the effort as well the importance DOI assigned it as part of its department-store approach to PR.

In parallel, DOI was working with OCD to develop its local speakers' bureau. For example, as part of a comprehensive PR plan for OCD prepared by DOI in September, it called for printing "a manual for speakers . . . on priorities, unemployment and other dislocations of civilian life."[12] Later that month, OCD distributed to its local officials some sample speeches to use in their appearances. A DOI staffer liked them, noting, "They fill the bill—they are well-written, simple, and often eloquent.[13] By late fall, DOI and OCD agreed to harmonize their respective speaker programs. They distinguished between speakers covering four categories of subjects: pronouncements and clarifications of policy; reports on progress; technical information; and general information. DOI would be responsible for speakers in the first category, and OCD's Bureau of Facts and Figures would oversee speakers in the latter three.[14] DOI would help OCD on those other three areas by providing "basic information about the defense program to be furnished to their speakers."[15]

Photos

During 1941, DOI continued trying to balance its desire to coordinate all federal photo activities relating to defense without triggering push-back from agencies protecting their turfs. A position paper in March 1941 indicated its thinking had evolved since the winter of 1940–41. First, the stills unit was trying to work with all executive branch agencies (including the military) to define more precisely the subject areas for which each would have exclusive responsibility. Second, it was accumulating the output from these agencies in a centralized DOI photo archive, but taking care that each picture was "properly captioned and credited to the particular agency." Finally, DOI sought to imbue a greater appreciation for photos that would serve historical documentation purposes in addition to their current use.[16]

The one-year anniversary of the defense production effort in May 1941 provided a news peg for publication of DOI stills by newspapers and other publications in what were called rotogravure sections (sometimes referred to simply as "roto"), that is, pages dedicated to photo spreads.[17] Requests to the Picture Office for multiple photos for the occasion came not only from the dailies in major metropolitan areas, but also from lesser ones such as the *Indianapolis Star, Murfreesboro (TN) Daily News Journal,* and *Duluth (MN) News-Tribune.* Specialized and foreign-language publications also requested them, including the *Jewish Daily Forward* (in Yiddish, based in New York) and *Corriere d'America.*[18]

By spring, the office began distributing a weekly roto (or mat) service of topical pictures to a mailing list of newspaper photo editors throughout the United States.[19] The mats were structured and sized for the convenience of newspapers. These were often timed to relate to a particular campaign that DOI was then implementing. For example, for the October campaign on conservation, it mailed out two roto layouts of relevant pictures.[20]

The Picture Office maintained an up-to-date list of all photos in its files to assist in responding to requests. When a request could not be fulfilled, the office forwarded it to the line agency that was likely to have it.[21] By October 1941, the photo office had responded to seventeen thousand requests for pictures from the daily press, news syndicates, picture agencies, and trade journals.[22] Most of the pictures came from federal agencies, but some were taken for DOI by photographers on contract or in-house talent.[23]

While DOI's photo office was oriented to serving a domestic audience, its stock was also used abroad. In one case, the office responded to a request from the British Press Service, which distributed the photos to newspapers in the United Kingdom to document the production of armaments being prepared for shipment to Great Britain. In return, it began supplying DOI with photos of US-made matériel being used in the war. These photos were prized by DOI because they were tangible visualizations for the domestic audience of the actual use of what the US workers were producing.[24]

Movies

As discussed in the previous chapter, Horton was determined that DOI would be free from dependence on the goodwill of the Hollywood studios for the production of shorts. By mid-1941, the infrastructure he had been building was in full operation and churning out product. "We have a complete production unit," he boasted to William Donovan, then the coordinator of information in charge of overseas propaganda (except Latin America, which was Rockefeller's office).[25] The Film Unit had grown to be something of a Hollywood-on-the-Potomac. At midyear, it had four shorts in distribution, one awaiting release, five in the cutting room, and three being shot.[26] From March to early December, DOI released about a dozen shorts that it had produced in-house. About five hundred to six hundred copies of each film were made, permitting each to quickly reach a very large audience.[27]

Some of the movies DOI released in 1941 were freestanding, in the sense of being topical, but unrelated to other, more comprehensive DOI campaigns. These included a nine-minute film on aviation training that was oriented to younger audiences as something of a recruitment vehicle;[28] *Army in Overalls,* on the work of the Civilian Conservation Corps (CCC) to prepare sites for new military installations;[29] *America Builds Ships,* on the defense work at shipyards; and *Food for Freedom,* on farmers' efforts to maximize agricultural production.[30]

The most acclaimed short that DOI released in this period was the one-reel (ten-minute) *Bomber* (sometimes called *Building a Bomber*).[31] It was nominated for an Oscar in the category of best documentary (but didn't win). Released in October, it depicted the construction of a B-26 medium bomber for the Army Air Force. One of the reasons for the attention it received was that the narration was written and spoken by famed poet (and Lincoln biographer) Carl Sandburg.[32] An entertainment columnist described *Bomber* as the "best" of all the national defense shorts released by the federal government.[33] Another said that it received an "excellent response."[34] According to the *Hartford Courant,* the movie "succeeds in getting over its message."[35]

DOI also figured out how to get extra life out of the shorts it produced. By Horton's calculation, there were eighteen thousand 16mm projectors in educational institutions in the United States, equal to the number of movie houses.[36] It was a no-brainer to convert as much of DOI's film stock as possible into a format for educational and civic screenings. After the theatrical release of *Bomber* was concluded, DOI recut it as a twenty-minute documentary called *Building a Bomber* and offered free loans of this and almost all of its shorts to education, civic, and defense groups.[37] Going a step further, for showings of *Building a Bomber* to educational audiences, DOI also published a companion forty-two-page study guide. It included suggested readings and biographical notes on Sandburg.[38]

Other DOI movie shorts were components of more comprehensive information campaigns of the division, which were organized to occur simultaneously through multiple media, including movies, publications, speeches, press releases, and radio. As discussed, worker morale at defense plants was emerging as a major concern for DOI and the production effort in general. Horton's adviser in Hollywood, Leo Rosten, suggested that DOI begin a new product line of films made expressly for industrial workers. He suggested the film unit issue a weekly newsreel-style short providing workers with a bigger picture of what they were involved in, such as factual updates on production and showing the finished products being used.[39] Given some other DOI film activities, including producing a dozen technical films on various production processes and the newsreel stock it possessed, this would not be much of a stretch, he felt.[40] In part, this would provide yet another way to reuse the same film for a different audience. For example, *Bomber* was used precisely this way, screening it at defense plants to show workers how the B-26 was assembled from the thousands of parts that they were manufacturing.

Political accusations that DOI-sponsored shorts and newsreels were pro-war propaganda were deflated by credible research results released in mid-1941. Using valid social science survey research methods of the time, USC psychology professor Floyd Ruch conducted a nationwide survey of moviegoers.[41] He asked, "Have you been annoyed by any propaganda in the newsreels and shorts you have seen recently?" Early results released publicly in August were 25 percent "Yes," 68 percent "No," and 7 percent "Don't know."[42] These results were widely interpreted within DOI as vindication of its film work.[43] At the end of the year, the refereed *Journal of Educational Sociology* published the final results of Ruch's survey research.[44] The wording of the questions and results were slightly different from those of the August press release, but still consistent with the earlier survey. Ruch asked if "there is too much propaganda in the newsreels and shorts you have seen recently?" The results were nearly two-to-one in the negative (when counting the "Don't know" answers as negative): 36 percent "Yes" and 64 percent "No" or "Don't know." Absent from the August press release was the information that the article had also asked the same question, but with a slightly different wording that might have invited an *affirmative* answer: "Do you agree with Senators Wheeler and Nye that there is too much propaganda in the newsreels and shorts you have seen recently?"[45] The "Yes" responses *decreased* to 32 percent, with 68 percent "No" or "Don't know."[46]

With Ruch's results, DOI staff need not worry anymore about fine lines differentiating supposed information from propaganda. The moviegoing public had expressed its comfort with straddling that boundary and discounting anything that might be viewed as over-the-top. The results were received as a full-speed-ahead endorsement, both for in-house productions or those created in Hollywood that Rosten was encouraging.[47] From scratch, Horton had made DOI into a major player in government films as a form of public relations, reporting, and persuasion. And the public wasn't bothered by the national defense focus of DOI's products, even if some claimed these were propaganda.

Posters

Similar to its movie and photo product lines, as an independent agency DOI undertook a quantum leap in its involvement in posters compared to the winter of 1940–41. It will be recalled that during the winter DOI had begun producing posters intended for workers at defense plants. The first one was largely text, with nearly no graphic design elements (see chap. 3). During 1941, DOI greatly increased its use of posters for industrial morale and expanded the brand to posters aimed at civilian morale. Each poster was a major undertaking, with DOI seeking both impact and quality. The division often obtained for free the designs of major graphic and cartoon artists around the country. Then, the standard print run for a poster was 75,000 sized 11" x 28" and about 35–40,000 larger ones, 30" x 40".[48] A review of prewar and wartime posters published in 1998 highlighted and reprinted several of DOI's prewar posters for their distinction and quality.[49]

By their nature, posters cannot be used to explain or report a public policy. Rather, like bumper stickers, they are limited to conveying slogans intended to influence public opinion and personal behavior. DOI decided to use posters to exhort the citizenry to support the defense mobilization and production effort and to convey the emergency at hand including the threat to Americans posed by events occurring far away. Horton directed that a general theme of the initial poster series be "What we are defending."[50]

Horton believed that before proceeding with the large-scale production of posters for workers and the citizenry, OEM needed to have an insignia and slogan that captured the defense production and mobilization effort.[51] Here was another early example of branding, long before the term entered common use. The brand was unveiled as part of the new masthead of the March 25, 1941, issue of *Defense*. It showed an eagle in flight, holding a cogwheel in its talons and flying over silhouettes of an airplane, tank, and ship. Circular dotted lines emanating from the cogwheel connected to the tank and ship. It looked dynamic, as though the eagle, plane, tank, and ship were all moving forward. It was an effective representation of OEM's mission: America (eagle) mobilizing its industrial capacity (cogwheel) to defend the country with arms for the Army, Navy, and (Army) Air Force.[52]

In late April, DOI released its next poster, intended for both factory workers and the public at large.[53] Almost the opposite of the text-heavy first poster for production workers in December 1940, this one had only six words: "'We the people. . . ' ARM FOR DEFENSE."[54] It was in red, white, and blue.[55] Horton was hitting the patriotism button just about as hard as he could: the American eagle in the logo, the quote of the first three words of the US Constitution, and the colors of the flag. He was equating the armament buildup with patriotism, not so subtly taking on the isolationists. This poster was definitely *not* covered by the propaganda exception of widely held values. Horton wanted to increase morale by persuading both industrial workers and the citizenry that the production effort was consonant with being a loyal American even if there were public voices—perhaps even among their own families or elected officials—who fervently challenged that stance. DOI distributed the poster as widely as possible, for display "in post offices, by manufacturers with defense contracts, and by State defense groups, and related organizations."[56]

Next came a series of six posters for exclusive distribution to factory workers. In seeking additional funding to cover this morale initiative, Horton wrote that "posters are a most important medium for this purpose."[57] The first was a large streamer with the slogan, "Time is Short."[58] It was followed a week later by a poster showing a powerful gloved hand with the slogan "America's Answer! PRODUCTION."[59] Through the rest of the summer and fall, DOI released four more in the series, all depicting the end products of the production effort. They were on the theme of "Keep 'em Rolling" and had the same basic design. Each featured a different form of armament: airplanes, boats, anti-aircraft guns, and tanks.[60] While the main purpose was to boost industrial worker morale, DOI welcomed as broad a distribution to the public at large as well. For example, it notified newspapers that two-column mats of the four-poster series were available upon request.[61]

Seeking further ways to improve industrial morale, DOI hit upon the idea of a variation on a poster, this time a large sign (6' x 4') that plants could place on outside walls and fences to proclaim publicly their role in the defense production buildup. With a large OEM logo, the signs read:

DEFENSE
PLANT
PART OF THE
ARSENAL OF
DEMOCRACY

Only plants utilizing at least half their productive capacity for defense could display the sign. In a cover letter, William Knudsen wrote that he hoped placing it for the public to see would make workers and managers "feel a closer personal relationship with the defense effort. . . . I am sure also that everyone will feel more keenly the tremendous responsibility of being part of the ARSENAL OF DEMOCRACY."[62]

Other exhortative slogans used in plant posters included "Don't Let Him Down!" (referring to a serviceman) and "United We Stand."[63] Before Pearl Harbor, DOI was planning to release on December 20 another industrial poster showing silhouettes of a worker at a drilling machine paralleling a soldier at a machine gun. The planned slogan was, "It Takes Both Barrels."[64] Only a few days after Pearl Harbor, DOI quickly changed the poster to "Give 'em Both Barrels" and circulated it as widely as possible, not just to defense plants.[65]

The increase in DOI's PR activities in 1941 was reflected not only through the expansion of its earlier activities, but also by getting involved much more deeply in PR products that had previously either been minor or nonexistent.

Publications

As previously discussed, DOI had issued a few publications in earlier phases of its existence, mostly limited to public reporting, a guidebook for public speakers, and the weekly publication *Defense*. Now, it greatly increased its attention to the potential of publications for disseminating information, whether to specialized and technical audiences or to the public at large. In March, Horton enumerated a dozen new publications that were under way. They included such diverse titles as *OPM Regulations, How to Sell to the Government, Housing Legislation, Analysis of Appropriations,* and *Price Stabilization: Machine Tool Priorities.*[66] By October, Horton estimated that DOI had distributed about 3 million copies of its publications.[67]

An example of a publication for specialized audiences was the April *Priorities and Defense: A Handbook on the Operation of the Priorities System.*[68] This sixty-nine-page booklet sought to help explain to manufacturers and producers how the new priorities preference and allocation system (headed by Edward Stettinius) to maximize defense production was to work. It contained general explanations, Q&A, examples of forms, text of the regulations that governed the process, instructions, and sources for additional information. To maximize distribution to the target audience, DOI invited trade associations to request a large number of copies for distribution to their members.[69]

DOI used a different publication approach when there were shortages and disruptions in the steel and iron supply. In November, OPM convened a one-day session with industry leaders. DOI staffed the meeting with stenographers and then quickly typeset and published a transcript. This was a way the information could reach as many people in that business as possible.[70] The same month, due to labor shortages and problems, DOI issued a twenty-two-page booklet on labor-management agreements in the shipbuilding industry that were helping to accomplish labor stability. The booklet included summaries of the national labor agreement, and DOI offered them as model pacts for other industries.[71]

A major new product line for DOI in 1941 consisted of smaller and shorter pamphlets for the public at large. This was an effort to explain the defense effort in general and the military production buildup in particular. The first pamphlet, *Guns Not Gadgets* (see chap. 4), contained an open attack on public figures who disagreed with the administration's policy, practically calling them traitors. Despite the hot rhetoric of that introduction, the content of brochure following it was much more in line with Horton's emphasis on disseminating factual information.[72] The twenty-one-page booklet had six short chapters summarizing different aspects of the production mobilization. It was an attempt to explain to consumers the reason for the increasing shortages of consumer products. It was presented as the first in a series of publications called "Arsenal of Democracy." The second in the series was issued in

November and titled *Materials for Defense*. With forty-five pages, it was twice as long as the first and had eleven short chapters explaining specifically which metals were being diverted from consumer production and for what military matériel they were needed.[73] Another, *Dollars for Democracy*, summarized the economics of the defense program.[74] It explained "the effects of our expenditures for defense on the national economy, and the ways in which we will raise the money."[75]

In general, DOI had become a mass pamphleteer during 1941, using print materials as a PR venue to explain OPM's work, especially why and how they were disrupting certain industrial sectors and, to the citizenry, why the sacrifice of consumer luxuries was necessary. DOI's ongoing focus on press relations could be termed wholesale PR because its purpose was to reach the citizenry indirectly, by dealing with an intermediate medium. The extensive publishing program that DOI adopted in 1941 was an effort to reach citizens one by one. It was retail PR in a *very* big country.

Radio

Besides continuing already existing radio efforts (including radio news releases and radio speeches), DOI focused especially on significantly expanding two radio products: retail distribution of radio programs and radio dramatizations. In March 1941, Horton formally established a DOI Radio Section and appointed Bernard Schoenfeld, who previously had worked at the Interior Department's radio studio, to head it.[76] Given the organizational fluidity over the previous year and potential confusion about power, Schoenfeld was explicitly given jurisdiction over all radio activities anywhere in NDAC, OPM, and OEM.[77]

DOI arranged to tape several series and other radio programs that were recycled from programs already aired on national networks. It developed a mailing list of local radio stations that welcomed receiving recordings (called at that time "transcriptions" or "the needle network") of DOI programs that the stations could air at their convenience, sometimes multiple times. This was a way "of reaching a large audience at the time large numbers of people are listening to the radio."[78] The topics for these radio series included labor training, raw materials and substitutes, and the twelve-episode *Building for Defense*. Another series sought to translate abstract and impersonal statistics about the defense mobilization into tangible terms that would be meaningful to individual citizens.[79] By summer, the Radio Section was distributing fourteen different series. Schoenfeld boasted that this "is almost double the radio being turned out by the Army and Navy."[80] In the fall, Horton reported that about five hundred radio stations had aired DOI programs thirty-one thousand times.[81]

A slightly different project was called "decentralized radio." It involved sending "skeleton scripts" of possible interviews to field personnel of OEM agencies. Those local officials could then try to interest local radio stations in their area, typically understaffed, to do an interview with them roughly following the skeleton script.[82] Schoenfeld also promoted distributing the recordings of radio programs to schools as well. This was a way to reuse radio programs that had already been aired. In the fall, an educator calculated that DOI's radio series *How We Build Airplanes* had been played to 41,512 students. He estimated DOI's radio programs, if distributed even more broadly to schools, could easily reach 2 million students.[83]

The most noticeable innovation by Schoenfeld was the radio play, called, in DOI's argot, a dramatization. These were original plays, written specifically for radio, which tried to convert news headlines into fictional stories that were meaningful and engaging to the audience. However, by their nature, the imperative for drama meant going beyond dry recitation of facts. Radio plays were perfectly suited, he felt, for citizens to *feel* the import of world developments, to get a "visceral understanding" of their implications.[84] Schoenfeld wanted "to stimulate the people to an awareness of a problem, clarify it for them, [and] suggest what they can do about it. For these purposes, I consider the dramatic form a superlative one." Further, he felt it was OK to take some liberty with the dry facts in the news or the ambiguities in official government policy that were Roosevelt's trademark, especially in 1940–41. Schoenfeld was willing "to take the bull by the horns and determine *what* was to be said as well as *how* to say it."[85] Horton wholly supported this innovation, wanting to pursue every means of convincing the citizenry of the seriousness of the world situation, even if it might be questioned by isolationists.

One of the first dramatizations to be aired was in May, as part of a larger one-hour report on the first anniversary of the defense program. It sought to convey "how far we have gone in building our defenses."[86] On the Fourth of July, a fifteen-minute play focused on "the need for renewed effort in the defense program."[87] It was followed later in the month with a "verse drama" titled *Highway for Americans,* which was intended to be inspirational about the American spirit and featured actor Paul Muni.[88] Other original radio plays later that year included the story of "a typical defense worker" in search of housing;[89] and two to encourage individuals to volunteer for civilian defense, *From Mr. Humphreys to Mr. Hitler* and *Eyes for America*.[90] Three dramatizations (two written by Schoenfeld) were considered of a quality deserving publication in a volume of one hundred radio plays published in October 1941.[91] A shortage of script writers limited the number of dramatizations the section could produce. Horton unhappily noted that some airtime opportunities were foregone due to staff shortages.[92] In the fall, the writers in the Radio Section began working on a multi-episode dramatization inspired by the recent book *You Can't Do Business with Hitler*.[93] The initial episodes were prepared before Pearl Harbor, but not aired until after the attack (see chap. 6).[94]

Commemorative Days

While a reporter by profession, Horton had an intuitive understanding of public relations. For example, he understood the benefit of commemorative days as a way to create a news peg for press coverage and feature stories as well as for civic events. These special days could break through the noise of the daily din and call attention to a larger idea, especially to link an individual citizen to it in the context of the defense buildup. Elements of observing such celebrations were infinite, including speeches, press releases, posters, radio programs, newsreels, and locally organized events. Horton encouraged DOI to help promote, sponsor, and even invent such commemorations.

One of those special events, Bill of Rights Day, scheduled for December 1941, was briefly discussed in the preceding chapter regarding difficulties getting OCD managers to make some basic decisions about a poster for it and that Eleanor Roosevelt mentioned the upcoming commemoration in her daily newspaper column.[95] Some of the side PR benefits of this observance included a spot news photo of the president signing the proclamation of the upcoming commemoration[96] and an agreement by the American Legion to support the event as a patriotic outlet for its members. The Legion's headquarters office agreed to send five copies of the poster to each of its twelve thousand posts for display and dissemination to other prominent venues in their localities.[97] This neatly co-opted the American Legion (relatively conservative politically) as a partner for a DOI/OCD PR activity.

An earlier event that year was the third annual "I'm an American Day" on

May 19, 1941. The president's proclamation for it stated that the event was to honor young people who were near the age of majority (twenty-one then) and naturalized citizens. Those two demographics could especially appreciate the benefits of being a citizen of the United States. This implied, of course, that Americans should not take their liberties for granted and that residents of some other countries didn't have such freedoms. A major rally took place at Soldier's Field in Chicago. Even the rabidly conservative, isolationist, and anti-FDR *Chicago Tribune* actively promoted the local observance, another indication of how such commemoration days could obtain the cooperation of unusual partners.[98] The pageant attracted seventy-five thousand people. Foreign-born Knudsen gave the keynote speech, which was broadcast live on a national network.[99] Besides its news coverage, the *Tribune* published two pictures from the rally on its picture page.[100] It was a PR man's fantasy come true.

The Fourth of July was a permanent commemorative day in the American calendar that didn't need advance PR to promote its observance. Instead, Horton made sure to try to redefine its meaning for 1941 by associating it as closely as possible with the defense buildup and the war abroad. Horton arranged that the president would give a short live radio address on the Fourth. He then worked with the National Association of Broadcasters to maximize the airing of the speech on all national networks and as many unaffiliated stations as possible. The association urged its members to participate, explaining that "it would be advantageous for the strengthening of civilian and soldier morale, and for the unity of the country if millions and millions of our citizens will, at identical moment, rededicate themselves to their country."[101] The *Post*'s headline previewing the holiday theme could have been written by Horton himself: "Greatest July 4 Program Yet Will Be Warning to Dictators."[102]

Everything worked out as DOI planned. The president gave a short talk from his Hyde Park, New York, home on the importance of preserving freedom and resisting tyranny. The Crown princess of occupied Norway and her children were seated on a sofa next to his desk listening (and a photo of that then released to the press). After his address, the microphones shifted to Estes Park, Colorado, where the US chief justice led the pledge of allegiance, with the radio audience encouraged to recite it along with him. In conclusion, the broadcast moved to Washington, DC, with the Marine Corps band playing the "Star-Spangled Banner." It was, according to the *New York Times* "an unprecedented nation-wide demonstration of unity" including a "solemn hush" in New York City.[103] Traffic stopped at Times Square, "the busiest traffic center in the world," with the president's speech booming out of loudspeakers.[104] Horton was one of the many speakers that day at local gatherings. He urged "an increasing acceleration if we are to be adequately prepared for any eventuality."[105] As mentioned in the preceding section, the Independence Day celebrations included a radio dramatization on a national network. In all, Horton had successfully hijacked the Fourth of July to make it about what he wanted.

Campaigns

An extension of the PR technique of commemorative days was the concept of comprehensive campaigns that would last longer than a day, sometimes weeks and months. As a centralizer of PR, Horton was not only able to see the big picture of defense information needs, but also had the in-house expertise to create and conduct these more complicated and layered PR projects. In fall 1941, he established a formal Campaigns Unit to plan, organize, and implement national campaigns for all OEM agencies.[106] Horton wanted "integrated" campaigns that included just about every PR technique in existence, including "press, publications, radio, newsreel, still pictures, motion pictures and speeches."[107]

This chapter has already mentioned several such DOI campaigns, including the request by OPM leaders to raise worker and citizen morale to appreciate the urgency of the production effort, aluminum collection, Civilian Defense Week, urging consumers in the South to reduce electric consumption, and, in the fall of 1941, a general campaign for consumer conservation of scarce materials.[108] There were many others in this prewar period, including urging consumers to buy and store the coal they would need for the winter during the summer months (when transportation capacity was more plentiful),[109] waste paper salvage,[110] rubber,[111] and volunteering for local OCD projects.[112]

The campaign to increase the subcontracting of defense production to small businesses is an example of the comprehensive approach that DOI used. This was also the longest-running of DOI's campaigns, beginning at about the time that DOI was created as an independent agency and extending into 1942. One of the major OPM efforts in 1941 was to increase the subcontracting of major defense contracts. This was a way to maximize the productive capacity of the industrial sector by using the potential of small- and medium-sized businesses. This was also a politically savvy effort to spread the wealth around from the Niagara of defense spending. The campaign was initially called "Farming Out" and later the catchier "Bits and Pieces." To handle the specialized mission, OPM created a Defense Contract Service. The field operation was initially conducted through the Federal Reserve System, which had twelve regional banks and twenty-four subregional branches. The ostensible reasons for using it included its extant field organization, the desire by the Fed to contribute to the defense effort, and the potential link between subcontractors obtaining new business and needing federal financing for start-up costs and operating lines of credit. Outreach efforts to a specialized audience (in this case, small business) were part of DOI's PR expertise. Recognizing that this was largely a publicity effort—increase awareness of the program, then draw potential customers to the local Federal Reserve office—DOI tried to educate the Fed's field officials on elementary publicity and promotion.[113] But this was hardly the way to succeed. DOI quickly realized that this was not a good structure. First, one official wrote to the assistant DOI director, "I think we are making a grave mistake in placing our whole reliance for the promotion of this program on the Federal Reserve officers. . . . They are not qualified to do the job of promotion." Second, the campaign had a targeted demographic and needed to focus on reaching that specific audience (to be "channelized" in the argot of the times) instead of publicity to the public at large.[114]

DOI therefore developed a broad-based campaign to make the subcontracting program well known to its potential audience, including through movies, publications, photo stills, and exhibits, both travelling and stationary. It produced a short called *Bits and Pieces* as a way to reach and recruit smaller workshops for the defense effort.[115] The movie was issued in two versions, a "short short" for theatrical screening and a longer one especially aimed at reaching businessmen, such as through screenings at meetings of chambers of commerce and civic groups.[116] To reduce confusion between the two versions, the latter was titled *Farming Out Defense Contracts.* For print media, DOI worked both sides of the street, issuing a publication explaining the Defense Contract Service for small businesses and a series of bulletins on farming out for labor audiences.[117] The division also released several stills to help visualize what the effort was all about.[118] Writing in midyear, a Harvard Business School professor judged the subcontracting PR campaign "definitely worth while" even though it "has not been without its weaknesses."[119]

To DOI's relief, the Federal Reserve System was gradually phased out of the effort. In September, the president signed an executive order recommended by OPM to create a freestanding Contract Distribution Division.[120] The division would have a headquarters staff in the capital and its own extensive field service. Upon its creation, Horton submitted to the division's first director, businessman Floyd Odlum, a new comprehensive plan for a PR campaign. It was a ten-point program including (besides the activities discussed above) radio, regional promotion, periodic press releases of contracts signed, and press conferences.[121] The new director accepted Horton's plan, with the provisos that his advance approval would always be obtained and that his division given the public credit when trumpeting accomplishments.[122]

The major new component of the PR plan was to create travelling and stationary exhibits that demonstrated what kinds of "bits & pieces" the federal government was buying and to staff them with contract officers to answer questions and even sign contracts. This was something that had never been tried before on such a scale. The concept, essentially, was to create a general and across-the-board local publicity effort about a short-duration event that would be a magnet for small businesses that otherwise were not on anyone's radar. The goal was to reach the unreached, find the needles in the haystack, draw them to a specific time and place, then link them to the right primary contractors and federal contract specialists.

DOI concluded that the most efficient way to reach the scattered pockets of small manufacturers was through travelling exhibits. Instead of small businesses coming to Washington (or to the local Federal Reserve office in only thirty-six cities), OEM would go to them. DOI organized three identical trains that would fan out from the capital and visit seventy-nine locations over a five-week period. Each train, called "Defense Special," was painted red, white, and blue and bore the official US seal. Each consisted of eight cars, six with exhibits of some of the sixty thousand products the federal government was seeking for the defense efforts and two for about thirty contract officers from the military, Maritime Commission, and OPM travelling with the train, as well as information specialists from DOI.[123] The three trains left Washington's Union Station on November 10 amid as much hoopla as DOI could muster.[124] One train headed to the Northeast, another to the Midwest, and the third to the West Coast.[125] They travelled between cities at night to maximize being open during daytime hours at each stop. The trains were not open to citizens because this was not a general *public* relations activity, rather outreach only for the specialized audience of manufacturers. Often leading civic officials, such as governors and mayors, welcomed the train to their town and tried to drum up as much interest by local businesses as they could. Defense spending meant jobs and prosperity. Everybody seemed to be for it. Visits by the trains to smaller cities were big news, including to Wilmington, Delaware; Trenton, New Jersey; Salt Lake City, Utah; Madison, Wisconsin; Poughkeepsie, New York; and Rock Island, Illinois.[126] The trains were scheduled to be back in Washington on December 19. By then, of course, Pearl Harbor had happened. In late December, Odlum estimated that fifty thousand small businessmen had visited the trains and that eleven thousand contracts would result.[127]

Parallel to the trains, short-term stationary exhibits were also set up in major cities, including New York, San Francisco, and Kansas City.[128] The Chicago event in a hotel ballroom had 3,500 visitors on the first day of its three-day run. The *Chicago Tribune* called it a success: "Prime contractors reported excellent potential facilities were uncovered and a large number of subcontracts will result ultimately." The governor and Odlum attended and spoke, indicating the importance of the event.[129] Los Angelino businessmen said the exhibit there was "effective beyond all expectations."[130] On the morning of Pearl Harbor, the *New York Times* published an article about the successes of the Bits and Pieces effort, noting that it especially helped reduce the predatory practices of so-called brokers, who claimed to have special connections and charged businessmen for linking them to government agencies.[131] That's exactly what Horton wanted. If information was power, then the Bits and Pieces campaign was part of a process to redistribute economic power. It conveyed important information to the little guy, the small businessman. He, too, could be in on the gusher of federal spending even though much of it originated in large primary contracts to big business. The rising tide could lift small boats, too. And no need for a middle man, either (such as a broker). For Horton, Bits and Pieces was a quintessential New Deal orientation for the production effort.

Displays

DOI similarly used displays for many other purposes besides Bits and Pieces. In particular, while the defense exhibits were for a limited constituency of manufacturers, many of the other displays that DOI was involved with were for the public at large and were part of the larger effort to explain the defense buildup and develop public support for it.

For example, a Civic and National Defense Exposition was being organized for New York City to run from mid-September to mid-October. When invited to participate, DOI agreed.[132] The timing was lucky because DOI and the Army were in the midst of planning a public display on the defense effort that could be moved from city to city. It would be a unified exhibit of multiple federal agencies involved in the defense effort, including (besides OPM and the Army) the Navy and Treasury Department. DOI's goals for public displays at venues such as this included: "To present to the nation an enlightening picture of the industrial and commercial activity for National Defense" and "The opportunity to educate the public on Civilian Defense through educational exhibits, graphic presentations[,] and demonstrations of their specific part in the Civilian Defense Program."[133]

This New York exposition would be the inaugural appearance for the display in which DOI participated. The exposition was oriented mostly to the public at large, to educate them about the national defense effort. It was staged on four floors of Grand Central Station, occupying about 175,000 square feet. The well-attended show gave DOI an opportunity to connect with individual citizens on the importance of the defense buildup.[134] (Going for a two-fer, OPM also held a three-day clinic on subcontracting for small manufacturers in conjunction with the exposition.)[135] The exhibit later moved to similar expositions in other cities and also was used on a train that would tour the country, planned for 175 stops.[136] This would be a train exhibit for the public at large, in contradistinction to the Bits and Pieces trains.

A different approach to public displays was the creation of a photomontage that was the size of an outdoor advertising billboard. Exiled French artist Jean Carlu designed it "at the suggestion" of DOI.[137] Measuring about 15' x 30',[138] one side was a montage of pictures relating to the theme of the Four Freedoms (Worship, Want, Speech, and Fear) while the other visualized the Arsenal of Democracy, including pictures labeled "Production" and "Fighting Power."[139] The mural was first displayed for a month at a major intersection in Washington beginning in mid-November. In another indication of DOI being able to work with unlikely partners to expand its PR for the production effort, one of the speakers at the dedication was from the Daughters of the American Revolution, a conservative (and racist) group.[140] (After Pearl Harbor, the mural was displayed in New York City and then toured the country, by then under the auspices of DOI's successor agency, OWI.)[141]

Field Offices

Based on his experience as a reporter and then PIO for the Maritime Commission, Horton knew that a major part of the news business was driven by *local* news. Sure, people generally wanted to know what was going on in the nation's capital or around the world. But, what they really cared about was their neighbors, their city, their state. The federal government announcing it was spending $X billion on defense supplies was an abstract story. On the other hand, the government signing a contract for a measly $1 million with a hometown company was of much greater interest to the news consumer. This localized news might *affect them,* directly or indirectly. Perhaps it raised the possibility of a high-paying job for themselves or someone they knew, or perhaps they would benefit from the economic ripple effect of the contract, and so on. Local was *personal.* While slightly more remote, state news still usually felt more relevant to citizens than national. Many Americans identify themselves as natives of a state and are proud of their state's heritage and reputation. Good news from Washington for one's home state was more interesting than national headlines.

Horton wanted to localize the flood of news DOI was announcing. One of the ways to do that was by providing state-by-state breakdowns of contract announcements and summaries. But that barely scratched the surface of the potential for DOI disseminating localized news. Just before the president re-created DOI as a freestanding agency in OEM, Horton began considering creating a field staff in regional offices throughout the country. One of the items that triggered his thinking was letter in mid-February from the *Miami Herald*'s shipping columnist to Horton's successor at the Maritime Commission. He said that a lot of the press releases from the commission were not being covered in port cities such as Miami because the local editors did not see the link between these national announcements and local impacts. They were simply disregarding the releases they were getting in the mail. The columnist said that he sometimes found those mailings helpful, especially if he had the time to follow up and identify a local angle. A light bulb went off in Horton's head. What DOI needed were information experts in the field who would routinely localize DOI's national announcements.[142] The key was local, local, local.

Horton's well-oiled machine swung into action, but even in the big-spending atmosphere of the defense buildup there were the normal constraints to bureaucratic growth, especially CSC's approval of the classification of these wholly new positions. In March, DOI Assistant Director Robert Straus promised an impatient Horton that the "new field offices will be brought into the system as rapidly as they can be developed," but these things took *some* time.[143] It took a month until the new position classification for "regional information specialist" was approved. The detailed list of responsibilities included "personally initiates informational projects of special interest to the area," which included the gamut of PR work that DOI conducted in Washington, such as press releases, holding radio interviews, engaging public speaking, and disseminating still pictures.[144]

Also helping with a fast start was DOI's work with the field information activities of the Farming Out campaign (discussed above). In retrospect, that had provided the agency with a kind of shakedown cruise, giving it some experience and expertise for its own regional structure. For example, it quickly adopted the same boundaries for its regions as those of the twelve Federal Reserve Banks, which had been the initial building blocks for the Bits and Pieces field structure. The initial goal was one PIO in each region. To expedite opening its local offices, instead of searching for office locations, DOI initially placed most of its regional PIOs in the Fed's regional bank buildings.[145]

By late May, about five of the twelve had been hired. The new men (almost always former reporters who had worked in that region) were brought to Washington to familiarize them with DOI's work and expectations. Once at their postings, the division made efforts to be sure to plug the regional officers into everything that was happening in Washington, including advance notice of press releases,[146] inquiries the headquarters office received from local radio stations,[147] and updates on relevant activities by OEM agencies.[148] By early June, the head of the nascent Field Section reported that it "already is showing results." Local newspapers were publicizing localized news as were radio stations. Visits by VIPs from OPM were getting more local coverage, including their talks on local radio stations.[149] When the regional office opened in New York City, the *Wall Street Journal* covered that as news, reporting that its role was "to supply data and answer questions on non-military defense activities."[150]

By August, DOI had ten of the twelve regional offices open and staffed.[151] Former reporter Marvin Cox was the information officer for the South, based in Atlanta. He gave talks to local organizations, localized national news, and visited other cities in his region.[152] Former reporter Larry Sisk (whose pen name was L. L. Sisk) headed the Texas office in Dallas. He provided information on defense spending in Texas, reported on decisions in Washington regarding local projects (e.g., a housing project for defense workers in San Antonio was not approved), and served as the spokesman of the federal government to local organizations.[153] Other regional PIOs helped promote visits by local businessmen to the Bits and Pieces train when they made local stops,[154] maximized local publicity for visits and speeches by senior OPM officials,[155] and inspected local defense activities.[156] Working with the Picture Office, they identified photos in the collection that were of production and other OEM activities in their regions and offered them to local newspapers.[157]

Besides their role to localize national news, the regional information officers also were to be official spokesmen for the activities of all OEM agencies in their region, paralleling the role of DOI in staffing each OEM agency in Washington with an information officer. However, the quest for autonomy by bureaucracies and turf rivalries sometimes made that difficult. For example, the Consumer Division of the Office of Price Administration and Civilian Supply (OPACS) only would concede, in a carefully worded memo, that its own field staff should "establish and maintain a continuing contact with these [DOI regional] representatives, and consult them freely when in need of factual information, advice on press inquiries, or other public relations matters."[158] It was not openly advocating a revolt against Horton's established status quo for OEM agencies, but it wasn't submitting to his primacy in the field either. In reaction, Assistant Director Straus had what apparently was a strained telephone conversation with a senior Consumer Division official. To prevent any later claims of misunderstanding, he wrote a short follow-up memo restating his concerns, including to "be sure that everyone understands the inter-relationship of the various agencies of OEM," an indirect reminder of the media relations monopoly DOI had with all OEM silos, including OPACS and its Consumer Division.[159] Similarly, the Chicago regional PIO reported that Frank Bane, head of the State and Local Cooperation Division (whom Horton had bested in control of the weekly *Defense* [see chap. 3]), had held a suspicious meeting in Chicago. Despite soothing reassurances of experiments and cooperation, it looked like Bane was trying to create own apparatus for dealing directly with midwestern radio stations, bypassing DOI entirely.[160]

Again showing his ambition for centralization and growth, Horton was hoping that DOI's regional PIO would take a lead role in coordinating the local PR activities of *all* executive branch agencies (not just OEM), but he was overreaching.[161] While that was a nonstarter, Horton kept pushing in other directions for the new regional organization. In October, Wayne Coy, OEM's liaison officer to the White House, approved expanding the field apparatus. He okayed opening fourteen new *branch* offices, in major cities that were not the "capitals" of federal regions. Each branch office would have two staffers, a PIO, and a secretary. Coy also approved expanding the staffing in four of the twelve regional offices, adding two more in New York, Chicago and Cleveland, and one more in Boston.[162] He turned down proposals for several more new branch offices, but indicated he might approve them in the future.[163]

The new regional staff were mostly engaged in outgoing communication, but sometimes also the inflow of information. They reported back on the local mood and how things looked from there. For example, in June, the weekly DOI in-house summary stated that regional offices had submitted a "report showing anti sentiment [in] S.F., apathy [in] Phila[delphia]."[164] During the aluminum collection campaign, they reported back that "general confusion prevails."[165] In October, the Boston staffer reported that one of the regulatory efforts "is unpopular and does not have the confidence of the people."[166] On at least one occasion, the headquarters office invited regional staff to report their assessment of civilian morale. This was an effort to get a grassroots-based picture of the national mood.[167] While these feedback and listening activities were relatively minor, they demonstrated the capability of the regional staff to engage in two-way exchanges of information, the basis for good communication and public relations. However, unlike the regular reporting by Mellett's OGR field staff to Washington, the potential for this feedback mechanism was never fully developed by DOI during this period.[168]

While local newspaper and radio stations largely welcomed localizing national news, OEM's regional structure drew the usual criticism from the Washington press corps. Always quick to complain about federal PR and propaganda, a nationally syndicated columnist criticized DOI for, among many other sins, recently establishing a regional information service.[169] Notwithstanding the somewhat predictable criticism, DOI had relatively quickly created from scratch a system of regional information offices that were helping implement the agency's now-emerging dual missions: *informing* the public about the defense buildup and *convincing* the citizens that these actions were necessary and justified.

Administrative Sketch

President Roosevelt's decision in late February to convert DOI into an independent OEM agency triggered a growth period for Horton's empire. The preceding chapters detailed the significant expansions and deepening of the categories of the PR programs that DOI engaged in pre-autonomy as well as the new activities it initiated during 1941. Adding impetus to these increases was the agency invisibly becoming a morale and persuasion agency above and beyond its mission of disseminating information. In all, this was boom time for Horton's DOI and a period of seeming institutionalization. The DOI staffer in charge of its newsroom commented that some of his functions were not being given adequate or quality attention, and that this was "another symptom of our growing pains."[170] The head of the Radio Section needed a quick turnaround on a request he made and feared that "Horton is much too busy to do anything about this."[171]

Horton wanted to inculcate an organizational culture that was adaptable, flexible, and fleet-footed, not only because of the changing needs of DOI's public relations mission, but also because of the near-constant tinkering by the president with the structure of the national defense buildup. So, for example, in August 1941, he reorganized DOI's structure to keep pace with external and internal developments. He wanted "closer integration and coordination as this [defense] program enlarges." Therefore, he created four basic organizational building blocks, called branches, within DOI: Production, Civilian, Campaign, and Field.[172]

One difficulty of presenting an administrative sketch of the agency is that DOI was such a dynamic administrative entity, growing quickly and unpredictably in parallel to the international situation and funding allocated to it from presidential national defense emergency accounts. Therefore, the kind of routine comparative administrative data for traditional executive branch

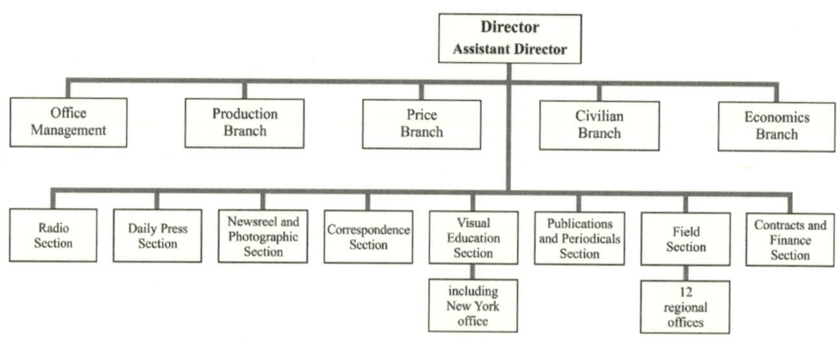

DOI Organization Chart, June 1941.

Folder: Personnel Regulations, Box 9, Entry 576A, RG 208, National Archives II.

agencies, such as changes in appropriations and staffing levels between fiscal years, cannot be applied easily to DOI.[173] Everything was constantly changing. Given those obstacles, the following information represents more of a series of administrative snapshots of the agency, taken at slightly different times, rather than fixed data covering the entire period.

Budgeting

It will be recalled that FDR's decision to convert DOI into an OEM agency helped maximize its legitimacy, especially for congressional funding. On June 17, 1941, Horton was one of the directors of OEM agencies to testify before a subcommittee of the House Appropriations Committee on the Second Deficiency Appropriation Bill, which the president had requested to further expand the defense buildup. For DOI, this bill was tantamount to its FY1942 budget bill, as it was funded not by the traditional annual departmental bills (which were limited to agencies created by statute). One of the major differences between the traditional appropriations cycle on Capitol Hill and this one was timing. (A reminder that the lump sum appropriation was to OEM as a whole, to be allocated at the president's discretion.) Annual departmental bills began being considered in January after the president's annual budget message, and then leisurely worked their way through the legislative process with a goal of being signed by the president in time for the beginning of the new fiscal year on July 1. For DOI and other nonstatutory emergency agencies funded by this deficiency bill, the timing was tight and the need to get it to the president's desk was more urgent. On the day of Horton's hearing, FY1942 was only two weeks away.

For FY1942, the president had submitted to Congress in spring 1941 his plan to allocate $750,000 to DOI from emergency funds under the president's discretion.[174] This budget figure apparently continued to be generally accurate through late calendar 1941, the midpoint of FY1942.[175] However, reflecting the fluidity of the situation, other sources in the fall of 1941 varyingly put the DOI annualized budget at $600,000,[176] $700,000,[177] $872,400,[178] and "close to a million dollars."[179] These differing figures do not necessarily reflect sloppy reporting, unintended errors, or malicious misstatements. Rather, they likely represent the difficulty of accurately presenting a moving target. An example of DOI's dynamic budget situation was mentioned in the section on posters. In midyear, BOB and OEM's Division of Central Administrative Services agreed to allocate an additional $41,000 to DOI to conduct a new campaign to improve worker morale at production and manufacturing factories through a series of posters.[180]

Staffing

Employment figures for DOI were similarly fluid and in constant flux. Formally, up to mid-1941, DOI was authorized to employ 201 people, with about a 25 percent increase to 249 to occur in the second half of the calendar year, that is, when shifting from FY1941 to FY1942.[181] Sources published in fall 1941 variously put DOI's employment at 200,[182] 220,[183] 225,[184] 240,[185] and 250.[186] In January 1943, a BOB examiner confusingly testified before Congress that DOI's staffing a week before Pearl Harbor (that is, thirteen months earlier) was either 207 or 249.[187] Regardless of the exact number, Horton's was a big empire, especially considering that he began with just himself in May 1940, and it was growing fast. For example, an October 1941 personnel plan expected to fill thirty-six new positions within sixty days, exclusive of the expansion of the regional staff.[188]

As DOI grew, it worked closely with the CSC to maximize the number of its employees holding traditional appointments in the classified civil service. This was not only a way to professionalize its workforce, but also contributed to stability and continuity within the agency. With a permanent civil service appointment, staffers had the assurance that they would be eligible to transfer to similar jobs elsewhere in the federal government. That kind of (future) job security, DOI hoped, might reduce turnover.[189] For example, Assistant Director Straus made sure that any DOI staffers who were temps or held nonclassified positions were aware that they could apply for an upcoming CSC exam for public information specialists.[190] On another occasion, DOI worked with the CSC to obtain approval for the new personnel classification of "Principal Information Specialist," in contradistinction to assistant, no-prefix, and head.[191] This would elongate the professional career ladder for people in that professional track.

In general, expanding the classified service to include such a broad array and quantity of public relations positions was a relatively new endeavor for the commission. Its efforts to professionalize and routinize the recruiting and selecting of qualified candidates were quite bumpy. It had several false starts. In the summer of 1941, the head of information at the Interior Department noted that the "Commission had to make three distinct attempts to formulate an examination that would yield desirable results before it succeeded in assembling workable information registers" of qualified candidates.[192] In the fall, still not enough of the applicants for information specialists and radio writers passed the CSC's examination to fill all the vacancies in the defense effort (in its entirety, not just DOI or OEM). With one hundred vacancies still to be filled, the CSC started yet another round of recruiting applicants and asked Horton to help write a new exam for candidates to take.[193]

Sometimes things were moving at DOI too fast for the CSC, no matter how cooperative the commission tried to be. (CSC had a reputation, partly undeserved, for being a slow-moving and punctilious bureaucracy.) For example, in June 1941, the division urgently needed some graphic and layout artists—in CSC argot, "visual information specialists." However, the commission didn't yet have a register of qualified candidates who had passed the recruitment process. Trying to be helpful, its executive director suggested that DOI hire some of the pending *applicants* for the position as temporary employees. Then, once the examination had been administered and the list of approved eligible candidates became available, DOI could either shift the temps to permanent status (assuming they passed the exam) or let them go and replace them from the new list of qualified candidates.[194]

Planning for 1942: A Counterfactual History of DOI If Pearl Harbor Hadn't Happened

Horton understood that by its nature, press relations was a reactive activity. A PIO was usually responding to events and developments that were out of his (all were men at that time) control, such as reacting to a major policy decision by issuing a press release as quickly as possible and replying to inquiries from reporters about news developments. Horton was determined to try to break out of that purely reactive mold, get ahead of the curve, and conduct proactive government PR. This meant *planning.* DOI was among the first government PR units to engage in longer-term planning. Certainly, as part of its new foci on commemorative days and campaigns, DOI staff were creating elaborate and detailed plans for rolling out a particular observance or project through multimedia venues. However, Horton also encouraged PR planning that went beyond these kinds of specific events. He believed that broader gauge (what would now be called strategic) planning could be done as part of providing PR services to government agencies. Several planning documents were circulated during the eight weeks before Pearl Harbor that describe what

DOI would have done in 1942 had the status quo of 1941 continued into the next year. In mid-October, an in-house document, probably authored (or at least certainly approved) by Horton, discussed organizing DOI around "The New Victory Program." It called for an "all-out" information effort to mobilize the public in support of the United Kingdom and opposition to Nazi Germany. This effort would focus on the "victory" theme, rather than the passive and reactive term of "national defense" used up to then. The campaign would have specific objectives (such as the Four Freedoms) and then concentrate on using those objectives to link events occurring abroad to their relevance and impact on everyday Americans. A key would be to depict a world in which Hitler had beaten the United Kingdom. How would that affect US citizens, such as farmers or workers in export-based factories?

In the new campaign, DOI's tone would change. Acknowledging that such a PR effort by DOI would be criticized as propaganda, the plan nonetheless called for a more aggressive informational stance, not just to provide facts but also "to point out truths and relationships and patterns." Horton suggested that currently this "is a war of the intellectuals. But it can't be fought or won by the intellectuals." Rather, the campaign needed to speak to the average American because "if it doesn't mean something to him in these [tangible] terms, then no amount of vague principles are going to appeal." Specifically planning for the future, the Victory campaign would have monthly themes. The planning document suggested that the theme for December 1941 be conservation and that for January 1942 it be "what Germany has done to free speech and Democracy."[195]

Bruce Catton, assigned by DOI to be press secretary to Donald Nelson (who was in charge of production) followed up on the New Victory memo. He suggested that the theme of all DOI information activities in 1942 be that "this is not simply a defensive campaign, but is an effort to bring the country through a crisis and into an era in which democracy can mean more concrete material benefits for more people." The moniker he suggested was "Production for Plenty."[196]

Catton's colleague Stephen Fitzgerald also responded to the New Victory memo.[197] He submitted a detailed plan for DOI's Production Branch for 1942, suggesting specific information themes for the first four months of the new year. January 1942 would be dedicated to emphasizing that "there is a real threat to America and every American." To implement that theme, he suggested a range of PR activities including radio talks on the subject; a booklet, *If Hitler Wins,* embedding the theme as much as possible in all regular press releases; and an essay contest. Fitzgerald proposed similar detailed PR programs to implement themes for the subsequent months. In February, it would be, "What we are doing about the threat"; in March, "How *you* can help"; and in April 1942, "What are we aiming for?"[198]

Not everyone agreed with Fitzgerald's suggestion of introducing a monthly PR theme in 1942. Leigh Plummer, who headed DOI staff for the Price Branch, questioned its effectiveness, writing to Straus: "I don't think that a 'schedule' of propaganda ideas is workable. The reason is that we don't know how long it will take to convince the country that a particular idea should receive general acceptance. . . . Instead, we should pick out a small group of ideas which are considered essential and try to incorporate them in everything suitable for propaganda we put out."[199] It was an interesting, if irresolvable, argument. Should DOI execute a PR agenda for a (not-at-war) United States in 1942 that would change monthly or focus on a short list of permanent and unchanging central themes?

Separately, DOI's staffer assigned to the Defense Housing Coordinator also submitted a six-month PR plan (although not in reaction to the New Victory memo). His plans for up to mid-April 1942 included decentralization by shifting the location from which press releases were issued from Washington to local and regional offices, a new exhibit to tour the country on defense housing needs and the government's response, and a new brochure on defense housing availabilities that could be designed to have localized information inserted in it.[200]

While hardly definitive, these documents suggest that DOI's senior leadership was planning a major intensification of its PR program in 1942, virtually blurring any distinction between the United States being a nonbelligerent in the war or a combatant. It was as though a declaration of war approved by Congress was not all that important. Horton and his deputies were seeking a more convincing framework to persuade individual citizens that they would be tangibly and negatively affected if Hitler won the war against Great Britain. Meanwhile, lower-level staff, such as the PIO assigned to the Housing Coordinator, were planning that 1942 would be something of a more-of-the-same-but-better approach to PR.

Summary and Commentary

The period from March to December 1941 was a very difficult one for President Roosevelt and his administration. While Congress had voted him funding for a robust national defense (with spending allocations largely subject to his discretion), extended the draft, and even approved Lend-Lease, the United States was not in a state of war. Even Roosevelt's declaration of an unlimited state of emergency in late May didn't change that basic fact. As chief PR man for the defense production buildup, Horton navigated this difficult political and governmental landscape aggressively. He was not significantly intimidated by potential or actual criticisms from isolationists, congressional conservatives, or the press. No shrinking violet of a PIO he, Horton was not wracked by *doubt*. He went full-throttle, growing his DOI into a very large government information apparatus. He flooded the country with news, reports, radio programs, public speakers, photo stills, film shorts, newsreels, posters, publications, commemorative days, and campaigns. Initially, all were factual. During 1941, however, DOI's messages gradually expanded from information to morale building and justifications for the national defense policies of President Roosevelt. Horton was using every communication medium at his disposal to convince the country—with facts *and* arguments—that the United States would be in danger if Hitler were to win and Great Britain be defeated. A half century earlier, the Women's Christian Temperance Union (WCTU), one of the leading national pro-Prohibition organizations, had used the public slogan "Do Everything" to guide its work.[201] That approach to persuasion seemed to be Horton's SOP, too. He did *everything* he could think of.

The normal rules of American political culture limited government public relations to information only, with limited exceptions for widely held values, presidential communication, and war. Horton blithely ignored the rules of the game. He was advocating for policies that were not widely held, and the United States was not at war. At most, he was elaborating on the president's views, although Roosevelt himself could at times be opaque and vague. None of these constraints seemed to limit how Horton led DOI. As far as he was concerned, it was DOI's responsibility to raise civic and worker morale and to mobilize the nation for a common goal, and it was the public's duty to accept sacrifices and significant changes in daily life as a means to that end. This was government public relations to the max, no holds barred. Given how significantly Horton violated the norms and consensus in 1941 about what was OK and not OK for government PR, it is somewhat surprising how relatively little criticism he provoked. He was adroit politically and communication-wise without being timid.

The other significant aspect of Horton's work in 1941 was how successful he was in maintaining DOI as a centralized PR office servicing about a dozen separate agencies, some virtually at war with each other. While the autonomistic imperative is buried deep in bureaucratic genes, Horton was largely successful at fending off persistent desires by agencies for their own PR unit. As a result, he was able to impose a coordinated and somewhat unified communications apparatus on a large swath of the burgeoning national defense bureaucracy. It was an accomplishment practically without parallel in modern American government at a time when the country was not in a state of war. Horton deserves recognition for attaining this against-the-odds accomplishment. During 1941, he was engaging in ultimate government PR, a record that probably would never be replicated in peacetime. Still, doing everything, and doing it on a centralized basis, didn't necessarily mean the needle was budging much on the public opinion meter. It was a *big* country. At times, Horton's work must have felt like shouting into a howling wind. If anything, 1941 showed the limits of propaganda and government PR in peacetime. But Horton certainly tried.

PART III

GOVERNMENT PR IN WARTIME

CHAPTER 6

AN OVERVIEW OF HORTON'S AUTONOMOUS DIVISION OF INFORMATION

December 1941–June 1942

Contrary to popular memory, Pearl Harbor was *not* a bolt out of the blue, although the location of the attack was something of a surprise. Largely sifted out of the standard historical narrative is that there were several major false alarms of impending Japanese attacks in the months preceding the real attack, including on July 25 and October 16, 1941. Also, on November 27, the Army and Navy sent war warnings to its commanders.[1] On Tuesday, December 1, Roosevelt told OPM's production chief, Donald Nelson, that he "wouldn't be a bit surprised if we were at war with Japan by Thursday," December 3.[2] These earlier false alarms and generalized war warnings explain partly why the behavior of some officials and commanders seemed, in retrospect, to have been somewhat lackadaisical in the hours immediately before the real attack began on December 7. There was no "this is it *for sure*" moment before the bombs began falling.

"A Date Which Will Live in Infamy"

That Sunday, December 7, Horton was at the Mayflower Hotel meeting with Garson Kanin and several other Hollywood men, trying to persuade them to make some shorts, including some for Army training.[3] As soon as the news broke, he rushed to the office. Horton told one of his staffers to call the residence of George Lyon, the PIO for DOI who was assigned to LaGuardia's OCD, to ask where the mayor was. Not able to reach LaGuardia promptly based on the information Lyon provided, Horton then personally called Lyon back and said it was imperative that he get in touch with the mayor to issue a statement on air raid precautions. Lyon asked what the urgency was. According to Catton: "There was a silence at the other end of the wire, followed by a chuckle. 'Oh. I take it you haven't had your radio on this afternoon? . . . Well, the Japs have just attacked Pearl Harbor and we're in the war.'"[4]

DOI's thirteen-part weekly radio series *Keep 'em Rolling* was due to have its regular airing on a national network that Sunday night. Horton quickly called the DOI production director, who was already at the studio in Manhattan, where the program originated. Again, Horton was the one to break the news about the Japanese attack. Horton directed him to rewrite the dramatization portion of the show (due to be aired live in a few hours) to reflect the new situation and to insert a time slot for Nelson to speak live.[5] Horton then contacted the other networks to arrange for Nelson's speech to be aired on all of them. Contradicting the mythology that the nation instantly coalesced that day, he "had a terrible time" during that afternoon trying to arrange it. Each of the other networks asked Horton for an exclusive right to air Nelson's speech. Horton was disgusted.[6]

Horton and Catton quickly wrote a six-minute speech for Nelson.[7] Nelson was the only senior administration official to give a public comment that Sunday, with Roosevelt withholding any statement until he would address Congress the next day.[8] They realized that what they wrote was significant. Nelson spoke forcefully, but reassuringly, to the nation. He focused on production, the subject on which he was the acknowledged government expert. Nelson urged each citizen to play a role in the war, whether through military service, in arms production factories, or through conservation in personal life. The most newsworthy aspect of his talk was his interpretation of the day's events: "We must keep in mind that though the attack has been made by the Japanese it is in reality an attack upon us by the Axis powers. It is, as you and I can see, part of a pattern. That pattern is designed to bring about, if possible, the extinction of democracy—of all freedoms everywhere. We are face to face with attack *directed primarily from Berlin*."[9]

Horton and Catton had put forward the Roosevelt view that the chief enemy was Germany. Yet, as of that Sunday night, the United States was only in a de facto war with Japan. It was not at war with Germany, nor was Germany at war with it. When the president asked Congress the next day for a declaration of war, he pointedly asked for it only against Japan.[10] Horton and Catton were already previewing what was to become the administration's mantra: "Germany First."

The lights burned late that Sunday night at all of OEM's agencies as they began making decisions to reflect the new war situation. The DOI staffers attached to each of them began preparing a slew of public announcements of those decisions.

DOI Goes to War

In a flash, everything had changed. After walking the tightrope of government PR in peacetime for so long, Horton could finally let loose. This was war. No more tiptoeing around to prevent criticism by isolationists. No more pretending that this was purely for *defense* and only that. Finally, Horton's PR could invoke the third exception to the ban on government propaganda: wartime. Ever since the German invasion of Poland in September 1939, Horton could argue that national defense was important, that US interests lay in Germany being thwarted, that Lend-Lease was a national priority endorsed by Congress, even that the president had declared the United States to be in a state of unlimited national emergency. But the United States was not in a state of war, and therefore the third exception to limits on government PR could not be invoked in an unqualified way. More than two years after Hitler's invasion of Poland, with Horton engaging in government PR when the world was at war

Table 5
Events when Horton headed the Division of Information (after Pearl Harbor)

TIME PERIOD	INTERNATIONAL	DOMESTIC
December 7, 1941–June 12, 1942	Pearl Harbor; British surrender Singapore and Hong Kong; Japan attacks Dutch East Indies; US garrison at Corregidor surrenders; Russian counteroffensive begins; Doolittle raid on Tokyo; United States wins Battle of Midway; Lidice massacre.	Congress declares war on Japan, then Germany; Churchill guest at White House; tire rationing ordered; National War Labor Relations Board created; price and rent controls; begin daylight savings time for duration of war; forced expulsion of Japanese Americans to concentration camps; War Powers bill signed; suspension of antitrust suits against corporations in war production; Board of Economic Warfare and War Manpower Commission created.

but the United States wasn't, the gloves were finally were off. The initial stage of the US role in World War II had begun, when the United States was largely on the defensive, not "winning" the war in any visible sense (see table 5).

One would expect that DOI's PR would be significantly more persuasion oriented and closer to the category of war propaganda than before Pearl Harbor. Specifically, *what* was different between DOI's prewar and wartime activities, and *how* was it different? For DOI's own public face, during that first week after the United State entered the war, Horton changed two things. First, he coined the phrase "Remember Pearl Harbor!"[11] It echoed the slogan "Remember the *Maine*" from the Spanish-American War. The phrase began appearing across the top of all DOI press releases on Wednesday, December 10.[12] According to the *New York Times,* "Immediately, the phrase was snapped up and is being used on the air, in the press and is sweeping across the land."[13] Second, on December 11, DOI's weekly publication of record, *Defense,* was renamed *Victory.*[14] The first issue with the new masthead was published on December 16.[15]

Horton understood that the declaration of war created a need for some feature-style press releases to give newspaper readers a broader perspective and bigger picture on daily news developments, especially relating to the events preceding Pearl Harbor and what the attack portended for the United States' future. So, for example, DOI released for the morning papers of Tuesday, December 9, a long piece entitled "Our Stake in the Pacific" (which conveyed the opposite message of Nelson's radio talk). Then, for the first Sunday papers after Pearl Harbor, DOI issued a feature-length article and photo of the US-built tanks being used by the British in North Africa against Rommel. Ten days after the Japanese attack, a long explanatory piece appeared titled "Shipping for Defense." For the second Sunday after the attack (and the last Sunday before Christmas), DOI released a very long feature piece (seven mimeographed pages) and photos explaining why the United States had an electrical power shortage and how that was affecting its ability to pursue the war effort.[16]

DOI quickly issued its first war poster. Consisting wholly of text, it was a quotation from the president's December 9 radio talk to the nation (the day after his speech to Congress):

WE ARE NOW
IN THIS WAR
We are all in it
all the way

> Every single man, woman and child
> is a partner in the most tremendous
> undertaking of our American history.
> We must share together the bad news
> and the good news, the defeats and the
> victories—the changing fortunes of war.[17]

As a manager, Horton made two decisions early on that would help convey to his employees how much the war had changed the status quo of their working conditions. He announced that DOI would not grant any employees Christmas leave because it is "necessary that each of you be on duty every working day that your health permits. . . . [I]f we can forego the holiday pleasures many of us had planned this year, we can trust that they may have far greater significance next year."[18] At the end of the month, he announced that New Year's Day would not be a vacation day, that the office would be open as usual and all employees were expected to report to work.[19] In fact, DOI issued a relatively routine press release on New Year's Day, dealing with changes in shipping and transportation due to the war.[20]

Horton had pivoted quickly to adapt to the new wartime situation. He had built DOI to be fleet-footed, and its initial post–Pearl Harbor PR products and activities reflected that. The declaration of war had significant impacts on DOI. Qualitatively, it could now openly engage in pro-war persuasion activities. Also, it was less restricted to matters dealing with the production buildup. Now, just about anything dealing with the civilian side of the entire political economy was within DOI's purview. Quantitatively, for every PR activity in which the agency had engaged before Pearl Harbor, Horton's message was simple: more, MORE, ***MORE.***

Press Relations

DOI's pre–Pearl Harbor flood of press releases now became a Noah's flood of words. Its press center was permanently open 24/7. And it was busy all the time. From the beginning of the war until DOI's dissolution in June, it issued 1,835 press releases in its PM (Production Management) series alone, for a pace of about nine per day, seven days per week. With the creation of the new War Production Board (WPB) in mid-January (replacing OPM), DOI initiated a new press release series for it. There were 932 releases in the WPB series between mid-January and mid-April, reflecting a pace of about ten per day. DOI also had several lesser series, including T (Transportation), DH (Division of Housing), and R (Radio). In total, from January 1, 1942, until its dissolution in June, DOI issued about 3,000 press releases, a pace of about sixteen per day, including weekends.[21]

It is hard to conceive of this flood of information pouring out of DOI's newsroom all day (and night). To assist reporters, DOI began issuing a formal daily "Summary of Press Releases." The summaries for the last week of February 1942 present a typical example of DOI's press releases after Pearl Harbor until its dissolution. It consisted of a light day (7 on Sunday, the 22nd), two heavy days (28 on Friday, the 27th, and 26 on Saturday, the 28th), and several medium days (21, 14, 18, and 18 on Monday through Thursday, the 23rd through the 26th).[22] The rate of its output increased later in the spring, with DOI incredibly issuing an average of 30 releases per day.[23]

Still, no matter how well organized DOI made its press releases to facilitate coverage by reporters, one gets the impression that the division was trying to pour too much product into too small a funnel. The news media simply couldn't digest that much information. But Horton was keeping his promise to maximize the release of news by OEM agencies. No reporter or anti-Roosevelt politician could credibly argue that Horton was being too tight-fisted with information on decisions and actions.

While many of DOI's releases, especially in the period immediately after Pearl Harbor, tilted to features and analysis, its routine daily output comprised mostly spot news releases on decisions of OEM agencies. Given the scope of the government's wartime control over the civilian economy, the topics of the releases included just about all economic activity.[24] An unusual release, neither spot news nor a feature, was an effort by OEM agencies to provide a unified front on the supply of rubber:

> Four leading war agency officials today joined in a statement designed to clarify the facts about the severe rubber shortage. Issued because many confusing and conflicting stories have been circulated about rubber, the statement points out that the shortage is extremely serious. . . . There has been a great deal of confusion about the rubber situation, much of it caused by optimistic stories about the availability of synthetic rubber at an early date, or the large amount of scrap rubber which can be reprocessed. But there is little real basis for such optimism. Our rubber shortage is one of the worst materials shortages we face.[25]

One of DOI's innovations in press relations during this period, compared to its earlier practice, was the inclusion of graphics in some of its releases. This was a way to convey relatively complicated matters in an easy-to-understand visual way. For example, a feature-oriented press release titled *The Geography of Rubber* included a global map of America's sources of rubber. It showed that 98 percent of all US rubber needs were met by rubber from the Far East, with only 1 percent coming from South America.[26] The lesson? The importance of controlling the Pacific Ocean and preventing Japan from monopolizing the rubber supply from Asia. Another time, DOI tried to explain why gasoline needed to be rationed. A map of the United States showed that shipping oil in tankers from wells near the Gulf of Mexico to the Atlantic states was no longer feasible due to German submarines. The shift to pipelines was causing shortages because of an inadequate pipeline network that could not handle any more volume.[27] Again, the graphic demonstrated that a picture was worth a thousand words.

Submission of fillers with short facts was a relatively common press relations activity. DOI modified such an occasional product after the War Production Board was established. The division began sending out a *regular* weekly release of fillers containing facts about the war supply situation. Calling them "Splinters," DOI also suggested to editors that the contents of the weekly release could also be used as a freestanding feature, as the basis for editorials or as ideas for cartoons.[28]

Horton also arranged for some of the reporters' bosses to be briefed on the war effort. On December 22, DOI organized an all-day briefing of business-paper editors and publishers, including a talk by Nelson. When Horton met with them, he emphasized the constructive role they could play in the war effort by sharing what would now be called best practices (on the business side) and promoting conservation by readers.[29] A second briefing took place on February 13. At that event, Horton said he was committed to helping them "carry sound information and advice to the people that you represent."[30] On both occasions, the editors and publishers were assured of the government's commitment to allocating adequate supplies to permit them to continue printing. Later in the spring, DOI helped organize a separate briefing in New York City for the labor press. There, Horton showed his New Deal colors when he "assailed the unfairness of the daily press in its treatment of labor news."[31]

In a time of war, Horton's consistent policy of issuing as much information as possible was easier said than done. There was some confusion by DOI staff in the first months after Pearl Harbor regarding what could be released publicly and what couldn't. Horton, therefore, distributed a memo that tried to give some informal in-house guidance. He compared the censor's official rules on what could not be released and the policies of the Committee on War Information (convened by OFF before OWI was created) on what should be. These were not necessarily in conflict and could be harmonized. He focused on two guidelines: not giving information that would be helpful to the enemy and that WPB was authorized to distribute information on the production effort without preapproval by the censor. However, he emphasized that information authorized for release by WPB could only be issued in written statements. That meant oral comments by WPB officials (and heard by the DOI staffer assigned to a WPB agency) were not automatically releasable. Yes, DOI should not give aid and comfort to the enemy. But, Horton symmetrically balanced that by emphasizing that "giving aid and comfort to the American people is also very important and that this must be done by a wide distribution of facts."[32]

A leading national reporter, neither pro- nor anti-Horton, described his daily interactions with Horton's press relations staff in 1941–42: "Of course, there were drones and incompetents and show-offs, as there are in any large organization, but if you worked from day to day with these men you were of necessity impressed with the number who were hard-working, efficient in the face of great odds, and terribly in earnest."[33] On the lighter side, *Newsweek* reported that the press officers challenged the reporters to a baseball game by posting this taunt on the bulletin board: "Whereas we, the Information Experts of the Division of Information have noticed an increasing tendency on the part of the 'newspapermen' and 'reporters' of the press room to compensate for their mental inferiority by bragging that they are at least our equals as men of action." The reporters accepted the challenge in the same spirit by attaching conditions: "That the game actually be played on April 26, and not, as is your invariable custom, three days later than originally promised. That after the decisions and results have been announced you do not, as usual, insist on sending out a correction, a complaint that you were misquoted, or a demand that the results be censored or held for release until next winter." The PIOs won, 20 to 18.[34]

In his column, Damon Runyon also made fun of the OEM releases he routinely received in the mail. He wrote how well-informed he felt on rubber and sugar shortages after reading the DOI releases. But he lightly chided DOI that only some of its releases were printed on both sides of the paper, while others continued to be one-sided, thus wasting paper, of which there also was a shortage.[35]

Public Reporting

DOI's public reporting activities in the first half of 1942 decreased somewhat from the previous period. While quantification is difficult, there were discernibly fewer products that would be categorized as reporting. Most activities were continuations of previous efforts, such as a detailed four-page press release summarizing production totals for airplanes (a sensitive subject ever since Senator Byrd's attacks in the summer of 1940);[36] a new radio series "to keep America well informed" as a follow-up to the just-concluded *Keep 'em Rolling* series;[37] two more movie reports, each covering multiple topics;[38] an updated version of the booklet explaining OEM's structure and role;[39] and two publications explaining the war production effort, one for broad circulation with brief text and another for more specialized audiences containing detailed information.[40]

DOI also prepared a retrospective report, "America from Dunkirk to Pearl Harbor: The Story of 599 Days." It was a comprehensive summary of the defense preparedness and production effort in the eighteen months before Pearl Harbor. Its theme was that "this story of what happened in America between Dunkirk and Pearl Harbor is worth studying. . . . If there is also in it some record of shortcomings—of chances missed, of time wasted, of important jobs left half-done—may it teach us, once and for all, never again to underestimate the size of the job or the extent of the effort which we must make."[41] The tone was apparently all wrong for the mood triggered by the Japanese attack, and the seventeen-page report was never issued.

The diminution of reporting activities perhaps appears starker than it really was, perhaps simply in juxtaposition to Horton's robust reporting record before Pearl Harbor. Another partial explanation could be temporal, namely that during the first few months of the war, there simply was not much retrospective and past performance information to report on yet.

Government PR as Persuasion: Widely Held Values, Presidential Communication, and War

Horton now had all three face cards, the three exceptions to the ban on propaganda in government PR: there was a broad consensus that the war should be won, President Roosevelt's personal wartime leadership, and Congress's formal declarations of war on Japan and then on Germany and Italy. If Horton wanted to convert DOI into a propaganda agency, like the Committee on Public Information during World War I, now was the time. But, Horton held true to what he had done before Pearl Harbor. Not much changed. He wanted to raise civilian and, especially, production worker morale, but largely by sharing facts. Yes, enthusiasm was good, banners were good, posters were good; but underlying them all was the goal of an informed citizenry and workforce for which Horton had generally been pushing since well before the Japanese attack on December 7.

According to H. W. Brands, "The American government encouraged patriotic thinking but declined to whip the public mood into the frenzy of the earlier conflict," that is, World War I.[42] A mid-1942 report by DOI confronted the choice head-on: "There has been a conflict of opinion in Washington over whether the emphasis should be on propaganda or straight reporting of facts. The Division of Information has subscribed to the fact-reporting theory."[43] Similarly, in a public talk in May, Horton specifically disavowed any interest in shifting DOI to a wartime propaganda orientation. He said that recently "our office is charged [by critics] with disseminating propaganda and the word propaganda has a connotation of fabrication. This is a gross untruth. We give only the facts as we see them."[44] Schoenfeld, DOI's chief of radio programming, defined propaganda similarly. He asserted that DOI's radio dramatizations about life under Nazism and fascism were part of the production effort because they helped *explain* the nature of the enemy: "Such information is not propaganda; such information, based on authentic sources, becomes as necessary and realistic as statistics and our shipping lists."[45] So, DOI's definition of propaganda was communication that was based on fiction rather than fact.

Horton's somewhat defensive comment about critics accusing DOI of conducting propaganda accurately reflected the times. The conservative coalition on Capitol Hill had condemned the growth of government PR throughout Roosevelt's presidency, as did the press.[46] After Pearl Harbor, this criticism increased noticeably in both amount and ferocity. This likely occurred as a *result* of the declaration of war. Fully aware of the unstated rules of government PR and the wartime exception, political opponents of Roosevelt knew they needed to act preemptively and vociferously to delimit that loophole before Roosevelt could rush in and exploit it. The war also gave them a new rationale for their views, namely that PR was a nonessential expenditure that needed to be curbed in wartime. Dollars for production, not for posters, press releases, and publications. It proved an effective line of attack.

Some of the broad denunciations of federal wartime propaganda (without singling out DOI) in the *Congressional Record* in February and March 1942 carried such titles as "The Government's Propaganda Bill," "Propaganda Expenditure," and "New Deal Propaganda."[47] An indication of the fever pitch of these attacks occurred on February 23, 1942. Senator Arthur Vandenberg (R-MI) endorsed an editorial just published in the *New York News* and *Washington Times-Herald*. The editorial had condemned the recent wartime expansion of federal information services because it "is building up in many people's minds a suspicion that this administration is putting together a propaganda ministry of the German, or Dr. Paul Goebbels' type, for use both during and after the war. From that suspicion it is an easy jump to a suspicion that this administration expects to be running some sort of totalitarian government either before or after the end of this war, and is prudently getting ready for same."[48] Vandenberg liked the editorial so much and it so captured his thinking that he inserted it for republication in the *Congressional Record*, making it more widely accessible to others. A senator's endorsement of this hysterical accusation about government PR helps capture the perspective of the conservative coalition against Roosevelt—war or no war.[49]

The increased frequency of such attacks on government propaganda immediately after Pearl Harbor sometimes focused specifically on DOI. In January, the first month after the attack and declaration of war, Congressman Richard Wigglesworth (R-MA) criticized DOI, saying that "Mr. Horton, of the O.E.M., runs one of the largest publicity set-ups in the entire Government."[50] Senator Robert Taft (R-OH), interested in running for president, in a speech in Tennessee "devoted nearly a quarter of his address to the publicity machine which the Government offices and agencies have set up in the Capital City." In Taft's list of seven such agencies, DOI came second, after OGR. "It is becoming propaganda, pure and unadulterated," he said.[51] In May, a newspaper story reported on Senator Harry Byrd's attack that "government outlays for travel expenses and publicity bureaus 'very nearly approaches a national scandal in the waste of public funds.'" He criticized "overlapping and unnecessary agencies conducting publicity or propaganda activities," including DOI's budget of $1.5 million.[52]

Later that month, Senator Millard Tydings (D-MD) characterized OEM's press releases as "frequently nothing more or less than pure propaganda articles" and a waste of money in wartime. He criticized the agency sending out fillers, such as about Venezuelan income taxes, paper conservation in England, and auto restrictions in the Canary Islands. In particular, he criticized a DOI release titled "How to Spend the Week-end without a Car." He said the release contained five suggestions for citizens:

1. working in the garden, where one could "dig for fun, for health, for good living, for economy and for patriotism";
2. organizing community discussion groups;
3. hiking, bicycle riding, and using streetcars instead of automobiles;
4. playing games; and
5. taking up a hobby such as "stamps, coins and autographs" instead of going for pleasure drives.[53]

On the Senate floor, he explained why he had zeroed in on that press release:

> That would not be so bad, perhaps, if it came from one of the old established orthodox bureaus or divisions of the Government not connected with the war; but here is an agency, an emergency agency, set up with millions of dollars to aid in the war effort that actually has high-priced newspapermen, publicists, press agents, or whatever one may want to call them, turning out this drivel, using up good paper and ink and machines which often cost two or three thousand dollars apiece, and employing a large number of people. . . in the midst of a great war, which we are told threatens civilization, to find that sort of drivel being turned out and sent to newspaper offices in the United States of America by the Office for Emergency Management.[54]

Tydings had struck gold. Editorial writers, ever ready to criticize government waste and the deluge of press releases coming out of Washington, had a field day. With great mirth and sarcasm, this example became exhibit A of the idiocy of the government employing flacks and of excessive federal spending, especially in wartime. Were these guys so out of touch with reality? Do we need to be told that stamp collecting is a way to spend free time on weekends? What a bunch of idiots![55]

As is usually the case in these situations, the headline and lead were more sensational than the actual details. Here, verbatim, are two shorter versions of the release that DOI supplied to newspapers as part of its regular informational columns. This was for housewives:

> Have you been wondering how to spend a week end without the family car to save tires and gas? Well, perhaps you will substitute a Sunday hike for the Sunday drive. More than likely you'll discover more about your community on foot than you ever did when you had the family bus at your command. Or if you are a stay-at-home week ender, try table tennis or badminton with the family and some of the neighbors. Some of you, having stored your car except for business, probably will join in the Victory Garden program. Other Mrs. Americas may discover ways of keeping their husbands busy repairing household gadgets over the week end.[56]

This was from an even shorter DOI summary of news from the home front: "There are plenty of ways to spend a pleasant week-end without the family car—If 30 American families pass up their Sunday afternoon auto rides, they will save enough gasoline to keep a bomber in the air a full hour—and save tires, too."[57]

While such a release is easy to ridicule, it was well-meant. With gas and tires being rationed and low-level grumbling going on around the nation about the disruption of daily lives, DOI was seeking to provide some concrete and tangible suggestions of activities to replace the tradition of the Sunday-afternoon drive. It may have been pretty elementary, but that was the nature of many advice columns. In fact, just a few weeks after the press clucking had died down, the *Washington Post* (which had led the effort to stop the building of OGR's US Information Center on Pennsylvania Avenue) ran a half-page photo spread titled "Here's How to Spend the Weekend," showing activities in the Washington area that could be reached without a car. It made no reference to DOI as the source of the idea for the story.[58] Also without attribution, the *Hartford Courant* published part of the original DOI release relating to noncar recreation opportunities in "our national parks . . . that have been inaccessible to automobile tourists."[59]

One is hard put to identify DOI products that a layperson would categorize as propaganda, namely communications that were misleading (if not overtly false), manipulative, and emotional. Yes, Horton continued trying to explain developments to citizens and workers, encouraging participation in the war effort, and maintaining morale. All these, though, were based on the facts of the situation. None involved fabrication. A few movie shorts were of the patriotic and flag-waving nature, such as Garson Kanin's *Ring of Steel* or *Keep 'em Rolling*. The former, narrated by Spencer Tracy, was a "historical summary and tribute to American soldiers who have protected our country since 1776, forging a 'ring of steel' around American democracy." The latter was a three-minute short of Jan Peerce singing a Rodgers and Hart song "against [a] background of scenes in war production plants."[60]

Similarly, some of the radio dramatizations, intended to make vivid the world under Hitler, focused on viscerally reaching the audience rather than with dry facts. For example, the radio series *You Can't Do Business with Hitler* was based on facts, but was dramatized and simplified. However, these programs were explicitly identified as dramatizations and mini-plays, making clear that they were fictionalizations based on known facts. There was no mistaking that these were live events or documentaries, preventing a "War of the Worlds"–type misunderstanding.

Perhaps the closest DOI came to propaganda was the ominous poster that read, "He's Watching You." It showed the outline of a German soldier from the nose up, wearing a military helmet and with large eyes staring forward.[61] To Paula Harper, the poster is "reminiscent in theme and composition of the World War I poster 'Beat Back the Hun.'" However, she argues that it was deliberately designed "in a schematic style which abstracts and sterilizes the image and makes it acceptable to a generation which was conscious of the propaganda excesses of the First World War."[62] So, the poster was, at most, something along the lines of propaganda lite. If this was the best Horton could do in terms of propaganda, it was an amusing failure. A survey of production workers revealed that they thought the helmet was the Liberty Bell and the message was that the country was depending on them. An alternate interpretation they offered was that the staring eyes were of the boss at the plant, reflecting tense labor-management relations.[63]

Nonetheless, a central dynamic of politics and public opinion is that perception is reality. The exaggerated complaints from the conservative coalition of government propaganda and the big play those accusations received in the press were working. This, eventually, led Roosevelt to conclude that he had better reorganize the wartime information services by executive order before Congress imposed a different solution on him by statute.

Horton's Centralized Structure for Government PR

Horton's philosophy of a centralized PR office servicing a large number of government agencies had some wins and losses during the first half of 1942. His biggest win related to the new organizational fulcrum for the war production effort, the War Production Board. On January 15, 1942, Roosevelt yet again reorganized the civilian side of the national defense (now war) effort. He abolished OPM and replaced it with a board that had a powerful single chair, Donald Nelson.[64] This was as close as the president was willing to get to appointing a single "czar" to run the economy during the war.[65]

Nelson was on good terms with Horton and thought well of him and DOI. Before WPB, Horton had detailed Bruce Catton as Nelson's *personal* press aide and speechwriter, separate from the DOI section that provided PR services to the part of OPM that Nelson oversaw. That structure worked well for Nelson, and he saw no reason to change it.[66] Also, as a former corporate executive, he understood the logic of one central PR office serving the entire corporation, rather than separate fiefdoms. On January 26, only two weeks after his own appointment by the president, Nelson in turn appointed Horton as head of WPB's information effort.[67] The next week, Nelson announced his decision to all WPB staff: "In the interests of good organization and procedure, and to assure accuracy and consistent expression of policy, it is desirable to centralize responsibility of all public material relating to the War Production Board. Pursuant to this, I have designated the Division of Information as the Division within this organization responsible for the handling and release of all public relations material. The Division is responsible to me for the proper handling of such material and will operate in accordance with policy."[68]

This gave Horton the power he wanted to implement his vision of a centralized government information service. However, the organizational relationship was confusing (exactly how Roosevelt liked things). In one respect, DOI was now one of the entities within Nelson's domain, including making Horton Nelson's subordinate. This is as it was depicted in organization charts and photos of WPB published in the media and in DOI's magazine of record, *Victory*.[69] Also, a postwar official history similarly listed DOI as a division within WPB.[70]

On the other hand, Nelson could not unilaterally overrule the February 1941 presidential letter that established DOI as an independent OEM agency.

Only the president would direct such a change. This did not happen. So, for example, in Nelson's memoir, when he listed the internal organization of his new WPB, he listed its line *and staff* divisions, but not DOI.[71] Similarly, the OEM organization chart in the official *US Government Manual* that spring showed boxes for WPB's divisions, but DOI was not among them. Instead, it was presented as a freestanding OEM agency.[72] Probably the most accurate description of Horton's role was that he headed an independent and unsupervised OEM agency, while at the same time DOI was "hired" by Nelson to handle WPB's external communications, somewhat akin to the relationship between a corporation that instead of having an in-house PR department would contract with an independent entity to provide all its PR needs. In twenty-first-century usage, Nelson had outsourced WPB's PR to DOI.

Horton had the best of all possible worlds and was on a roll. Besides WPB, his centralization philosophy led to other expansions of his domain in this period. In February, Leon Henderson, head of the Office of Price Administration (OPA) permanently transferred OPA's consumer publications office to DOI. In explaining his decision, Henderson said he liked Horton's suggestion "that the scope of the work should be broadened to include information which demonstrates the impact of the war on the average citizen," rather than the current more narrow focus on prices and consumers.[73] In May, Horton picked up two new clients: the Alien Property Custodian and the War Relocation Authority.[74] On June 1, 1942, DOI was serving and staffing seven independent OEM agencies (including WPB) and conducting information liaison work with ten other OEM entities. Within WPB, it was providing PR services for its ten divisions (or their administrative equals). Finally, within WPB's Division of Industry Operations, DOI was serving seven branches.[75] Trying to avoid double counting, the sum total would be about thirty-three distinct administrative entities.

But that spring there was subtraction as well as addition. The continuing problems with OCD and LaGuardia (discussed in the previous chapter) were becoming untenable. LaGuardia and his successor, James Landis, wanted OCD to have its own PR office.[76] Horton at first fought it, claiming to BOB that Landis simply wanted an office he could control with men loyal to him personally. However, at the same time, Horton conceded to BOB that from a personal standpoint, he would be glad to let go of it.[77] This would have been a very reluctant conclusion for him, as it undercut everything he had been preaching about PR centralization. The divorce was announced to DOI staff on February 7 and to the press the next day.[78] Seven DOI staffers transferred to OCD and joined about two dozen other OCD employees who were already there as a kind of de facto PR unit.[79]

Horton hoped the loss of OCD was merely a one-off event, but as a good bureaucratic in-fighter he knew it created a precedent that could corrode the infrastructure he had built. The next shoe to (almost) drop was housing. As discussed in the previous chapter, Defense Housing Coordinator Charles Palmer had hired Howard Acton as a special assistant for PR, and Acton immediately began pushing for PR autonomy from DOI. In early January, 1942, Acton met with DOI Assistant Director Straus. Acton insisted that Dana Doten, the DOI staffer detailed to the Housing Coordinator be withdrawn because "he does not measure up to our present requirements." Straus and Horton refused. Acton also asked that Doten be replaced by two new staffers from DOI, a reporter and a writer. They would work to implement Acton's own "present public relations objectives as we now see them and our proposed approach to their attainment."[80] As it turned out, the president unintentionally resolved the matter in February. By executive order, he reorganized all housing-related entities in the executive branch into a new National Housing Agency. OEM's Coordinator of Defense Housing unit was dissolved and its functions transferred to the new agency. Palmer was politely fired, with the president naming BOB Assistant Director John Blandford Jr. to head it.[81] With the new agency outside of OEM and EOP, DOI no longer had any PR jurisdiction. Horton wrote Blandford that, if Blandford wanted, the two DOI staffers who had been assigned to the Housing Coordinator's office (including, still, Doten) could remain at the new housing agency for the interim "to carry on any purely service functions which would aid you in your work" until Blandford was ready to make permanent decisions about PR staffing. Horton poked Acton in the bureaucratic eye by including Acton in the list of people to receive carbon copies of his letter to Blanton.[82] For Horton, not losing the PR duties for an *OEM* agency was a win. Horton had one other loss, which occurred just three weeks after Pearl Harbor. For reasons that are obscure, effective January 1, 1942, DOI's Public Service Unit within the Distribution and Correspondence Section was transferred into OPM's (later WPB's) Inquiry Section. This entailed ten clerks and typists who handled in-person and mailed inquiries and requests for information.[83]

In general, Horton's PR centralization philosophy held strong for the first half of 1942, the first six months of the war. Trying to describe to the sprawling and growing OEM workforce what it did, DOI presented front and center the rationale for Horton's centralization philosophy: "The focussing in one Division of all the information work of OEM—with the exception of the Office of Civilian Defense which on February 9 established its own information section—eliminates duplicating and non-essential informational activity within the war agencies and permits one office to coordinate requests with relation to each other as well as to similar activities of the non-emergency agencies."[84] Horton had no doubt that this was the best organizing principle for government public relations. His commitment to the centralization of PR services had survived the initial wartime flush relatively intact. He had some defections, but also some gains. Horton realized how natural it was for a government agency to want to control its own PR office and fought as fiercely as he could against it. The principle of centralization was still in place, although somewhat tenuously.

CHAPTER 7

THE DIVISION OF INFORMATION'S PROGRAMS AND MANAGEMENT

December 1941–June 1942

Besides the most traditional government PR functions of press relations and public reporting, other now-standard DOI activities accelerated after Pearl Harbor, simply much, much more of what it had been doing before. Just as the gusher of press releases had turned into a flood, the same held true for DOI's other ongoing PR products. But now Horton could also expand the scope of a wartime DOI to as many additional PR activities as could be conceived. He wanted to do *everything*. This was more than merely a broad approach to government PR.

This was curb-to-curb external communications to the max, with its only historical comparison in US history being World War I's Committee on Public Information (CPI). In early summer of 1942, Rex Harlow, one of the few professors of PR at the time, concluded that the government's current PR, while somewhat disorganized, was better than CPI's had been: "Citizens are far better informed about this war, in all its aspects, than they were about World War I. They also know far more about the general workings of government."[1] While not directed specifically at DOI, Horton could justifiably bask in the compliment, which exactly described his goal.

Speeches

DOI continued its relationship with the Junior Bar Association and other organizations that provided volunteer speakers in their localities. To keep the speakers as up-to-date as possible on developments, DOI arranged for them to receive on a complimentary basis its weekly publication, newly retitled *Victory*.[2]

After the war declaration, Horton personally assumed a somewhat higher public profile. He became more of a spokesman and senior official making public statements about the war effort than just a behind-the-scenes bureaucrat. Besides those already mentioned, other public talks Horton gave that spring included a discussion of OEM's approach to making documentaries after a screening of some of its shorts in a movie theater in New York City;[3] an address titled "What It Means to Be in a TOTAL War" to an industrial conference in Chicago;[4] and a speech to the Kiwanis International convention in Cleveland.[5] He was one of three OEM officials to discuss the rubber crisis live on a national network radio program called *Town Meeting of the Air.*[6] His comments were considered newsworthy enough to be included in an AP national wire story summarizing the on-air discussion.[7]

Even without the news peg of a speech, Horton was also relatively frequently quoted or mentioned in newspaper stories. For example, excluding coverage of rumors of Roosevelt reorganizing wartime information agencies, Horton was quoted interpreting the president's remark that "parasites" should get out of town;[8] interviewed by the *Baltimore Sun* on DOI's burgeoning regional information activities;[9] mentioned in several nationally syndicated news columns;[10] covered in the *Washington Post*'s daily column for federal workers;[11] and quoted on the conversion of pencil erasers into gas masks.[12] DOI's involvement with the entertainment industry through its film and radio activities also made Horton something of a minor figure worth covering. That included mentioning his role as head of the Film Unit;[13] a gossip column recounting a meeting he had with Garson Kanin;[14] the potential role for actor Melvyn Douglas in civilian defense PR;[15] and of two entertainment business executives who flew from LA to Washington to meet with him.[16]

In all, after Pearl Harbor, Horton was becoming a newsmaker through speeches, radio appearances, and news coverage. He was emerging as more than just a faceless official running a PR agency. This was in sharp contrast to his (apparently former) mentor, presidential assistant and OGR director Lowell Mellett, who abhorred coverage of himself and tried his best to minimize it. Still, Horton was no publicity hound. The vast majority of DOI news releases, which all could have led with "DOI Director Robert Horton announced today," did not use that formulation. Instead, they sometimes quoted the head of the OEM agency involved in the news being announced. Often no one was named at all. Many began simply, "The Office for Emergency Management announced today."

Photos

An article in the April issue of *Popular Photography* provided updated statistics on the activities of the Photographic Unit since Pearl Harbor. The eight photographers were trying to document the war effort in ways not covered by the news media. The unit by now had 2,500 photos in its file and was responding to about three hundred domestic requests a week. (Statistics for requests for international use that came from Rockefeller's Latin American office and Donovan's Coordinator of Information office were not provided.) Two or three times per month the unit sent a bulletin to a mailing list of national media outlets with a roster of all new pictures since the last mailing. The magazine article was extremely complimentary about the quality of the staff photographers, referring to "the dramatic pictures turned out by a little staff of crack cameramen and editors." The office "has injected some new ideas into government publicity" and was generating "excellent shots" of the war effort. The spread included eleven photos, including one that the magazine selected as its "Picture of the Month."[17]

By late spring, the unit had expanded to thirteen photographers and sixteen clerks. For the first six months of 1942, it distributed 18,371 prints.[18] However, a BOB report was critical of its operations, stating that "the unit was run on a more lavish basis than a commercial shop would be and took many more photographs than an average photographer would take on any job."[19]

Movies

DOI released about a dozen shorts in the half year between Pearl Harbor and June 1942. They included movies for OEM and related agencies, including *Homes for Defense* (Housing Coordinator), *Fighting the Fire Bomb* (OCD), *Lake Carrier* (Transportation), *For the Common Defense* (Rockefeller Latin American office), and *Men and the Sea* (War Shipping Administration and Maritime Commission).[20] In late December, DOI released *Women in Defense.* It attracted significant attention partly because it was released only a few weeks after Pearl Harbor and partly because of star power attached to it: Eleanor Roosevelt had written the script, and Katherine Hepburn narrated it. The ten-minute movie showed the many different roles women were playing and should play in the war including doing research, volunteering, working in factory jobs that traditionally had been held by men (such as munitions production), helping the Red Cross, donating blood, and making sure their families ate nutritiously. In particular, the movie called on women to help win the "Battle of Production."[21] The *Washington Post* called it "an excellent straight-forward exposition" that received "a round of sincere applause" from an audience.[22] Looking back a half century later, Thomas Doherty criticizes the message of the movie in that "traditional gender associations were reinforced and merely moved out of the domestic sphere and into the industrial workplace."[23] Another movie, *Tanks,* attracted attention, too, because it was narrated by Orson Welles, his first screen work since *Citizen Kane.*[24]

Posters

DOI also went into high gear with posters, producing thirty-four in the first six months of 1942.[25] The posters and streamers were produced partly for DOI's client agencies, including WPB, OPA, OCD, Defense Housing, Defense Transportation, and even two for OFF.[26] Some were targeted to the specialized audience of production workers, while many others were for larger segments of the population, such as consumers, participants in collection and conservation campaigns, and the citizenry-at-large. Besides the ones already mentioned, they included:

- Production workers: "The Knockout Blow Starts Here: Fellow Soldiers"[27]
- Consumers: "Mrs. America Buys Clothes with Care"[28]
- Participants in collection and conservation campaigns: "Get in the Scrap: America's war industries need metals, paper, old rags, rubber. Get it back in war production."[29]
- Citizenry at large: "The enemy is listening. He wants to know what *you* know. Keep it to yourself.[30]

In January, another photography magazine, *U.S. Camera,* announced that in cooperation with DOI it would run a monthly competition for the best photos for use in OEM posters. There were two categories, submissions by amateurs and by professional photographers. The jury for the monthly selections was chaired by famed photographer Edward Steichen. He was initially identified as "photographic advisor to the O.E.M." and a month later more formally as "Colonel Edward Steichen, Consultant in Photography to the Office for Emergency Management." Another esteemed photographer, Margaret Bourke-White, was a member of the jury panel.[31] This was truly a blue-ribbon group. The winning submissions for the first round were printed in the April issue. One showed a pair of hands with the slogan, "Your Weapons, Guard Them." Another used DOI's slogan, "Let's keep 'em rolling," showing a team of horses pulling an artillery gun.[32] The August issue included in the professional category a photo of smoke billowing out of an industrial smokestack with the motto, "Time to go to work, America!"[33]

Writing that spring in a political science journal, a federal PIO whose work was not connected to DOI praised the posters and DOI's other graphics. He judged that "the quality of the output is exceptionally high; the graphics production, especially noteworthy."[34]

Publications

DOI's publications section issued five categories of materials: booklets, pamphlets, leaflets, fliers, and miscellaneous. Between January and June 1942, it published forty-six booklets and pamphlets.[35] Most were based on the particular needs of WPB and other OEM operating divisions. The section published a stream of technical, regulatory, and specialist publications, such as *Plant Efficiency* and an update of the authoritative *Priority Orders in Force.*[36]

There were also lay-oriented publications for the public at large. For example, in early 1942, DOI issued another pamphlet in its "Arsenal of Democracy" series. This one, titled *Conversion: America's Job,* was a thirty-six-page brochure with six sections on the efforts to transform the civilian production capacity to serve the country's war needs.[37] Other lay publications were also in the category of public reporting (and were mentioned earlier).

Some DOI publications reflected Horton's emphasis on reusing the same material as many times as possible. Already mentioned was the transcript of a meeting with business editors and publishers.[38] Similarly, after a two-day briefing for county government officials in Washington, DOI published a transcript that it distributed to thousands of (nonattending) local government officials who were equally interested and affected by WPB policies. The published transcript also included Q&A. This helped address the practical and specific issues that were on the minds of all county officials.[39]

Radio

Horton "took the view that radio was one of the most effective media for dissemination of government information." While he supported production of headline-style stories, he thought that longer and dramatic programs had a greater impact on explaining the complicated production and war picture to the citizenry.[40] Therefore, the radio section put greater focus on the latter products. These were sometimes regular weekly broadcasts on programs sponsored by private corporations, such as *The Firestone Hour* and *The General Electric Program.* Another format was a radio series on national networks produced by OEM itself with the air time donated by broadcasters. These network programs were often a mix of interviews, addresses, Hollywood star appearances, and radio dramatizations. Another major product was what the section called "transcriptions," which were recordings of programs sent to individual radio stations that had requested them for broadcast at each station's convenience. Finally, the emerging regional information network focused significantly on local radio stations, especially interviews based on suggested scripts the section sent them.

In January 1942, the Radio Section estimated 75,000 separate broadcasts of its programs had been aired since it was organized in spring 1941, including 382 different scripts.[41] Considering that there were about 850 radio stations in the United States at the time, this indicated deep market penetration.[42] Other statistics for the WPB era of DOI's radio activities came in its summary for FY1942. The Radio Section enumerated about a dozen *ongoing* programs. Examples included 350 stations airing the *Building for Defense* series, then up to 124 episodes. *Keep 'em Rolling* was a weekly half-hour national network program with twenty-six parts. Another network weekly half-hour program was a new, post–Pearl Harbor series called *Three Thirds of the Nation.* It was then in its tenth week. Additionally, fifty radio stations asked to be regularly sent recordings of each program so they could also air them at other times. The Radio Section also produced programs on more specialized topics, based on the requests and needs of DOI's client agencies. For example, it produced radio programs for WPB's operating divisions and OPA on salvage, waste paper, rubber, rent control, and gas rationing. Sometimes the specialized programs were targeted by audience, such as for airings to production workers or to opinion leaders in each locality.[43] Counting slightly differently, in the first six months of 1942, the Radio Section produced 234 different programs, either live or as transcriptions.[44]

The Radio Section's most successful and high-profile series was based on the book *You Can't Do Business with Hitler.*[45] As previously discussed, the section began preparing the dramatization before Pearl Harbor, but it did not begin airing until after the attack. It was initially released in January "with no advance fanfare" and then went on to break "best-selling broadcasting records."[46] By June 1942, more than 90 percent of all radio stations in the United States requested DOI to send them the program, as well as stations in Puerto Rico, Hawaii, and Canada.[47] By mid-1942, thirty weekly installments had been produced.[48]

The section also experimented with a way to turn radio into an interactive two-way communications medium with a program called *The People Speak to the President*. It recorded citizens around the country describing how the war effort was affecting them. Schoenfeld edited the interviews down to thirty minutes and then arranged to play it to the president. As Schoenfeld explained, the project ostensibly was intended to "reassure and inspire President Roosevelt, as his radio talks have reassured and inspired the people of the country." In turn, DOI sent copies of the thirty-minute program to three hundred radio stations that had requested them for broadcast.[49] This was actually a double two-way loop: Roosevelt's radio fireside chats prompted the audience to give their views, which were then played for the president and subsequently broadcast, with the public seemingly listening in with the president. That, in turn, presumably led to the president incorporating his impression of public opinion into his decision making and subsequent radio broadcasts.

Campaigns

When Donald Nelson appointed Horton as WPB's information director, it was partly to set the groundwork for the biggest and most comprehensive campaign that DOI had ever conducted. Nelson, Archibald MacLeish, and Horton wanted the centerpiece of WPB's new wartime effort to be a national "War Production Drive."[50] It would focus especially on labor-management cooperation in factories. They felt that if the ingrained suspicions and distrust that usually existed between corporate managers and unions could be transcended and workforce morale raised, this would significantly contribute to a much-increased production outcome. Crucially, they decided that the plan should have national performance measurement goals and similar metrics for individual companies and workers.[51] That approach would give a concreteness to the effort in lieu of empty sloganeering, exhortations, and cheerleading. The division created an extensive and elaborate plan for as large and comprehensive a campaign as its staff could imagine. The Production Drive would be bigger and bolder than anything they had done up to now. For DOI, this would be the mother of all campaigns.

Nelson announced the drive in a national radio speech on March 2.[52] It was followed up by thirty-one regional meetings with total attendance of about fourteen thousand people, and letters inviting participation to about ten thousand contractors. By June, several national unions had signed on, about nine hundred labor-management committees had been created encompassing about 2.5 million workers, slogan contests had been held, and individual award programs announced.[53]

DOI was the central agency to implement the PR aspects of the drive (although OFF had policy supervision in case of disagreements). The division's outputs included plan books, report books, military speakers at plants, exhibits, photographs, material for plant newspapers, and stickers for accomplishments. For example, for the kickoff of the drive, the Radio Section produced a thirty-minute dramatic program called *Production Now* that explained the importance of the campaign. After the national broadcast, 350 radio stations aired it again from copies sent them by the section. Then, on about a weekly basis, the section created (through June 1942) eleven war production recordings that encouraged labor-management cooperation, and distributed them on a regular basis to each labor-management committee. When Nelson made a follow-up speech a week after the kickoff, his speech was translated into French, Spanish, Polish, German, and Yiddish and sent to three hundred foreign-language radio stations as well as to factories with large populations of foreign-language speakers.[54] The Publications Section created six fliers, four booklets, three types of award certifications, and one pamphlet for the drive.[55]

A great amount of internal Sturm und Drang occurred during the spring regarding what production information could be released on the results of the drive without compromising military security. After months of meetings with the military, the first report was scheduled for July, to cover statistics for June. Although DOI no longer existed when the report was released, the official BOB history credits it as having "paved the way for the first general production report."[56] That first report, released on July 25, 1942, showed that production in June was three times that of the previous November (the last full month before Pearl Harbor).[57] Horton and DOI had done their part of the job well.[58]

Field Offices

It will be recalled that Horton's plan for a regional information structure was largely in place before Pearl Harbor. He envisioned a DOI field staffer in each of twelve federal regions along with some branch offices within regions. After the attack, Horton was able to construct an even deeper field staff. Only a few weeks after December 7, James Secrest, the Washington-based head of the regional staff, reported on the extraordinary increase in desire for localized news. It became so persistent that regional offices paralleled the operations of DOI's press room in Washington, namely needing staffing nearly twenty-four hours a day. Therefore, DOI sought to expand its major field offices to three professionals each to handle the nearly continuous news cycles.[59]

As with the pressroom in Washington, Horton had a firm policy of hiring reporters for the field offices. He wanted staff who were inculcated with the journalistic dogma of fact-based information, even if occasionally it made the government look bad. So, for example, DOI's Texas spokesman plainly stated that a side effect of tire rationing was an increase in tire thefts.[60] Another time a regional DOI spokesman matter-of-factly confirmed that there was some vandalism at construction sites of new defense housing.[61] A journalism background was also necessary because sometimes the regional information officer served as national spokesman on local events of national interest. For example, during a welders' strike at shipyards in San Francisco, DOI regional officer Dean Jennings was widely quoted in the national media with updates on the situation.[62] Another time, the information officer in Ohio was quoted in a national wire story about seizures of metal scrap.[63]

Another condition for selecting field staff was that they were already working as journalists in that region.[64] Horton did not want to parachute strangers into a media market. Rather, he wanted men who already knew the region, could hit the ground running, and had credibility with the local news media. Horton thought it was vital that DOI regional staff "hold the confidences of the newspaper editors and radio station managers with whom they are in constant contact."[65] Two exceptions to hiring male reporters stood out: DOI appointed a male Hollywood *screenwriter* as assistant regional information officer for the western regional office and a woman to staff its Arizona field office.[66]

By April, DOI had twelve regional offices and eighteen additional offices in major population centers (that were not "capitals" of federal regions).[67] The expansion was happening so fast that, at first, the clerical personnel hired for the new offices were inadequately trained and consequently hampered the smooth operation of those offices.[68] The growth spurt also prompted negative newspaper coverage. The subheadline of the front-page story of the *Baltimore Sun* said it all: "Capital Publicity Mill Augmented by Far-Flung Setup Giving out Data Already Available to All."[69] At its peak, in mid-June 1942, in addition to the twelve regional offices, DOI also had two formal subregional offices (Chicago and Seattle), twenty six offices in other major cities (including some in state capitals and a few where major federal installations were located), and about another dozen were in the process of being opened. The field staff had 166 employees, divided about fifty-fifty between professionals and administrative support.[70]

Field officers were expected to function in their area as DOI did in Washington, namely they were to coordinate and act as clearinghouses for information being released to the public by the field staff of all OEM agencies

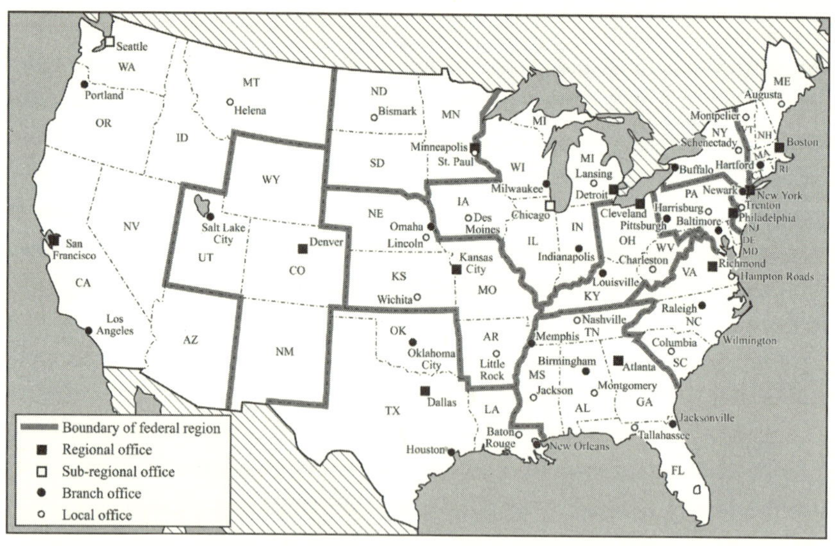

DOI Regional Offices, Spring 1942.

Folder: Information Services, Box 13, Entry 576A, RG 208, National Archives II.

(except OCD). Hence, the PR structure in regions, states, and cities were reflections of the centralized structure that Horton had developed for DOI in Washington. As in the federal capital, DOI field offices were the one-stop shop for the media, civic groups, and individual citizens to obtain authoritative information about all aspects of OEM's war effort. So, for example, they were local spokespersons for the subcontracting effort,[71] coordinated the scrap iron salvage project,[72] explained OPA's gas and sugar rationing for all citizens,[73] and provided information on OPA's price rules for retailers.[74] Other activities by field information officers reflected the panoply of DOI's PR roles, including talks to groups,[75] liaising and coordinating with local government defense agencies,[76] and serving as the representative of the federal government for collection campaigns.[77]

One of the primary duties of the field staff was to provide useful products to radio stations seeking localized news of the war production effort, not national statistics already broadcast on the networks. The Radio Section in Washington produced some programs that were neither broadcast nationally nor distributed directly to radio stations. Instead, they were sent to the field staff, who then worked with local radio stations to determine if they were interested in that particular offering. For example, the radio office sent out 225 copies of a talk explaining rent control and 350 copies of two programs explaining price control.[78] It also continued sending the field staff "skeleton scripts," often in Q&A format, to facilitate locally based interview programs. Often, the federal official being interviewed was not the DOI information officer but rather the local rationing administrator or area priorities manager.[79] Early in 1942, it became apparent that regional press relations for spot news (especially the print media) involved different tasks, pacing, and expertise from liaison with radio stations. As a result, DOI then worked to add to the personnel formula of its major field offices a radio expert who would concentrate on that aspect of local public relations.[80] For example, by May, the regional office in San Francisco for the seven western states included a full-time staffer in charge of "radio information."[81]

In June 1942, the Radio Section estimated that DOI programs distributed solely by its regional PIOs were broadcast 1,500 times *per week*.[82] With about 850 radio stations in the United States at the time, this would mean that on average, every station aired two programs per week supplied by the regional staff.[83] Reflecting Horton's constant pushing to do more and better, in May 1942 DOI staff assessed which radio products were being aired and which were not. They concluded that the primary customers for the regional offices were small, rural stations. These stations especially welcomed skeleton Q&A scripts and transcriptions (recordings) of programs. On the other hand, they rarely had the capability to produce a dramatization based on a script provided from Washington. Therefore, in early June, DOI began cutting back on writing and distributing scripts of dramatizations to the smaller radio stations and emphasized doing more Q&A scripts and recorded programs.[84]

New Programs

By the time the United States joined the war, Horton had developed DOI into a mega-mall of PR services. He had wanted his agency to cover the waterfront of external communications, and indeed DOI grew in the first half of 1942 to become that. While Pearl Harbor had had some impacts on the content of DOI's messages and the agency's size, there wasn't much in the PR grab bag that DOI wasn't already doing. Two initiatives represented how little was left undone.

Paintings

Moving fast, only eight days after Pearl Harbor, DOI announced a competition for original art on the war. Complementing the separate competition by *U.S. Camera* for war photographs for posters, the *O.E.M. Art Bulletin No. 1* of December 15, 1941, invited artists to submit works in the traditional categories of watercolors, oil painting, drawings, and prints. While the subject was broad, DOI in particular invited submissions on several specific topics relating closely to OEM's missions, including: (1) "Impressive manufacturing and defense operations, where accessible without special permission"; (2) "Production of foods, in the home and at canning centers"; and (3) "Defense construction and housing." This was a rush effort, with the submissions due only a month later, on January 15, 1942. Like the *U.S. Camera* effort, this was a real competition in the sense that it was juried and prizes were awarded.[85] There was extensive and positive coverage of the competition in Sunday arts sections and in a monthly arts magazine.[86] However, one artist complained that the financial prizes were too low for original art.[87]

About five thousand pieces were submitted.[88] On February 2, the supervisor of the campaign reported to Horton that the final decisions had been made, with 109 works selected and nearly $2,500 awarded, which was more than the initial plan of $2,000. This suggests that the quality and quantity of work was higher than expected and the jury felt it necessary to expand the award pool by 25 percent.[89] To round out the scope of the collection, DOI also commissioned eight artists to submit paintings of restricted sites requiring Army or Navy permission.[90] Thirteen submissions by five of the artists passed muster and were added to the final collection.[91]

The results were unveiled at the recently opened National Gallery on February 7, 1942. In the catalogue for the *War in Art* show, written by Forbes Watson (a former art critic who worked at the Treasury Department's arts program for federal buildings), he "giddily predicted the advent of 'the post-Pearl Harbor period of American art.'"[92] The art critic for the *Washington Post* pronounced the exhibition an "inspiring showing,." with "a fresh and vigorous style" and of "such high caliber."[93] After closing in late February, the exhibition traveled to the prestigious Museum of Modern Art in New York City.[94] It then went on a national tour of other major art museums, including Chicago, Milwaukee, and Denver.[95]

Survey Research

Much had changed since Horton's first frosty reaction to the creation of OFF in October 1941. Archibald MacLeish was not an empire builder like Horton and did not have strong feelings for or against Horton's centralization philosophy. The turning point in their relationship came in February 1942, when MacLeish recommended to Donald Nelson that DOI be responsible for PR for WPB's War Production Drive (previously discussed). Horton now understood that MacLeish was not interested in competing with him or in growing OFF into an *operational* PR agency. Instead, MacLeish was interested in message, policy, and strategy, leaving to Horton to do the heavy lifting of the PR itself. Horton could live with that.

In a sense, Horton was doing PR's equivalent of lower-end, blue-collar, manual labor, while MacLeish's vision was higher-end PR, white-collar and cerebral. For example, in the two years of DOI's existence, Horton almost exclusively focused on a flow of outgoing information and products, rarely using DOI in a listening mode. To MacLeish, conducting survey research on public opinion was a sine qua non of effective communication. OFF staff collaborated with the National Opinion Research Center at the University of Denver on several polls. Two related to the government's information activities. In late January, OFF issued an internal report titled *How the Populace Regards the Government's Handling of War News.*[96] Two months later, it released the results of a related, but separate poll, in a report titled *People's Attitudes toward the Government's Information Policy.*[97] Both used the professional standards of survey research at the time and included cross-tabulations by geography, gender, age, religion, education, and economics. The results showed general support for how the government was handling war news, with casualty information being handled especially circumspectly and generally avoiding news that could help the enemy. But the results also reflected customary American impatience, with citizens wanting more news faster and showing some skepticism about what news the government was releasing or withholding.

The polling was eye-opening for Horton. A week after receiving the results of the second survey, he sent MacLeish ("Dear Arch") twenty-three follow-up questions in which his staff were interested. Horton hoped OFF could include them in future polling. As would be expected, the questions tended to the practical and pragmatic, with DOI looking for guidance on how to be more effective in its outgoing information. Most of the questions were thematic, such as how people felt about news on production results, rationing, wages and prices, and salvage efforts. Some questions were about how citizens preferred to get their news: newspapers or radio? Weeklies or dailies?[98] Had DOI existed longer, this new cooperation with OFF could have produced survey research that may have led to major revisions in DOI's information program. It would no longer have been communicating quite as blindly and broadly as it had until then.

Managing the Division of Information after Pearl Harbor

From an administrative perspective, these were DOI's salad days. Business, budgets, and staffing were booming. It was almost as though the sky truly was the limit.

Budgeting

Oddly, authoritative budget information—a standard statistic and document practically synonymous with public administration—was scarce to nonexistent for DOI during this period. This could be because such information was very tightly held to tamp down the inevitable congressional criticism of a propaganda machine and/or because funding levels were changing so quickly that there never was an annualized FY1942 budget that captured the total picture of the agency.[99] After DOI no longer existed, congressional testimony by OWI deputy director Milton Eisenhower revealed that based on BOB's allotment to DOI for the last quarter of FY1942, its annualized spending going into FY1943 (that is, as of June 30, 1942) was $2.6 million.[100] DOI was larger than OGR ($2.4 million) and OFF ($1.6 million). It was the largest civilian domestic information agency in the federal government. This explains, in part, why it attracted such fierce criticism by the conservative coalition and the press. They simply followed the money. The fatter the target, the better.

Staffing

At the beginning of FY1942 on July 1, 1941, DOI had about 250 employees. A year later, when it closed its doors on June 30, 1942, it had "over 600 persons" on its payroll, a 240 percent increase in a year.[101] As a proportion of the overall budget, about 60 percent of DOI spending was on payroll.[102] Another stark indicator of DOI's growth during FY1942 is based on its higher-salaried positions. Congress required the CSC to submit to it an annual report on senior administrative and supervisory staff in federal employment (based on salary). CSC's annual report as of May 1, 1941, listed DOI with two employees in that category, Horton and assistant director Straus.[103] A year later, there were 18, showing a one-year growth rate of 900 percent.[104]

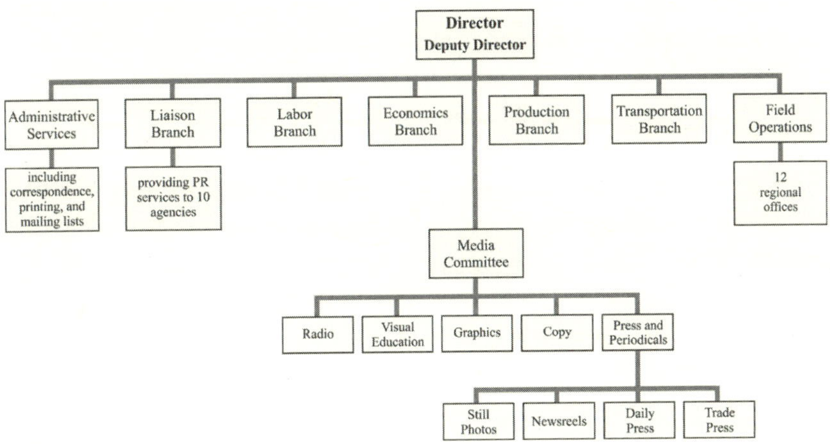

DOI Organization Chart, Spring 1942.

Chart after p. 5, Binder: Division of Information Report, July 1941–June 1942, Box 14, Entry 576A, RG 208, National Archives II.

With war declared, Horton used personnel policy as a way to convey to his burgeoning staff how much had changed in the agency's intensity of operations. Horton had announced that no Christmas leaves would be approved (see chap. 6). That announcement was considered significant enough to be mentioned the next day in the *Washington Post*'s column for federal employees.[105] Similarly, New Year's Day was a regular workday. No skeleton crew in the press center; this meant *everyone*.[106] Same for Washington's Birthday.[107] Horton also reduced the formula for calculating vacation days, eliminating any for employees who had worked at DOI fewer than six months, and setting a maximum of six days per year for veteran staff (with no rollovers or accumulations above the six days). Anticipating requests for temporary help when staff took leaves, Horton preemptively announced that "Units or Sections must be prepared to carry on *without additional assistance* during any employee absences from duty."[108] A desire not to burden one's colleagues would be a built-in restraint on taking maximum time off. Again, this was deemed sufficiently important for mention in the *Post*'s column for federal employees.[109] Later in the spring, as wartime work became more routinized, he slightly eased the vacation policy. However, it still had many limitations, such as requiring them to be coordinated and staggered (so no office would be significantly short-handed) and that they began and ended on Tuesdays, Wednesdays or Thursdays, "to help prevent train and bus congestion" on Mondays and Fridays.[110]

Continuing his desire to maximize the number of staff in the classified service, in February Horton approved expediting the handling of position descriptions and final classification sheets for submittal to the CSC for approval.[111] By April, about half of the headquarters staff had civil service status. Another 10 percent were eligible for post-DOI civil service positions, such as the right to return to the federal department where they previously had worked, and others held Ramspeck Act rights (as former congressional staffers).[112] Horton kept pushing to assure employment security for as many of his employees as possible.

Summary and Conclusions: DOI at War

The gloves came off after Pearl Harbor. Given the three exceptions to the ban on government propaganda—widely held values, presidential communication, and war—Horton now could do just about anything he wanted. If he wanted to whip public opinion into a frenzy in the way that the Committee on Public Information (CPI) had done in World War I, he could. But, he didn't. If anything was being whipped into a frenzy after Pearl Harbor, it was congressional criticism of federal propaganda.

While CPI is often compared by historians to OWI, this is probably the wrong linkage, given OWI's weak mandate. If anything, CPI's equivalent in World War II would more appropriately be DOI from Pearl Harbor to June 1942. It was the largest federal wartime PR agency, had the broadest scope, and had the dual missions of news and morale. If this historical comparison has validity, then, given Horton's refusal to go all out on a persuasive propaganda effort akin to CPI's, it was his own PR philosophy that prevented DOI from being the CPI of World War II.

With war declared, the budget and staffing floodgates opened. DOI more than doubled from December 1941 to June 1942. It was now doing more, just as Horton wanted, but that was true mostly quantitatively. Qualitatively, not all that much changed. Yes, Horton wanted to increase civilian and production worker morale. Yes, he wanted the Production Drive to be a success. But his propaganda-style campaigns seemed pallid compared to CPI and the specter of the Nazi-like propaganda campaigns invoked by congressional opponents and the conservative press. Some DOI radio dramatizations were quite oversimplified and some posters seemed rah-rah, although most were developed for a tangible purpose, such as conservation and production. These PR products were quite tame compared to true propaganda.

Horton was first and last a reporter who wanted the facts. He believed in contributing to an informed citizenry in a democracy and didn't see much difference between his early work as a reporter and his work as a government information officer. In his worldview, fiction did not provide an acceptable basis for government PR. Notwithstanding the free hand DOI now had to generate wartime propaganda, it was largely lacking in the division's war operations. There was surprisingly little qualitative difference in DOI's prewar and wartime communications. While the world around Horton had changed drastically, his approach to PR had not.

CHAPTER 8

HORTON AND GOVERNMENT PR AFTER THE DIVISION OF INFORMATION

June 1942–June 1946

About a month after Pearl Harbor, Roosevelt asked Milton Eisenhower of the USDA Office of Information to prepare a study of wartime information needs. Working closely with BOB, Eisenhower surveyed the existing defense-related PR apparatus and recommended replacing most of them (except OGR, which Roosevelt had put off-limits) with a single temporary wartime agency. Eisenhower was not a fan of Horton or his centralized model, which he called the "city-editor system."[1] When he submitted his report in late February 1942, he could have recommended that DOI become the core of a wartime information agency, but he quite overtly did not.

In the meantime, attacks by congressional conservatives on PR spending increased in intensity. Several White House advisers, including Lowell Mellett, Sam Rosenman, and BOB director Harold Smith, felt the president needed to get ahead of the curve or be faced with Congress imposing a statutory war information agency on him. By March, they had prepared a draft executive order reflecting Eisenhower's study. They submitted it to him. He let it sit on his desk. He wasn't ready to make a decision.

The Denouement of the Division of Information

It was the worst-kept secret in Washington. Rumors began circulating and were reported in the press as early as March that Roosevelt was on the verge of reorganizing the information agencies into one.[2] Press accounts of the just-around-the-corner event continued all spring.[3] The openness of the rumors served FDR well. It had the effect of somewhat tamping down congressional and press criticism of government PR, given that a major reorganization was apparently imminent. In the meantime, the president didn't actually have to take any action. But the rumors didn't totally eliminate press and legislative criticism of federal PR. The blowout battle over the construction of OGR's US Information Center on Pennsylvania Avenue near the White House tipped the political scales, even though Roosevelt got his way in launching it. (Critics dubbed it "Mellett's Madhouse," and the term stuck.) The president knew he had to act, but he continued dithering.[4] Partly, he was waiting until he found the right candidate to head the new agency. He also wanted to wait until the FY1943 appropriations for existing information agencies were largely in place, so as not to give Congress a chance to zero out funding for information activities before a new agency would come into existence. He wanted Congress to face the fait accompli of a new agency with all funding transferred from the old ones before it began the next appropriations cycle. Finally, he wanted to be sure the US Information Center was up and running first. It opened on May 4, 1942.

This all made for a demoralizing work environment. Horton and the DOI staff knew they were on the chopping block, but they didn't know when the changes would occur or what exactly would change. The uncertainty extended for an agonizingly long time. In late May (nearly three weeks before the executive order was eventually signed), Horton called a highly unusual staff meeting for all headquarters personnel. His terse memo notifying them of the meeting made it clear that attendance was not optional: "All employees of the division are expected to be present."[5] Only the auditorium at DOI's office building was big enough for such a large number of people. This was no intimate meeting. Horton would have filled them in on what he knew (not a lot), assured them that whatever happened, their jobs were most likely to continue unchanged (partly because of their CSC status, partly because the new entity would need them), and asked that they keep concentrating on doing to the utmost their current projects because the need was as valid then as on any other day of the war.

Horton wanted the job, but probably knew he was unlikely to get it. Roosevelt was authentically undecided about who would get it until nearly the end. A journalist's assessment, published in fall of 1942, noted that "jockeying for key propaganda jobs has consumed a scandalous amount of time."[6] According to an academic account issued in February 1943, "It was obvious that there was not room in Washington for the three super-information agencies such as the units directed by Mellett, Horton and MacLeish."[7] Mellett knew he was damaged goods, especially after publicly calling Senator Byrd a liar for Byrd's accusations relating to the nascent US Information Center.[8] MacLeish was not ambitious to run a large bureaucracy. He preferred dealing with strategy and policy. And he already had a job, Librarian of Congress.

Horton wanted it, but FDR's behavior was a signal. Horton had had little direct contact with Roosevelt since the 1940 election campaign, even though he claimed that the president was the only boss he had. After setting up DOI as an independent and centralized information agency in February 1941, Roosevelt proceeded to undermine Horton's claim of primus inter pares of national defense information. Seriatim, FDR created OCD largely as a morale agency, created OFF, assigned the *wartime* US Information Center to OGR, and called on Milton Eisenhower to study wartime information needs. Each of those actions undercut Horton's assertions of being *the* centralized information agency. Allan Winkler suggests that this pattern clearly demonstrated "the president's reluctance to assign central information work to Horton" beyond his original decision to create it.[9] Horton was disappointed by each of Roosevelt's decisions, but continued nonetheless asserting DOI's role based on the original presidential letter setting it up.

At last, Roosevelt was ready. On Saturday, June 13, in time to dominate the news for the big Sunday papers, he signed the final version of the executive order creating the Office of War Information (OWI) within OEM.[10] He simultaneously named reporter and radio commentator Elmer Davis to head the new agency. With the stroke of a pen, DOI was dissolved, along with OGR and OFF.[11] However, OWI did not inherit DOI en masse. Instead, the executive order carefully gave OWI only DOI's "general public information" role, while transferring to OEM's individual agencies those DOI staff who provided them "press and publication services."[12] In other words, OWI would not be a powerful centralized PR office like DOI in providing services to multiple agencies.[13] Instead, the default template of federal information snapped back into place, with each OEM agency now controlling its own PR. Horton had lost, both personally and conceptually.

DOI's professional staff (that is, not secretarial and with annual salaries of $2,600 or more) did not fare well in OWI. Of the 225 who were transferred in on July 1, 1942, only about half (109) were still there in May 1943.[14] None of Horton's managers were named to management posts in OWI, with those positions dominated by former OFF officials.[15] Horton got a few encomiums from the media for his DOI work. The *Washington Post*'s columnist for federal employees wrote an article (separate from his column, an unusual occurrence) titled "In Defense of Government Press Agents." The article's last sentence read, "The OEM information section [*sic*] got off to a poor start but it's now the most effective division in the city."[16] The *New Republic* editorialized positively about "Robert Horton, whose name wasn't mentioned often in the gossip columns, but who played a big part in Washington."[17] *Life* magazine complimented Horton for making DOI an information agency "where public relations was not a notable part of the war effort."[18]

Horton at Other Agencies, 1942–1946

OWI symbolized a rejection of Horton's fierce support for centralization of government PR services. He had won some battles early in America's participation in World War II, but ultimately lost the (PR) war. OWI was a repudiation of everything he believed in. It was a blow to the ideal he had worked for, pushed for, and argued for ever since NDAC had hired him two years earlier.

Now what? Horton still believed in Roosevelt and the New Deal. Most of all, he believed in the war. Hurt feelings aside, he couldn't imagine walking away, not participating in the war effort. He was very briefly chief of OWI's News Bureau (June–August, 1942), but he didn't fit in Davis's new regime or as someone's subordinate. Beginning in September, he had a short and stormy term as deputy administrator for information and education for Leon Henderson's OPA. The argument at the time was how heavy or light OPA's enforcement and regulation of price controls should be. In a backhanded compliment, a reporter grudgingly acknowledged that Henderson and Horton's more aggressive approach worked, but was unpopular: "What Henderson obviously needed was someone to curb his pugilistic tendencies, and here was Horton who, if anything, was more cocky than his boss about beating folks over the head to make them comply with OPA edicts. So Horton only egged Henderson on. Two more stalwart patriots could hardly be found in Washington, but if their zeal exceeded their wisdom, at least they made price control work in a crude sort of way."[19]

Plenty of citizens did not welcome being inconvenienced by the war and always found fault with how OPA affected them. Their complaints were encouraged, repeated, and amplified by conservatives. Senator Kenneth McKellar (D-TN) criticized OPA's regional PR as "propaganda stuff." Congressman John Taber (R-NY) said OPA's decisions were "Hitler orders."[20] By late 1942, Henderson knew he had become a political liability to FDR and resigned. Principled, Horton followed him out.

Interior Secretary Harold Ickes then appointed Horton as special assistant to the secretary and later director of the department's Division of Information (February 1943–February 1944). That, too, was a mixed experience. Eventually, Horton returned "home" to where he had started, as MC director of information, simultaneously serving in the same role at MC's wartime sister agency, the War Shipping Administration (WSA) (March 1944–June 1946).

He expanded the two agencies' wartime PR work, including promoting observances of the annual Maritime Day and Victory Fleet Day. For 1945's Maritime Day, he prepared a how-to kit for local activists, listing such "proven methods" as "Your local retail stores and outdoor displays are powerful publicity outlets"; "Plan spectacular window displays. They create greater community enthusiasm"; and "Your local newspaper is your best bet for promotion and publicity."[21] *Victory Fleet*, the newsletter his office published, included ideas for local observances, including insert materials for other publications, a flier for shipbuilding workers, and graphics.[22] There was a special Maritime Day poster with a quote from the president on the importance of the merchant marine.[23] Horton arranged for a travelling exhibit of art by seamen and sent public speakers to events in twenty-eight cities.[24] Afterward, his newsletter declared that 1945 "was probably the widest observance of National Maritime Day since the day was designated in 1933."[25]

Horton vigorously promoted naming ships after small towns and cities in the heartland, which otherwise had no tangible link to oceanic shipping. This became a bonanza of parochial publicity. For every stage along the way, the hometown press covered the process: nomination, decision, and launch. Some headlines, often front-page, capture how successful the naming project was: "Victory Ship to Carry Name of Brigham City" and "Liberty Ship Jefferson City to Be Launched Next Month."[26] Similarly, naming ships for prominent local historical figures or universities prompted similar rounds of self-congratulatory and positive coverage, such as "Ship May Yet Be Named for McLean" and "Ship to Be Named for Brown [University]."[27] The wartime activities of a ship named for the founder of a labor union were of ongoing interest to the union's magazine.[28] For government PR, this was about as good as it could get.

After VJ-Day, Horton participated in the demobilization of MC and WSA and the disposal of its now-surplus equipment. A commission poster looked like an ad for a big sale at a department store: "It's *Easy* to Do Business with the Maritime Commission! Fixed Prices! Fair Dealings! Direct Action! Early Deliveries!" It listed seventy-two categories of equipment that the commission was trying to unload.[29] One story attributed to Horton the solution to the Navy's unsuccessful efforts to dispose of large rafts. After it gave up, Horton "got his staff together and talked it over." The result of their brainstorming was that vacation resorts used rafts. His staff quickly designed a poster and descriptive material and sent them to a mailing list of resorts. Presto, all sold.[30]

Postlude: Horton after Government PR, 1946–1993

Horton resigned from the federal government in the summer of 1946, as WSA was being disestablished and MC was shrinking. He left Washington and never looked back. He and his wife returned to Vermont to run a family-owned hotel called the Sudbury Inn on Lake Hortonia in Sudbury. In Catton's pithy phrasing, "he lives in the mountains of Vermont, operating a summer hotel and meditating on the errancies of government life."[31] They advertised in the *New York Times* Sunday travel section, with small ads describing it as "A Vermont Country Inn and Farm on sparkling lake in green hills under management of Robert W. Horton former Washington newspaper correspondent and Lola G. Horton, cookbook and cooking column author."[32]

He engaged in only a handful of activities that built on his career. As a consultant, he helped Volkswagen create a German-American cultural exchange program for boys.[33] In 1948, he was described as a news commentator for a talk he gave to a woman's club in Hartford, Connecticut, titled "1947–1950: The Critical Period."[34] He contributed a historical article to *Yankee* magazine on Emma Willard, founder in 1821 of the Troy Female Academy (renamed the Emma Willard School in 1895), the first coed institution of higher education in the United States.[35] In 1959–60, he worked with the Center for the Study of Democratic Institutions (based in Santa Barbara, California), contributing a study on pay TV and serving on two panels about the media.[36] That work also led to an article in the *Reporter* on the economics of TV.[37] But that was about it. For a noted government PIO from whom so many words had poured forth between 1938 and 1946, it was like coming to a screeching stop. One gets the impression of a person who was burned out and used up after the intensity of his Washington experience.[38]

Horton had little interest in reliving the past. When Catton sent him an early copy of his 1948 *War Lords of Washington* that came close to hero worship, Catton's cover letter noted they had not been in touch in a long time and that the prominent role he had given Horton in the book might come as a surprise. Whether the surprise would be welcome or unwelcome, Catton was not sure: "I willfully neglected to take the precaution of showing you the copy in advance. If you don't approve of what I had to say about you I am quite sure that you will let me know pronto—and, as I say the prospect has me just a shade worried. In any case, I want you to have a copy of it and to realize that every word in it which refers to yourself grew out of a profound admiration for the finest guy I ever worked for and a very deep and permanent affection for same."[39] Horton did not respond to Catton, at least not in writing.[40]

In 1974, the director of the Vermont Historical Society wrote in the society's magazine that he had just read Catton's book and wondered: "What became of Robert Wyman Horton? Does anyone know his whereabouts?"[41] The society's files and subsequent issues showed no response from Horton or any other readers. Horton never wrote any memoirs or contributed his personal papers to an archive.[42] The only known occasion when he reminisced about his Washington experiences was in 1987, when author Richard Ketchum, also a resident of Vermont, went to some length to track him down.[43] A New Dealer to the core, Horton's strongest recollection of the prewar buildup and the war itself was the self-serving and anti-Roosevelt work of the dollar-a-year corporate suits, such as Edward Stettinius. He made an exception for William Knudsen, the Scandinavian-born patriot who didn't care about politics when the president asked him to help his adopted country in a national emergency.

Horton died in obscurity, at age ninety-one, in 1993.[44] If not for Catton's melodramatic telling of the flinty Vermonter who told it like it was and believed in a centralized model of government PR, Horton's story would probably have been lost to history.

CONCLUSION

ROBERT HORTON AND THE PRACTICE OF GOVERNMENT PR

One of the two central themes of this inquiry relates to the issue of propaganda versus information in government public relations. As a general rule, the political culture that gradually emerged in Washington had a grudging acceptance of dissemination of information as an inherent aspect of public administration. Information activities might be part of the mission of the agency, such as USDA sharing the newest techniques with farmers, the Bureau of Labor Statistics tracking unemployment, or the Census Bureau releasing census results. At other times, the information being released might be routine reports on agency performance, activities, and results. Contributing to an informed citizenry in a democracy was an acceptable PR activity.

The ban on propaganda was ostensibly a prohibition on persuasive information, of trying to convince the public that the agency's position or action on some matter was justified and correct. The assumption was that agencies should not be active players in contentious public policy issues, whether trying to persuade Congress, attentive publics, or the citizenry-at-large. However, the generally accepted template of government PR recognized that persuasive communications, aka propaganda, were permitted when relating to widely shared values, presidential communication, and war.

Some of Horton's PR activities were at base informational, such as press releases and public reporting. Others were more overtly persuasive, but generally fell within the acceptable exemptions. Between Roosevelt's reelection and Pearl Harbor, DOI was pushing the PR envelope quite strongly when trying directly and indirectly to persuade public opinion that an active US role in World War II was right. While his efforts were generally consonant with FDR's foreign policy positions and, therefore, falling within the exemption for presidential communication, Horton was at times out ahead of the president, such as planning for a "Victory" program *before* Pearl Harbor.

A Conservative Critique of Horton and Government PR, circa 1940

The long-running argument about government PR was well summarized by *New York Times* columnist Arthur Krock in a column in 1940. During the heated political imbroglio that summer over airplane production statistics, he incisively criticized Horton's role in it. Krock suggested that Horton's work was emblematic of a larger problem caused by the professionalization of public relations in federal agencies, putting the blame squarely on Roosevelt (even though it actually had begun earlier).[1] Krock presented four arguments against PR in public administration:

1. "These paid publicity agents have, of course, interest in demonstrating that the particular agency to which they are attached is making a great success of its work."
2. "They are primarily concerned with winning public opinion to the side of the administration as a whole."
3. "Now that the head of the administration is a candidate for a third term, they are virtually members of the campaign committee."
4. "When the [National Defense Advisory] commission was set up a strong effort was made to isolate the commissioners and their staff from the press. The requirement was that all such inquiries be made through the publicity agent."[2]

These observations capture four criteria for analyzing the appropriateness or inappropriateness of Horton's PR work. As framed by Krock, government public relations was an unwelcome development in executive branch departments and agencies because it was inherently (1) self-serving to the bureaucracy; (2) advocacy oriented, seeking to influence public opinion, especially in favor of the presidential administration in power; (3) political, in advancing the interests of a president running for reelection; and (4) an obstacle to good journalism, interposing itself between the news media and agency officials. In this detailed historical inquiry into Horton's government PR leadership, these four criticisms deserve to be examined in some depth, either regarding their application to Horton's record or more generally regarding the role of public relations in public administration.

1. *Is Government PR Inherently a Self-Serving Activity by a Bureaucracy?*

In some respects, the answer is yes, but the context of the answer is crucial. Are government agencies the political equivalent of children in the Victorian age? Should they be seen and not heard? In this command-and-control version of modern government, civil servants are to presidents and Congress what privates are to generals. Their role is to salute and promptly implement all legal orders—no thinking, no questioning, no doubts. In this model, when a legislator criticized a federal agency, it would inappropriate for an agency official to defend the agency publicly.

A closely related issue was actively considered during Horton's government career. On October 23, 1940, this very point was discussed at a (closed) NDAC meeting. According to the minutes: "Mr. Nelson presented to the Commission an invitation he had received from 'America's Town Meeting of the Air' to participate in a debate on December 19, on the affirmative side of the question 'Is America Rearming Efficiently?' Mr. Stettinius stated he did not think it was dignified for Mr. Nelson or any Commissioner to publicly argue that the Commission is doing a good job."[3] The commissioners were, indirectly, agreeing with Krock's column, published just two months earlier. In a sense, they were articulating the cultural norm of the ancien regime and of the old-line business aristocracy, that good deeds were all that counted. Puffery was to be disdained. Gentlemen did not stoop to argue with the hoi polloi.

But the Office for Price Administration (where Horton briefly worked in 1942–43) had the opposite attitude. While, indeed, it was the right of every American to criticize government, "it was OPA policy to react vigorously . . . to criticism believed to be unjustified, and to misstatements of fact; and the agency defended its right to keep the record straight."[4] To Krock's way of thinking, OPA's approach was a perfect example of a bureaucracy trying to put a positive spin on its work. However, if a government agency is comparable to a business corporation, that corporation is legally a person. Like a person, a corporation would be expected to defend itself from criticism, to present its version of the truth. If that is appropriate behavior in business administration, then surely some rough comparability would also occur in public administration.

There is another reason for government public relations to be, in Krock's phrase, "demonstrating that the particular agency to which they are attached is making a great success of its work." This is the function of public reporting in public administration. Public reporting was a communication activity inherent to government itself. A public-sector agency had a duty to report to the public on its record of activities and stewardship of taxpayer funds. That these reports would generally focus on the positive and on the value that the taxpayer received from these expenditures is inherent in the reporting process: "Here's what we did, how much we spent, and what results we got." Reporting can be done indirectly through the press (as Horton did with press releases) and in direct reporting to the citizenry (as Horton did through publications and film shorts). From Krock's perspective, this was the epitome of wasteful public relations that always puts the agency in a good light. Yet it is hard to conceive of public administration sans public reporting. There is no one else who is in a position and has the incentive to gather the information, process it, and produce a summary report. The voice of an agency stating what it accomplished is merely one of many voices in the public square. It is an asymmetrical relationship. When an agency engages in public reporting, it in no way is drowning out criticism. But, conversely, the diversity of views in the public realm would be distinctly unbalanced and incomplete should a public sector agency be banned from public reporting. Reporting, as a form of legislative oversight, overlaps with public reporting. Annual reports to Congress were long a feature of the federal government before the emergence of a large professionalized civil service in the executive branch.

Certainly, the work of government PR can extend to defensiveness and rationalization. When it happens, it can be called out. But it must be remembered that congressional critics of an agency *always* claim that agency responses are inappropriate for some reason or other, viz. Senator Byrd's repeating of claims about inadequate airplane production regardless of what Horton or, for that matter, the president said. Byrd was using a selective collection of facts to pursue a larger ideological and political agenda. His attacks continued regardless of what the other side was saying. And who is the "other side"? Can only a president argue publicly with another elected official? This seems unreasonable. And when the response comes from an agency spokesperson, it may well be self-serving in justifying the work of the agency, but it is a response. In a democracy, the free exchange of divergent views is assumed to contribute to an informed citizenry. One of the ancillary problems is, of course, that there are virtually no active participants in the public square who have the credibility to adjudicate between self-serving agency rationalizations (propaganda) and fact-based public argumentation (information). Krock could certainly not credibly present himself in that role.

2. *Is Advocacy-Oriented Government PR Objectionable?*

According to the Constitution, "The executive Power shall be vested in a President."[5] A less frequently cited provision states that the president "may require the Opinion, in writing, of the principal Officer in each of the executive Departments, upon any Subject relating to the Duties of their respective Offices."[6] These provisions make clear that executive branch agencies are accountable to the president, because the president is the chief of the executive branch. Using more contemporary management argot, department heads are the president's direct reports.

Notwithstanding this constitutional environment, Krock appears to be claiming that executive branch agencies are not part of the president's domain. David Rosenbloom has argued that, beginning in 1946 (six years after Krock's column), Congress gradually constructed a "legislative-centered public administration."[7] While the *legal* basis and standard operating procedures for an agency are set by laws (with the reminder that a president plays a role in the lawmaking process by signing or vetoing bills), even laws did not trump the president's *constitutional* powers. These are not arcane legalisms, but rather occur in the context of democracy. A president is an elected official and, therefore, seeks to be successful politically, even as a lame duck during a last term. With executive branch agencies within the president's constitutional embrace, it is axiomatic that the public voices of agencies would be in harmony with the administration, facilitating a president's desire for approval by public opinion. This explains why Congress's efforts to ban agency propaganda, employment of publicity experts, and criminalization of agency lobbying have been for naught.[8] They conflicted with the president's constitutional role, not just agency self-interest.

Krock's critique also seems more generally to condemn efforts by agencies to influence public opinion, whether in support of an administration's positions or for other, more agency-specific purposes (not conflicting with the administration's policies). This, in effect, is the exclusion of propaganda from the consensus and normative template for government PR. The introduction presented the generally accepted framework for external communications by federal departments and agencies, namely that while providing neutral information was an acceptable activity, providing propaganda was not. There were three relatively broadly accepted exceptions to the ban on agency propaganda: widely held values, presidential communication, and war.

This comprehensive inquiry into Horton's PR activities demonstrates the template in operation. At the Maritime Commission, he was engaging in persuasive communications for a widely held value that the country should have a viable merchant marine. Heading PR for NDAC, Horton felt his role was to show the public that NDAC decisions were necessary for the defense of the country, even though the United States was not at war. DOI was the public voice of the production effort, regardless of its many reorganizations. After the publication of Krock's column, in 1941, Horton continued to communicate about the *president's* national defense policy and how it was being implemented.

A president's policies are by definition the nation's policies unless overturned by Congress. This parallels diplomatic service, where a US ambassador represents the *president* to that foreign nation (and serves at the president's pleasure), even though confirmed by the Senate. At no point in the pre–Pearl Harbor national defense buildup did Congress flatly overturn a presidential policy that Horton was explaining and seeking to persuade the public was justified. (Even Roosevelt was careful not to stretch his actions beyond a reasonable interpretation of existing law, such as the limits on aid to the United Kingdom before Congress approved Lend-Lease.) Finally, in a time of war, Horton was seeking to raise and maintain civilian and worker morale, partly by flooding the country with information, partly through persuasive communications. These PR activities, before the election and after, before Pearl Harbor and after, were clearly efforts to influence public opinion about the rightness of the administration's positions and policies.

Krock appears to be arguing that federal agencies should not engage in persuasive communication, period. He does not seem to acknowledge any exceptions, not for widely held values, presidential communication, or war. Therefore, DOI's status as an agency within the Executive Office of the *President* would not, from this perspective, allow it any more leeway than what would be granted to a run-of-the-mill agency in the executive branch. The detailed examination of Horton's PR indicates repeatedly the impossibility of separating propaganda from information, persuasive communications from fact. All information is inherently persuasive, based on how it is presented and the context.

Still, one must be careful not to write history in a way that confirms the rightness of the actions of the winners. While Horton's record may appear to be justified, if only by the passage of time and the end results, Krock's concerns have valid and contemporary application. Was President George W. Bush's administration justified in 2002–3 when it tried to craft the publicly released information from several agencies about Iraq's supposed possession of weapons of mass destruction and its purported role in 9/11 to underpin its central argument that an invasion of Iraq was justified?[9] In that sense, Krock's argument continues to raise important issues about partisan and ideological perception affecting judgments. If where one stands depends on where one sits, then disagreements over Krock's point become situational and temporal, driven perhaps mostly by partisan affiliation. In that sense, the arguments about government propaganda versus information and about the politicization of agency PR are perpetual ones that cannot be settled objectively.

3. *Is Government PR Inherently Political during a Presidential Reelection Campaign?*

Notwithstanding the modern-day receding of the rigid strictures of the federal Hatch Act, civil servants are expected to avoid engaging in campaign activities during their working hours. The taxpayers have a right to expect that their money is not used for explicit campaign purposes. In that respect, the federal bureaucracy is to be neutral and apolitical. For example, Senator Sam Ervin (D-NC), who chaired the Senate Watergate Committee (1973–74), wrote in his memoirs what he considered one of the major transgressions of Nixon's 1972 reelection campaign: "They deemed the departments and agencies of the federal government to be the political playthings of the Nixon administration rather than impartial instruments for serving the people, and undertook to induce them to channel federal contracts, grants, and loans to areas, groups, or individuals so as to promote the reelection of President Nixon rather than the welfare of the people."[10]

Krock's specific point was that Horton's role in August 1940 went beyond the bounds of public relations in public administration. Horton most definitely was an active accomplice of FDR's campaign for a third term. At a presidential news conference in July, Roosevelt referred to "Bob" being there with more information on a subject than what the president covered. A few days later, FDR concluded a short press conference by sending reporters to the Cabinet Room to talk to Press Secretary Stephen Early and Horton for more information. On a third occasion, Early convened reporters to hear from Horton more information on airplane production rates. These were high-visibility activities by Horton *in the White House* when FDR was running for an unprecedented third term. Krock questioned Horton's role, feeling Horton had crossed a red line. Had Horton shifted from executive branch employee to de facto campaign staff?

An answer depends on a close examination of the personnel category of Horton's job. Most of the positions in DOI were in the classified civil service. Horton's, however, was not. Therefore, he was not "Hatched." He was not violating any law, rule, or standard of conduct by engaging in overt activities that benefited FDR's reelection campaign. Horton served at the pleasure of his appointing authority and could be discharged by same without cause.

That he was appointed by the joint action of the members of the National Defense Advisory Commission is clear, but with the demise of the commission, it became unclear who was his supervisor. Horton insisted it was the president. The OEM liaison officer said he had supervisory authority over Horton, but he never tried to exercise it, even in lesser matters than firing. If at any time Horton's higher-ups were dissatisfied with his performance, he could theoretically have been discharged by formal joint action of the Defense Commission certainly, by the OEM liaison officer perhaps, or, if absolutely necessary, by the president. As an appointee serving at the president's pleasure, Horton was in the president's official (and therefore political) family. The office he held was most akin to a subcabinet position, comparable to a departmental assistant secretary. The only difference was that assistant secretaries had to be confirmed by the Senate and Horton did not.

If the analogy to an assistant secretary is roughly right, then what is the appropriate role of a subcabinet member when a president is running for reelection? The general answer is that they are part of the president's *political* team and can be expected to promote the administration politically, even to engage in some campaign activities. This is similar to the role of their bosses, the cabinet secretaries (but without expending tax dollars for overt campaign activities). As these officials do not punch a clock or have formal work hours, it is hard to pinpoint a time of day when campaign activities are absolutely inappropriate.

Krock was not raising the question so much from a generic perspective of the office one occupied, but more specifically wondering about its applicability to senior PR men like Horton. If the analogy to the subcabinet rank is about right, then what is the appropriate role of an assistant secretary *for public affairs* in a presidential campaign? The first assistant secretaryship for public affairs was created in late 1944 by Roosevelt. He nominated Archibald MacLeish, whose term as Librarian of Congress was about to expire (and was no longer affiliated with OWI).[11] Hence, the new position came into existence during Horton's service in government PR, while at MC and WSA. If Krock was raising in 1940 the generic question of the appropriate role in a presidential campaign for (what later became) a formal subcabinet officer for PR, the answer was provided three presidential elections later. In 1952, Truman had chosen not to run for a second full term, instead endorsing and campaigning for Democratic nominee Adlai Stevenson, the governor of Illinois. Assistant Secretary of State for Public Affairs Howland Sargeant filled in for President Truman at a campaign appearance in Washington by reading a partisan and combative speech on behalf of the Democrats.[12] Nary a word of complaint was voiced by Krock, then still writing his column.[13]

Unless the analogy between Horton and a subcabinet PR position is fundamentally wrong, then Krock was arguing that in the *spirit* of the Hatch Act, Horton should have avoided campaign activities, *especially* because he was a PR man, a position that seems tortured and untenable. Perhaps the most charitable interpretation of Krock's point is a reminder of its context. In the 1930s and 1940s, propaganda was thought to be a highly effective form of mass persuasion that was practically impossible to defeat. If so, then perhaps Krock was suggesting that PR men holding government offices held a secret professional knowledge that should not be shared with any political campaigns.

Krock's point needs be considered even more broadly. By extension, Krock was commenting on Horton's PR staff as a synecdoche for PIOs in any federal agency. Some of Horton's staff were "Hatched" by their civil service status. That they worked for an agency in the Executive Office of the *President* made no matter, because that distinction meant only that they worked for the *institutional* presidency. So, hypothetically, was a classified employee in Horton's office in 1940 violating conditions of civil service employment due to DOI's apparent involvement in support of the president's reelection? The answer is probably no, because they were not working on PR campaigns that explicitly called for the reelection of the president. Rather, they reported on the work of the production buildup, which indirectly probably led some voters to conclude that Roosevelt deserved reelection. That DOI's messages were in harmony with the president's reelection campaign is little different from its messages being in harmony with the administration's overall policies (as described in the discussion of Krock's second objection).

4. Does the Intermediary Role of Government PR Create an Obstacle to Good Journalism?

Krock's objection to the interposition of PR officers between government officials and reporters expressed a long-standing complaint by journalists. The professional culture of American journalism had a fixed antipathy to PIOs. Understandably, reporters preferred to talk directly with the official in charge rather than the spokesperson. Elsewhere in his column, Krock was more specific about his objections to Horton's role vis-à-vis NDAC. He highlighted "the difference between a press conference conducted by a responsible official, particularly one in the position of the commission volunteers, and a press conference conducted by a publicity agent." From Krock's perspective, PIOs hurt democratic governance because senior officials could somewhat escape accountability and responsibility by letting the PR man be their spokesperson and never having to *personally* state and defend their work to a reporter. It is understandable that Krock wanted direct access to newsmakers. Almost every reporter in Washington felt that way and perceived PIOs as obstacles to such access. This harkened to the so-called good ol' days when supposedly any reporter could wander into any office and talk to the boss. There were several factors that make Krock's ideal unrealistic, all relating to the core reasons why government PR emerged the twentieth century, especially during FDR's presidency.

First, the practical factor was that if officials acceded to all requests for direct access, they would not have time to do their jobs.[14] When an official spent a few minutes briefing the PIO, the PIO then became a force multiplier by briefing dozens of reporters. This was expedient and efficient. Further, the PR officer wanted to prevent grumbling that some got preferential treatment. Horton's general modus operandi was for officials to have occasional press conferences, but otherwise for PIOs to be the routine source for reporters.

The second reason that Krock's criticism is unrealistic is that some officials were better at press relations than others. Media skills, such as staying on message, avoiding hypotheticals, declining to speculate, and generally being guarded and careful, were not possessed by all senior managers, whether they came from business or other backgrounds. Press skills were quite different from line executive ones. Most of the senior officials in the production buildup were perfectly glad to leave press relations to Horton. In particular, PIOs had the skills required to translate relatively arcane and detailed information into lay language that would be understood by generalist reporters and even more generalist readers. They could also hone in on nuggets of real news in official decisions buried in eye-glazing official documents. Notwithstanding reflexive professional grumbling, most reporters could not do their jobs without the assistance and mediation of PIOs.

A third reason for Horton's strict controls over press access—to Krock's consternation—was that during most of the buildup the effort was headed by more than one person. Until Roosevelt appointed Donald Nelson as the supposed production czar in January 1942, the arms production effort had first been overseen by a commission and then by the two-headed OPM. It was awkward and difficult, if not impossible, for all the commissioners to hold a joint interview in which they all expressed the identical position. Having a PIO state the final decision of a multiple-member body was a way to condense many officials' views into one cogent and accurate statement to the press.

Fourth, Horton was familiar with the journalistic tactic of creating conflict by interviewing one official, then going to another and claiming that the first official had said X, and what did the second official think about that? By forcing all reporters to go though his press staff (or at least to have a division PIO present when officials talked directly to reporters), Horton could prevent those artificial conflicts from occurring. Finally, in 1940 Horton was in the midst of institutionalizing his novel model of a centralized press office for multiple government silos. This had the effect of diminishing competition and rivalries between different agencies, much to the disappointment of reporters. While Horton did not prevent disagreements from going public, he did monitor whether any agencies were taking positions that went against a general and declared policy. No agency could go rogue in Horton's centralized PR world. If they tried, Horton could cut off the oxygen to the hothouse of official Washington that the press so liked. Still, in this case, Krock's generic objection to Horton speaking for agency heads instead of the officials themselves was not much of an obstacle to him as the Washington bureau chief of the *New York Times*. In his autobiography, Krock counted Nelson, Stettinius, and Knudsen as ongoing sources for his reportage.[15]

Krock's column was, of course, published before the United States declared war. But, the comparison of DOI's pre– and post–Pearl Harbor work disclosed only two totally new PR activities: paintings and survey research. Otherwise, what DOI did after the United States entered World War II was unchanged. The differences were in intensity and magnitude, with almost all categories of PR work expanded and accelerated. However, for example, the *goals* of the worker and public morale efforts were not significantly different. This may be something of a surprise, considering that one would expect a declaration of war to change everything. Perhaps the way that Roosevelt (and Horton) inched toward a combatant status, such as the declaration of an unlimited state of emergency, the draft, destroyers-for-bases, Lend-Lease, and the production buildup, fuzzed up the expected stark differences between peace and war.

The Failure of Horton's Centralized Model

Between mid-1940 and mid-1942, Horton created and maintained an anomaly in the history of government public relations. The traditional template was then (and continues to be) that each agency had its own office for external communications, thus giving it control over its public voice. Keeping PR in-house is more than merely a standard operating procedure. Rather, it derives from the bureaucratic imperative for autonomy, with public relations a key instrument in attaining and keeping it.[16] Horton's model was a threat that went to the heart of this institutional desire to protect itself.

However, it is unlikely that Horton's motivation for centralized PR was based on such an abstract and theoretical concept. After all, for all his insistence on centralization, Horton did not use the leverage it gave him to force all agencies to submit to his will and get them to "sing from the same hymnal." He was perfectly comfortable letting honest disagreements between agencies be public. A desire to use centralized PR to control the public voices of the different silos would have come from a motivation that mixed politics and professional public relations (or, at least, the cynical perception of it), namely the need to *look good* so as to influence public opinion and power politics. This latter approach was precisely what Horton was *against*. Sydney Weinberg independently confirms the underlying theme of Catton's colorful tale: "Although the administration wanted Horton to present a picture of unity in Washington, he refused. Horton acted on the premise that an information agency must tell the truth about the activities of government agencies with or without their approval. The war information program, he contended, must not be a 'sales job.' The disorganized state of the agencies during the early months of the war led government officials and businessmen alike to regret Horton's intractable devotion to the truth."[17]

For Horton, credibility with the press was the sine qua non of government PR. His was an early manifestation of what later came to be called transparency. (However, an analysis of Horton's motivation needs to include his activities in the summer and fall of 1940 to help Roosevelt's reelection.) Horton understood intuitively to what the opposite approach would lead. In the mid-1960s, President Johnson's administration developed a credibility gap due to its PR efforts to spin the news from the Vietnam War in upbeat and positive terms. Besides the importance of credibility in daily press relations, Horton had another practical reason for his centralized PR model: economies of scale. From a managerial perspective, it made sense that he could employ highly specialized personnel, such as poster artists or photographers, who would not be needed on a full-time basis by any individual agency. By aggregating the fractional PR needs for expert services of each agency, Horton's centralization was an efficient way to provide one-stop services to multiple agencies. In this view, this was simply good management, PR or otherwise, government or otherwise.

Considering bureaucratic realities, Horton almost miraculously succeeded in creating and protecting a full-service PR bureau that was not only vertically integrated (that is, providing all services, from soup to nuts), but also horizontally, a central one-stop shop for about a dozen agencies. Horton had to fight to keep it, with the autonomizing imperative constantly snapping at his heels. He won some (gaining new clients, such as the Custodian of Alien Property), but lost some, too, like OCD. He accomplished a lot in those two years, demonstrating the viability of a different approach to the structuring of government PR. Horton stretched his model as far as he could and for as long as he could, but finally couldn't hold back the tides. For a brief moment, he reversed the inexorable autonomism of government bureaucracy and provided, for history, a glimpse into what could have been, a counterfactual history of the organizational structure of PR in public administration.

Perhaps the last word belongs to Gosnell, a political scientist at BOB, who studied DOI in 1944. He concludes with some understated and backhanded compliments about the division's record, considering the difficulties of functioning as a central PR provider:

> If an administrative agency has its own information unit, then it cannot blame an outside service for any deficiencies in its information program. Considering the difficulties involved, it is to the credit of the OEM Division of Information that it was not subjected to more criticism than it received.
>
> The OEM Division of Information operated under a mandate which was vague and restricted, and it soon found itself in competition with rival information agencies which were given the various segments of the general task of coordinating war information. The staff of the Division was not large enough to furnish adequate information services to all the emergency agencies. Under the circumstances, the boldness and initiative of the staff enabled the Division to accomplish as much as it did.[18]

Horton as Government PR Manager

Horton's managerial strengths were simultaneously his weaknesses. In that sense, he was his own worst enemy. That was partly a factor in his downfall. He was a polarizing figure: intense, impatient, competitive, combative, sure of his journalistic, political, and bureaucratic judgment, and self-righteous in his commitment to the New Deal and to getting the United States into the war.[19] Some loved him, some hated him, but few seemed neutral, Elmer Davis told him.[20]

Descriptions of Horton's leadership and management style focused on his personality. They included such negative characterizations as "hard-boiled and short-tempered,"[21] "aggressive,"[22] blunt,[23] and that "his temperamental nature is his principal weakness."[24] Some of those same traits were at times described neutrally or positively, including "not the kind of person who sits back and waits for something to happen,"[25] "a hustling young man,"[26] "able,"[27] and "thorny, difficult, and spiritually incorruptible."[28] Similarly, Horton was criticized and praised for his press relations. He was subjected to withering criticism from some newspapermen (usually conservative columnists), but an academic source contradicts that, saying he was "was popular with newsmen."[29]

Some of his detractors also accused him of being bureaucratic. An OFF staffer (and former reporter) who admired MacLeish and disliked Horton's competitiveness toward MacLeish, described Horton as "of the carpet-carafe variety" of government PR managers, meaning that Horton was more of a bureaucratic empire builder than an information officer, epitomized by liking the perks of a well-appointed office.[30] The "Washington Merry-Go-Round" column referred to Horton as "a red-tape past master."[31]

Horton certainly didn't play well with others, especially when he disagreed with them or suspected their motives. He openly showed his disdain for corporate PR men and for the dollar-a-year executives who, he felt, were undermining the gains of the New Deal. His insistence that he was accountable only to the president was more of an assertion than authentically true. The liaison officer for NDAC and then OEM had some supervisory power over Horton and could have insisted on exercising it. Had that happened, in all likelihood Horton would have left.

One does not get the impression that Horton's being "difficult" was due to grandiosity, egomania, hunger for power, bureaucratic empire-building, or aggrandizement for its own sake. Rather, Horton's behavior reflected his certainty that his untraditional model was better for government PR, for good government, for democracy, and for winning the war. That's why he fought so tenaciously nearly every day for two years to build and protect the centralized PR structure in which he so fervently believed. Clearly, he had strong opinions about how government PR should be conducted, and he wasn't reluctant to voice disagreements. He was not a diplomatic person in terms of building alliances for future power struggles. By mid-1942, he had apparently used up all his political capital and had so many enemies in the media and bureaucracy that it was out of the question for him to run OWI. His quick flight from a midlevel OWI position to OPA also indicated that he liked running things, not having bosses to second-guess and direct his work.[32] In his post-OWI positions, he was always the agency's senior PR official (except for February to July 1943, when he was special assistant to the secretary of the Interior).

Horton's departure from federal service in mid-1946 had overtones of someone who was worn out and no longer wanted the stress and pressure. The prospect of serving in government PR in a period of normalcy after the adrenalin rush and satisfaction of contributing to winning the war probably felt anticlimactic. Returning home to Vermont to run the family hotel certainly displayed a radical break with his past. That he never wrote about his wartime experiences and only talked about it on the record once (to Ketchum) also gives the impression of someone putting his past behind him and out of mind. His low-profile postwar countenance suggests that he had come to terms with his roller-coaster experience in the federal government. In his interview with Ketchum, one catches a glimpse of the Washington Horton: fierce, passionate, unrelenting, uncompromising, a perfectionist, controlling, ambitious, and always pushing. But, by then, the embers were burning low. Horton seemed fatalistic and detached when recounting his rise and fall.

Debunking the "Mess in Washington"

This inquiry has focused on the external communications of the prewar and wartime production effort. However, it is sometimes hard to separate the public relations for something from the thing itself. Therefore, some tentative observations about the matériel buildup as a whole rather than just its PR are offered here. The consensus of American historians is generally that Roosevelt mishandled the production effort to the point of harming the war effort. For example, H. W. Brands concludes in his biography of FDR that Roosevelt made three major mistakes, notwithstanding his admirable and successful leadership in World War II. They were Pearl Harbor, the delay in opening a second front in Europe, and the production effort. Regarding the latter, Brands opines that "the insufficient coordination of America's war production impeded the efforts of the armies of the Grand Alliance."[33]

Perhaps the key to explicating the prevalent negative historical conclusion lies in a perspective offered by the biographer of another controversial and wartime president, James Polk. Like FDR, Polk was loudly and vehemently opposed during his term of office. Those criticisms then echoed into his historical legacy. Robert Merry suggests that "Polk's historical standing seems trapped in the arguments and controversies that swirled around him during his momentous White House years."[34] If journalism is the first draft of history, then even a casual reading of newspaper coverage in the prewar and wartime years highlights the ongoing political claim of the mess that Roosevelt was making. Politicians struck gold by focusing on the "mistakes" the president was making in the defense and then war effort, a goal that they, of course, supported. This was catnip for reporters. There were seemingly endless stories, all variations on the same theme. This anti-FDR news angle was wryly characterized as "damning him for not being perfect."[35] For example, Senator Byrd's 1940 criticism was that FDR's leadership should be questioned because of the small number of combat planes then under signed contracts. In that case, Roosevelt vigorously fought the charges not only through Horton as his surrogate, but also personally in a press conference. The president's involvement in that case was out of the ordinary, driven by the unusual circumstances of running for a third term.

More often than not, FDR left it to the agency heads to fend for themselves. Roosevelt understood that actively involving himself against every attack added stature to the attacker, who was important enough to elicit a response from the president. For example, the conservative coalition, in its continued assault on OPA's perceived misdoings, always aligned itself with a population segment that felt aggrieved, such as by tire rationing. While Roosevelt would often be asked at his twice-weekly press conferences about the attack du jour, he usually fobbed them off and avoided getting seriously involved. For example, regarding Elmer Davis and OWI, Roosevelt never defended what OWI was doing and never fought congressional cuts to its budget.[36] It was sink or swim in FDR's political world.

In that context, regarding the larger themes of the prewar and war periods, Roosevelt continued as the master communicator he had been during the Great Depression, with his adept turn of phrase, fireside chats, and consummate public relations. But when it came to the details of the production and economic mobilization, he seemed to prefer relying on the public's judgment of his deeds, not his words. So, for example, he relatively frequently tinkered with the organization of the civilian economic management effort before and during the war, often in response to public criticisms—so the dizzying shifts from NDAC to OPM to WPB. Similarly, he decided to reorganize the information effort to co-opt and deflect criticisms from congressional conservatives. He preferred to respond through actions, not verbally As a result, Roosevelt did not leave much of a verbal or print defense of the economic mobilization.

Catton's usual melodramatic style vividly evokes the political atmosphere caused by the ceaseless criticisms from Capitol Hill that Roosevelt was bungling the prewar and war efforts:

> The we-hate-Roosevelt people were successful beyond their dreams during the war, and 1942 was the year of their first big triumph. Their strategy was simple, and it was all the better for being purely instinctive rather than rational. It began with the excellent assumption that any action which the ad-

> ministration might take (other than those actions directly concerned with military matters) was sure to be unsound and ill-advised and was more than likely to be revolutionary; thus they always had something to criticize, and the criticism never had to be documented since it was based on an axiom rather than on facts and reasoning. Better yet, this created a game in which both ends could be played against the middle; for the very fact that this criticism was being made could then be used as a basis for further criticism, the idea being that there must be something terribly wrong or the administration wouldn't be under so much attack. . . . The tragedy was that the administration wasn't able to stand up against it.[37]

Besides the political game that was afoot, plenty of production controversies were real, in the sense that the senior officials had thankless zero-sum choices to make, with the losers convinced they had been wronged. They quickly appealed the supposedly wrong decision to the press and Congress, playing the role of victims of stupid, senseless, and ill-conceived bureaucratic diktats. The production effort (and organizational structure) looked complicated because it *was* complicated. The messy administrative complex of numerous alphabet agencies reflected the realities of the US economy: a complex decentralized economic engine with many moving parts that were very difficult to coordinate and where choices almost always triggered unintended consequences. So, understandably, it looked like a problem. In his memoir (partly ghostwritten by Catton), Donald Nelson describes the seemingly interminable coverage of all the "wrong" decisions he made:

> Some quirk of news evaluation always blew up each of our intra-mural arguments into a show a little larger than life-size. Nobody ever pays much attention to disagreements on the respected floors of the Senate and the House of Representatives, where they are habitual, or in Congressional committees, where they are the rule rather than the exception, or in business organizations, fraternal orders, or even in the governing bodies of churches. But any difference of opinion in a government agency, especially during a period of emergency, somehow gets to be a full-bodied sensation calling for the suspicious glance, the published rumor and innuendo, or an investigation of high, low, or middle voltage.[38]

The dynamic of journalism was tilted to an inherently negative tone in the coverage of the policies and decisions by leaders of the production effort.

In that sense, the ideological congressional coalition and the nonideological journalistic culture worked hand in glove to depict ceaselessly a mess in Washington.

The story of Horton's PR work also alluded to the ongoing warfare within the administration between New Dealers and dollar-a-year businessmen. Each felt the other was totally wrong in its preferences and recommendations, convinced that the other group was sabotaging the war effort by dogmatic ideology. They seethed with animosity toward each other. Hence that hostility was deeply seared into the collective memory of the prewar and war experience.

Another largely forgotten contributor to the negative view of FDR's production mobilization is the resistance in segments of the citizenry to regulations and rationing. The romantic given narrative of the domestic front in World War II is of a unified and mobilized public, everyone in solidarity putting shoulder to the wheel and accepting shared shortages and sacrifices without whimper. A casual reading of newspaper coverage shows the opposite: howls from those affected by rules and regulations, fervently arguing that they should not be impacted by the war effort; these included owners of racetracks, cars (some were veterans after all!), nightclubs, movie theaters, and seemingly all other tiny specks of the political economy. All seemed unembarrassed to suggest that they be excluded from the impact of the economic mobilization.

A related factor is the built-in political dynamic associated with winners and losers. Generalizing from the experience of Prohibition and its repeal, Daniel Okrent quotes one of the leaders of Prohibition saying that "a minority that has lost something will register its protest, . . . but 'the majority who have won the fight turn to other tasks.'"[39] Losers were unwilling to accept silently decisions with which they disagreed. Their voices echo down through history, while the winners or those unaffected moved on to other things.

So, in part, the ongoing historical perception of a wartime production mess echoes the political noise, partisan attacks, adversarial journalism, substantive disagreements, and democratic dynamics of the time. That image has persisted, somewhat unfairly. Perhaps one reason it has gone on so long and gained its own momentum is because it is an ambiguous accusation that is well-nigh impossible to disprove. How does one prove that the domestic mobilization did not make mistakes or have some false starts? Nonetheless, there is a small revisionist perspective that presents a more positive conclusion. In his history of the European Theater, British historian Norman Davies asserts that "nothing could compare to the miracles achieved by the wartime economy of the USA."[40] Perhaps his view will gain additional adherents over time.

In the meantime, the lingering negativity associated with the civilian and economic mobilization parallels somewhat the argument about the appropriate role of government PR. The debate over propaganda versus information is a perpetual one, but given American political culture's antipathy to government, those who assume the worst about bureaucracy hold the upper hand. In debate, an accusation of propaganda easily trumps a defense of "just factual information"; similar to the dominant historical narrative of the disorganization of the production buildup. In the end, definitive and unanimous conclusions about both topics are probably a mirage. Horton's choices about the practice of government PR were clear to him. He was sure he was right regarding what was and was not propaganda, what was and was not information, and the right and wrong organizational structure. But history's judgment is dynamic and will vary by the predilections of the narrator and the cycles of history telling. Either way, what Horton did was interesting, valuable, and unusual. He deserves some historical credit for that, rather than obscurity or Catton's hagiography.

NOTES

Abbreviations Used in the Notes

AP: Associated Press, a news wire service
CR: *Congressional Record*
CSM: *Christian Science Monitor* (published in Boston)
CT: *Chicago Tribune*
HC: *Hartford Courant*
LAT: *Los Angeles Times*
NYT: *New York Times*
WP: *Washington Post*
WSJ: *Wall Street Journal*

Preface

1. Lee, *First Presidential Communications Agency;* Winkler, *Politics of Propaganda.*

2. A recent article indicated some ongoing interest in the short-lived agency, but a comprehensive book-length academic biography of OFF has yet to be written (Girona and Xifra, "Office of Facts and Figures").

3. Lee, "Origins of the Epithet."

4. Catton, *War Lords.*

5. Earlier in 1941, Horton had assigned Catton to be Nelson's personal public information officer while still part of Horton's agency. Nelson was presumably Catton's main source for the story. Nelson and Catton worked so well together before and during the war that Catton later helped ghostwrite Nelson's memoir, before writing his own (*Arsenal of Democracy,* xviii). While helping with Nelson's book, Catton would have access to Nelson's appointment calendar, which would have listed the correct date.

6. Catton, *War Lords,* 9. Knox was not talking out of school or giving these VIPs any secret information. In the Navy's routine annual report for FY1941, which was released on December 6, 1941, the day before Pearl Harbor, Knox wrote that "the American people may feel fully confident in their Navy. . . . On any comparable basis, the United States Navy is second to none" ("Navy Is Superior to Any, says Knox," *NYT,* [December 7, 1941], 1).

7. Catton, 10, 12, emphasis in original.

8. Catton to Horton, October 6, 1948. Folder: Correspondence, 1948, 1949, 1952, Box 9, Bruce Catton Collection, American Heritage Center, University of Wyoming.

9. Catton, 181, emphasis added. Another indication of the power of this storytelling is that a third party chose to include it in a volume of Catton's best writings (Jensen, *Bruce Catton's America,* 205–7).

10. Downing, *Sealing Their Fate,* 279–80; Halper, "Supermarket Use," 458–59 (misquoting Catton's wrong date); Ketchum, *Borrowed Years,* 724–25; Lobdell, "Frank Knox," 706. In general, Catton's book has been widely cited in the historical literature and accepted as authoritative, despite its lack of documentation, melodramatic storytelling, and overt author bias (Lee, "Origins of the Epithet," 392–93).

11. *Diary of Henry Wallace, January 18, 1935–September 19, 1946,* Reel 1, Volume 12, November 28, 1941–Friday, Papers of Henry Wallace.

12. Lee, *Congress vs. the Bureaucracy.*

13. Richard Ketchum, "Interview with Robert Wyman Horton," December 30, 1987, 5–6. Papers of Richard Ketchum.

14. Shesol, *Supreme Power,* 235–36.

Introduction

1. Brewer, *Why America Fights,* 4; Ellul, *Propaganda;* Walton, *Media Argumentation,* chap. 3. The origin of the word was religious, as in "propagating the faith."

2. Fellows, "'Propaganda,'" 186; Sproule, *Propaganda and Democracy,* 224.

3. Fulbright, *Pentagon Propaganda,* 9.

4. Berry, *Voice for Nonprofits,* 51–52.

5. Safire, *Safire's Political Dictionary,* 581–82.

6. Okrent, *Rise and Fall of Prohibition,* 59, 100, emphasis added.

7. Jackson, "Earned Media," 112.

8. In something of a double standard, especially during the Cold War, Congress permitted, even encouraged, federal agencies to engage in propaganda aimed at foreign audiences.

9. Lee, "Congressional Controversy"; "Case Study of Congressional Hostility."

10. Kosar, "Executive Branch and Propaganda"; Lee, *Congress vs. the Bureaucracy.*

11. Friel, "Toot Your Horn."

12. Weiss, "Public Information."

13. Kumar, *Managing the President's Message.*

14. Maltese, *Spin Control.*

15. Axelrod, *Selling the Great War;* Winkler, *Politics of Propaganda.*

16. Rich, *Greatest Story Ever Sold.*

17. Besides the sources already cited, other references since 1980 (i.e., at least twenty-five years after the war): Bird and Rubenstein, *Design for Victory,* 24, 29, 35, 66; Kennett, *For the Duration,* 104–5; Koppes and Black, *Hollywood Goes to War,* 52; Shale, *Donald Duck Joins Up,* 22; Steele, *Propaganda in an Open Society,* 73–74; and "Great Debate," 71; Troy, *Donovan and the CIA,* 121; Winfield, *FDR and the News Media,* 157–58.

18. Lee, *Congress,* chap. 1.

19. Lamme and Russell, "Removing the Spin."

20. Allison, "Public and Private Management."

21. Friedrich and Cole, *Responsible Bureaucracy,* 26; Plant, "Carl J. Friedrich," 474.

22. Lee, "Intersectoral Differences."

23. Lee, Neeley, and Stewart, *Practice of Government Public Relations;* Lee, "Return of Public Relations."

24. US DOI, *Priorities and Defense,* 18; organization chart, *Victory* 3:4 (January 27, 1942): 5. Archival references to "Information Division": organization chart, June 18, 1941. Folder: Personnel Regulations, Box 9; Memo from Robert Ware Straus, Assistant Director, November 7, 1941, n.t. Folder: Memos-Straus, Box 7. Both in Entry 576A, Record Group 208, National Archives II, College Park, MD. *Note:* All subsequent archival citations are from Entry 576A of RG 208 (OWI), unless otherwise specified.

25. "D. of I.": Weekly update from Robert Ware Straus to Horton, July 7, 1941. "D of I": Weekly update from Straus to Horton, June 7, 1941, 2. Both in Binder: Weekly Round Ups/Box Score, Box 13.

26. "A Job for Elmer Davis," editorial, *New Republic,* June 22, 1942, 847.

27. Steele, *Propaganda,* 73ff.

28. Troy, 121.

29. Title of Folder: WPB-ID Responsible for Information Work, Box 6.

30. Published sources: Larson, "Publicity for National Defense," 249 and "Official Information," 69; US CSC, *Official Register, 1943,* 154; Catton, 10. Archival sources: Memo To: All Division Heads, From: Robert Wyman Horton, Subject: Information Service, March 25, 1941. Binder: Functions and Operations of Division of Information, 1941–42, Box 13; "Information Division," n.d. (about December 1940). Folder: Information Div., Box 13. Also *US Government Manual* (Summer 1943): 297 (Winter 1943–44): 304.

31. *Congressional Directory:* 76th Cong., 1st sess., 1st ed. (December 20, 1938): 395; 76th Cong., 1st sess., 2nd ed. (March 23, 1939): 395; 76th Cong., 3rd sess., 1st ed. (December 19, 1939): 390; 76th Cong., 3rd sess., 2nd ed. (June 6, 1940): 393. Also *US Government Manual* (October 1939): 435, (February 1940): 435.

Chapter One

1. Miller, *Story of Ernie Pyle,* 48; "Personal," *Marine Engineering and Shipping Review* 43:9 (September 1938): 434; "Robert Horton" (obituary), *Addison County (VT) Independent* (September 20, 1993).

2. Baldasty, *E. W. Scripps,* 106–12.

3. A columnist hostile to Horton's later government PR work described Horton as "a second rate reporter, a plodding, hard-working newshawk with neither vision nor imagination. He was, however, the office pet of Lowell Mellett, then his managing editor" (Ray Tucker, "Washington Letter" [syndicated column], *Sandusky [OH] Register-Star-News,* August 31, 1942, 4).

4. "So That's How the Farm Bill Works," *Nation's Business,* January 1930, 27–29, 162; "Washington Letter," *Canadian Forum* 14–15, nos. 164–75 (May 1934–April 1935).

5. "Current Favorites as Seen by the Radio Cameraman" (photos), *WP,* February 14, 1937,

TR6; Drew Pearson and Robert Allen, "Washington Merry-Go-Round" (column), *Charleston (WV) Gazette*, May 16, 1937, 6; "On the Air Today," *WP*, March 10, 1937, 14; C. E. Butterfield, "Radio Day by Day," *Cumberland (MD) Evening Times*, June 17, 1937, 9.

6. "Not Too Much for a Negro," *Nation*, December 11, 1935, 674–76. The DA who sanctioned the torture was John Stennis, later a US senator (D-MS). In 1937, Horton wrote two more articles for the *Nation:* "Death in the Air," January 23, 1937, 94–95; and "Congress Looks Toward 1938," June 5, 1937, 638–39.

7. Ketchum, "Interview with Robert Wyman Horton," December 30, 1987, 1–2. Papers of Richard Ketchum.

8. However, contrary to the given narrative, FDR's was not a *qualitative* break with President Hoover's own focus on agency PR, but rather a quantitative increase (Lee, "Government Public Relations during Herbert Hoover's Presidency").

9. "Blueprints: Notes on Some Increasingly Significant Federal Machinery," *Tide* 14:10 (May 15, 1940): 18–20.

10. Bishop and Mackay, "Federal Government Reports on Defense," 4. For a list of former reporters in federal PR, see "Defense Program Draws Newsmen to Capital," *Editor & Publisher* 74:43 (October 25, 1941): 20.

11. "Horton Heads Section of U.S. Maritime Body," *WP*, August 18, 1938, 2; "Union Jack Leads on Ships Coming to Boston in July," *CSM*, August 22, 1938, 11; "Personal," *Marine Engineering and Shipping News* 43:9 (September 1938): 434.

12. For MC's history, see Lane, *Ships for Victory;* Land, *Winning the War with Ships.* The shrinkage in US-flagged *passenger* ships after World War I was partly due to Prohibition. It was interpreted as prohibiting US-flagged ships serving alcohol at all, while foreign ships were prohibited only when in US territorial waters.

13. That 1936 was an election year is worth noting. Legislators were working hard to do things that would be popular and noncontroversial. This bolsters the viewpoint that the goals embodied in the act reflected widely held values.

14. 49 *Stat.* 1985.

15. During Roosevelt's first term, he appointed Kennedy as the initial chair of the new Securities and Exchange Commission. Kennedy served about a year and then resigned in September 1935.

16. Subsidizing the merchant marine reflected the shipping lobby, an active political constituency of shipbuilders, shipping lines, and labor unions. They tended to be successful on Capitol Hill regardless of the isolationist-internationalist arguments. While they represented a minor portion of the population, they achieved a political standing comparable to that of farmers, evoking an anachronistic historical idyll that was thought to be important to preserve even if uneconomical and with an unsustainable business model. Also, there was no anti–merchant marine lobby to neutralize the supposedly patriotic advocates for federal maritime subsidies and spending.

17. Paul Mallon, "News behind the News" (syndicated column), *Danville (VA) Bee*, May 24, 1937, 6.

18. Kennedy was one of his first major clients. By October 1938, Kennedy was already getting negative publicity about his diplomatic work and views (this a year before his somewhat defeatist views about the war between Germany and the United Kingdom). He brought Stringer to London temporarily to help him repair his image and standing (Paul Mallon, "Joe Kennedy

Under Fire in State Dept.," *HC,* October 27, 1938, 3). Kennedy's sons accompanied him to London, including, John F., the future president, and Robert and Ted, the future senators.

19. US MC, "Text of address delivered by Mr. Bon Geaslin, General Counsel of the US Maritime Commission, before the Federal Bar Association at the National Press Club, Wednesday, February 8, 1939," PR-305, 1.

20. Lee, *Congress,* 142–57.

21. Lane, 760.

22. US MC, "Text of an address delivered by Vice Chairman, Thomas Woodward of the US Maritime Commission over radio station WMAL at 10:30 P.M., October 31, 1938," PR-254, 1.

23. Ibid., 2, 4.

24. US MC, "Address delivered by Rear Admiral Henry Wiley (Retired), member of the US Maritime Commission, over the Columbia Broadcasting System, Station WJSV, Washington [DC], Tuesday, November 29 [1938] at 10:45 p.m.," PR-265, 4; "Address delivered by M.L. Wilcox, Director, Operations and Traffic, US Maritime Commission, at the annual dinner of the New York Freight Forwarders and Brokers Association, Tuesday evening, January 10, 1939," PR-287, 3.

25. US MC, "Text of address delivered by Rear Admiral Emory Land, Retired, Chairman, US Maritime Commission, at the thirty-fifth anniversary banquet of the Alumni Association, New York State Merchant Marine Academy, in New York, Saturday evening, February 4th, 1939," PR-303, 2.

26. Ibid., 11.

27. Ibid.

28. US MC, "Text of an address delivered by Vice Chairman, Thomas Woodward," 6.

29. US MC, *America Builds Ships,* n.p.

30. Charles Cohan, "Fact and Comment" (column), *LAT,* May 26, 1940, E3.

31. US MC, *New Ships for the Merchant Marine.*

32. US MC, *General Information on the United States Maritime Service,* and a revised edition released in January 1940. As an indication of the fast pace of developments, the original publication was followed by three revised versions with updated text and photos within a one-year period. Four of the pictures from the March 1939 version were later used in a newspaper story: Leigh S. Plummer, "Training Men for U.S. Maritime Service," *WSJ,* March 31, 1939, 26. Plummer later worked for Horton in DOI.

33. US MC, "Text of address delivered by Bon Geaslin," 4.

34. US MC, "Address delivered by M.L. Wilcox, Director, Operations and Traffic, U.S. Maritime Commission, at the Traffic Club of Baltimore, Tuesday evening December 6, 1938," PR-269, 6.

35. US MC, "Text of address delivered by Rear Admiral Emory S. Land, Retired, US Maritime Commission, before the fourteenth Women's Patriotic Conference on National Defense, at the Mayflower Hotel, Washington, D.C., January 26, 1939," PR-298, 5, 10.

36. US MC, "Text of address delivered by Bon Geaslin," 1, emphasis added.

37. Lee, *Congress,* 29–83.

38. For example, these references to an unnamed MC spokesman were likely to Horton: "Collapse Is Seen for Our Shipping," *NYT,* November 5, 1939, 40; "Drive to Lift Ship Ban Opens," *LAT,* April 10, 1940, 7.

39. AP, "Ghost Fleet Being Repaired," *LAT,* October 5, 1939, 3; "Tour Heads Back 'Travel America,'" *NYT,* January 20, 1940, 32.

40. US MC, "Text of address delivered by Rear Admiral Emory Land, at the thirty-fifth anniversary banquet of the Alumni Association, New York State Merchant Marine Academy, February 4, 1939," PR-303.

41. US MC, "Speech delivered by Admiral Emory Land, Chairman, US Maritime Commission, over the Columbia Broadcasting System, Station WJSV, Washington, D.C., Friday, September 16, 1938 at 9:45 p.m.," PR-236.

42. US MC, "Text of address delivered by Emory Land, at the thirty-fifth anniversary banquet of the Alumni Association."

43. AP, "Phoenician Gets Shipping Post," *(Phoenix) Arizona Republic*, December 1, 1939, 6.

44. Lee, *History of Public Reporting.*

45. Lee, *First Presidential.*

46. "Ship Construction Contracts," *Traffic World* 66 (July 13, 1940): 93. Published about a month after Horton left the MC, he would have been involved in its preparation.

47. For example: "Bureau Forecasts Rise in U.S. Tonnage," *NYT*, July 26, 1939, 41.

48. US MC, "Speech delivered by Emory Land, Chairman, US Maritime Commission, over the Columbia Broadcasting System, Station WJSV, Washington, D.C., Friday, September 16, 1938 at 9:45 P.M.," PR-236, 1.

49. Ray Tucker, "News behind the News," *Piqua (OH) Daily Call*, February 22, 1939, 10.

50. Hartley, "Sight and Sound," 225.

51. MacCann, *People's Films*, 95.

52. US MC, *American Flag Services.*

53. US BOB, *Budget . . . for the Fiscal Year Ending June 30, 1940*, 97.

54. "First Inter-American Travel Congress," *[US State Department] Press Releases* 20:496 (April 1, 1939): 258; "Press Director to West Coast," *Army Navy Journal* 76:33 (April 15, 1939): 775; "Tours Heads Back 'Travel America,'" *NYT*, January 20, 1940, 32.

55. US BOB, *Budget . . . for the Fiscal Year Ending June 30, 1940*, 97.

56. Lane, 758.

57. US House, *Independent Offices Appropriation*, 578.

58. Ibid., 522.

59. *Congressional Directory:* 76th Cong., 1st sess., 1st ed. (December 20, 1938): 395; 76th Cong., 1st sess., 2nd ed. (March 23, 1939): 395.

60. Land, "Building an American Merchant Marine," 48.

61. Tucker, "News behind the News," 10

Chapter Two

1. Brownlow, *Passion for Anonymity*, 428–29.

2. Roosevelt, *Public Papers*, 8:490–96.

3. Brownlow, 429.

4. US NDAC, *Press Releases*, PR-254, 1.

5. Wills, *Necessary Evil.*

6. Patterson, *Congressional Conservatism.*

7. Burns, *Roosevelt*, 435. At the time, newspaper coverage reported the FDR's response as, "I

guess I will be" (Joseph Alsop and Robert Kintner, "The Capital Parade" [syndicated column], *Atlanta Constitution,* September 5, 1940, 8). Brownlow's quote did not have the hedging: "I am" (431).

8. 3 *CFR 1938–1943 Comp.* 1320.

9. Brownlow, 429.

10. Fesler et al., *Industrial Mobilization,* 28–29. The argument about having a czar of defense mobilization dated back to the post–World War I era, with the Army and Navy creating several versions of an Industrial Mobilization Plan. FDR would have none of it (Lee, *First,* 48–67).

11. Gosnell, *Division of Information,* 8.

12. US NDAC, *Press Releases,* PR-2. PR-1 announced the appointments of a staff of experts to assist a commissioner. The acronym title of the series, "PR," was an abbreviation of "press release," not "public relations."

13. Gosnell, 24.

14. Horton to Sidney Sherwood (NDAC Assistant Secretary), memo, June 27, 1940, n.t. Folder: Memos–Sherwood, Box 7.

15. A week after his appointment, Horton was already the subject of unflattering coverage. In their column "Washington Merry-Go-Round," Pearson and Allen wrote that NDAC's commissioner for industrial production, William Knudsen, had ignored Horton, who was standing in front of Knudsen's desk waiting to talk to him. Knudsen was absorbed in reading a report about tank production. When Knudsen finally noticed Horton, he barked at him, "Can you make tanks?" Horton said no, at which point Knudsen rudely dismissed him (*Laredo [TX] Times,* June 11, 1940, 5). *Time* magazine plagiarized the item (without attribution) in its next issue, referring to him as "handsome Publicityman [*sic*] Bob Horton" (June 17, 1940, 17). Horton wrote a letter to the editor stating that the story was false:

> Sirs: Thanks for the ad. A rebuke for bad reporting. Mr. Knudsen did not summarily dismiss the undersigned. He did not say: "Then I won't be seeing much of you."
>
> Instead, he smiled at his preoccupation with one of the vital problems which he has to solve and we went on with business, which Mr. Knudsen conducts in a way that makes it a pleasure to be his associate.
>
> No bureaucrat, Mr. Knudsen has none of the mannerisms of one.
>
> Robert W. Horton
> Director of Public Relations
> The Advisory Commission to the Council of National Defense

In what passed for a formal correction by *Time,* three issues later it published Horton's letter along with the editorial comment, "*Time* was misinformed about what Mr. Knudsen said, was right about his being earnest and preoccupied" (July 8, 1940, 7).

16. Horton, "Handling the Preparedness Orders," letter to the editor, *Industrial Marketing* 25:7 (July 1940): 114.

17. Catton, 51–52.

18. US NDAC, *Minutes of the Advisory Commission,* 68.

19. Ibid., 17.

20. Ibid., 20. For Horton's three-page draft, see Document 1b, Roll 1 (US NDAC, *Numbered Document File*).

21. US NDAC, *Minutes*, 27.

22. Ibid., 32.

23. Ibid., 34.

24. Ibid., 56, emphasis added.

25. Ibid., 80.

26. Ibid., 32, emphasis added.

27. Ibid., emphasis added.

28. Ibid.

29. Gosnell, 24.

30. US NDAC, *Press Releases*, PR-32.

31. Roosevelt, *Complete Presidential Press Conferences*, 16:40–47.

32. AP, "Reports by the Defense Commission," *NYT*, July 17, 1940, 10; Joseph Harrison, "U.S. Defense Gains Reported by Commission," *CSM*, July 17, 1940, 7.

33. "Defense Publicity Agency Reported," *WP*, June 29, 1940, 2.

34. Roosevelt, *Press Conferences*, 16:78–80; US NDAC, *Press Releases*, PR-52.

35. The next day, a newspaper ran a one-paragraph article on the pulp news versus its fourteen-paragraph story on the president avoiding engaging in political comments at that press conference (AP, "Keeping Pulp Price Down"; "When President Says 'No News' Even Rooseveltian Snort Is Out," *CSM*, July 31, 1940, 3).

36. Horton was often called "Bob," including in print (for example, in Jerry Kluttz, "Federal Diary" [column for federal employees], *WP*, September 24, 1941, 21). FDR was routinely familiar toward people, even when he didn't know them well. Later that fall, Horton asked Knudsen whether it was true that, as a Republican, Knudsen would resign before the election to show solidarity with Republican nominee Willkie. Knudsen replied; "Me resign? Me quit the President? Why—why, *he calls me Bill!*" (Catton, 69–70, emphasis in original). This was no small matter. After the campaign, Willkie told *Times* reporter Arthur Krock that Knudsen's and Stettinius's refusal to resign "had cost him the 1940 election" (*Memoirs*, 196).

37. The pulp crisis faded as fast as it came. A month later, NDAC announced that there was no shortage of wood pulp (US NDAC, *Press Releases*, PR-88). Only the *Wall Street Journal* covered it, the subject having reverted to hum-drum business news ("No Wood Pulp Shortage Likely during 1941," August 31, 1940, 1).

38. Walter Trohan, "Reveal Muddle in Air Plan," *Chicago Tribune*, July 28, 1940, 1, 13.

39. David Lawrence, "Today in Washington" (syndicated column), *Syracuse (NY) Herald-Journal*, August 2, 1940, 18.

40. Roosevelt, *Press Conferences*, 16:84, 93.

41. August 3, 1940: "Defense Work Delay Denied by Roosevelt," *WP*, 2; AP, "Facts Given on Aircraft Production: Defense Commission Spokesman, at Roosevelt's Request, Reports On Present Status," *HC*, 2; United Press, "White House Denies Defense Is Stalled," *NYT*, 7. Written by three different reporters, these stories contained almost no direct quotes from Horton. A condition of the briefing may have been that the information was public, but that Horton could not be quoted directly, a relatively common White House practice then.

42. AP, "American Car & Foundry Building 1,156 Tanks for U.S.," *WSJ*, July 3, 1940, 2.

43. "Airplane Production," editorial, *San Antonio (TX) Express*, July 5, 1940, 2A.

44. US NDAC, *Press Releases*, PR-60, 65.

45. Ibid., PR-66.

46. "Reports Year Rate of 10,800 Planes," *NYT,* August 9, 1940, 2.

47. "Going Awfully Well," editorial, *LAT,* August 13, 1940, A4.

48. US NDAC, *Press Releases,* PR-72, 73, 76, 79.

49. *NYT,* August 15, 1940, 13; *WSJ,* August 19, 1940, 1, 6, 8; AP, *NYT,* August 24, 1940, 28.

50. "Byrd Seeks Inquiry on Defense Delay," *NYT,* August 25, 1940, 1.

51. Everything about the report was so vague that the last question the reporters asked Horton was its title. Should they call it "A report from the Defense Commission to the President?" Yes, said Horton (Press Conference Folder, Early Papers, 4). The report could not be located at the Roosevelt Library (e-mail from Virginia Lewick, archivist, June 8, 2010, author's files).

52. Knudsen was in Seattle inspecting a Boeing plant (United Press, "On Tour of Airplane Production Plants," *NYT,* August 27, 1940, 11).

53. Bertram Hulen, "6,747 War Planes Ordered for U.S.," *NYT,* August 27, 1940, 10.

54. "Report of the Defense Commission to the President" (transcript), August 26, 1940, Press Conference Folder, Early Papers.

55. Horton's conducting a White House press conference led to a gossipy item about him in the "Washington Merry-Go-Round" column. Without providing a precise date of the event being referred to, in late 1940 a column stated that the "swankiest newsman at the White House press conference is Robert Horton, press officer for the Defense commission, who, while most of the others are hoofing to their offices after the conference, drives away in a limousine with a chauffeur" (Pearson and Allen, *Laredo [TX] Times,* January 1, 1941, 7). This was probably a reference to his August 26 press conference, which the columnists held to use later as filler.

56. August 26, 1940: AP, "Contracts Let for 6747 U.S. Warplanes, F.R. Told," *Oakland (CA) Tribune,* 2; United Press, "Roosevelt Given Defense Reports on Plane Orders," *Altoona (PA) Mirror,* 1–2.

57. Willard Edwards, *CT,* August 27, 1940, 5; *CSM,* August 27, 1940, 7.

58. George Bookman, "President Lays Plane Delays to Congress," *WP,* August 28, 1940, 1.

59. Roosevelt, *Press Conferences,* 16:150–61.

60. "President and Knox Paint Brighter Defense Picture," *CSM,* August 29, 1940, 1.

61. "Data on Air Defense Barred to Sen. Byrd," *NYT,* August 29, 1940, 12.

62. After the election, General (ret.) Hugh Johnson weighed in. (He had headed the National Recovery Administration for Roosevelt, but broke with him in 1937. An isolationist, he had endorsed Willkie in 1940.) Johnson denounced the "Horton publicity machine" and Horton's control over what national defense information would be released. Johnson slightly exculpated Roosevelt personally, writing that "the President *was persuaded* to make a report" with the optimistic and misleading statistics ("Dollars Won't Defend Us!" *Hearst's International* 109:6 [December 1940]: 20–21, emphasis added). Johnson's implication that Horton had practically forced a passive, even reluctant, Roosevelt to hold the August 27 press conference is incredible.

63. US NDAC, *Press Releases,* PR-101, 104, 108, 115, 123, 132, 135, 143, 163, 167, 171, 225.

64. Ibid., PR-101.

65. Ibid., PR-188.

66. The subject was still touchy a year later. Airplane production numbers had come to symbolize the production effort. In October 1941, the OPM Council urged FDR to begin treating plane production statistics as confidential because of their usefulness to potential enemies (US OPM, *Minutes of the Council,* 63–64). Roosevelt agreed with alacrity.

67. *Baltimore Sun:* "Timetable of the Aircraft Defense Program," August 27, 1940, 10, and "Official Statements Which Still Have Defense Obscurities," August 29, 1940, 12. Also "The President on Defense," *HC,* August 29, 1940, 14; "NDAC's Airplane Figures," *Oakland (CA) Tribune,* September 11, 1940, 32.

68. Pearson and Allen, "Washington Merry-Go-Round," *(Reno) Nevada State Journal,* August 9, 1940, 4.

69. AP, "Defense Board Looks Back on 3 Months of Progress," *CSM,* August 28, 1940, 6.

70. US NDAC, *Press Releases,* PR-64.

71. Ibid., PR-66.

72. "Reports Year Rate of 10,800 Planes," *NYT,* August 9, 1940, 2.

73. US NDAC, *Minutes,* 55, emphasis added.

74. US NDAC, *Press Releases,* PR-98.

75. For example, ibid., PR-334.

76. Ibid., PR-158, 1, emphasis added.

77. As would be expected, the radio studio of the Interior Department was controversial with the conservative coalition in Congress, who saw it as yet another venue for pro–New Deal publicity (Lee, *Congress,* chap. 8).

78. Horton to Shannon Allen, Director, Radio Section, Division of Information, Department of the Interior, August 6, 1940; Allen to Horton, August 13, 1940. Folder: Radio, Box 5.

79. "Radio Transcriptions on Defense," *Defense* 1:5 (September 27, 1940): 8.

80. US NDAC, *Numbered Document File,* Document 112.

81. Ibid.

82. Editorial page: September 10, 1940, 4; September 17, 1940, 4; September 21, 1940, 4. Classified ads page: September 13, 1940, 13; September 20, 1940, 15.

83. September 4, 1940, 5; September 5, 1940, 11; September 28, 1940, 17.

84. August 5, 1940, 6.

85. "Censorship on Defense Reorganized" (syndicated column), *HC,* September 10, 1940, 3.

86. Epstein, *Big Picture,* 3.

87. Mercey to Mellett, memo, July 26, 1940, Subject: National Defense "Newsreel Special" Series. Archival copy includes a handwritten note (probably by Mellett): "forward to Mr. Horton." Folder: Newsreel (Miscellaneous), Box 5.

88. Mercey and Robert Collyer to Horton, memo, August 27, 1940, Subject: Newsreel and Topical Motion Picture Program. In August 1940, the Office of Education asked for help to instigate a newsreel story on FDR's call to college-age students to register for college and stay in school until drafted. Mercey's reaction was that a newsreel story would work only if it had "a little more action" than merely a talking head, even if the head was the president's (Mercey to Mellett, memo, August 16, 1940, Subject: Education Registration; Memo from Mercey to Horton, August 17, 1940, Subject: Educational registration). All in Folder: Newsreel (Miscellaneous), Box 5.

89. By mid-1940, newsreels on national defense were common, but not popular with some theater owners. The industry's president made a public appeal to members not to delete defense items from the newsreels ("Movies Asked Not to Cut Reels on Defense of U.S.," *NYT,* June 10, 1940, 8).

90. Janet Mable, "The Wide Horizon; Flying: A Career for Women?" *CSM,* August 7, 1940, 20.

91. AP, "Dewey Scores Defense Idling and New Deal's 'Tragic Blunders,'" *LAT*, October 18, 1940, 7. More generally, Republicans complained that films produced by federal agencies and available for free rental were partisan propaganda ("U.S. Films Used by New Dealers, Dirksen Charges," *CT*, September 27, 1940, 13).

92. Harmon, "Motion Picture Industry," 703.

93. US NDAC, *Press Releases*, PR-223, 1.

94. Ibid., PR-228, 1–2.

95. Lee, *Congress*, 4–12.

96. Horton to Navy Secretary Knox and War Secretary Stimson, August 12, 1940. Folders: K, S (alphabetical series), Box 9.

97. "Navy Moves to Buy 17,000 Air Engines," *NYT*, August 30, 1940, 11.

98. John Norris, "Army Curbs Plane Data," *WP*, October 5, 1940, 1, 3.

99. Horton to Directors of Information, All Federal Agencies, memo, n.d. (probably early September), n.t. Folder: Radio, Box 5. In November, two months after Horton's memo, a Harvard professor who specialized in government and communication indirectly endorsed Horton's effort, stating the need during the defense emergency for presidential coordination of all federal agency requests for radio time (Friedrich, *Controlling Broadcasting*, 23–25).

100. Pearson and Allen, "Washington Merry-Go-Round," *Charleston (WV) Gazette*, September 15, 1940, 25.

101. Paul Mallon, "Censorship on Defense Reorganized," *HC*, September 10, 1940, 3. The month before, Mallon complained about Horton's PR work twice. He described Horton as the cork in a bottleneck of releasing defense information, calling it a "Hitlerized publicity system" (*Portsmouth [NH] Herald*, August 1, 1940, 1) and criticized Horton's airplane figures as "lopping over into the field of more dangerous statistical deception" ("Hitler Marks Sept. 15 for Final Victory," *HC*, August 30, 1940, 3).

102. Warren Francis, "Defense Moves Being Hampered by Confusion in Nation's Capital," *LAT*, September 29, 1940, II–5.

103. Joseph Alsop and Robert Kintner, "Capital Parade," *Atlanta Constitution*, September 5, 1940, 8.

104. US NDAC, *Minutes*, 68.

105. Ibid., 68–69, emphasis added. Harriman, son of railroad baron E. H. Harriman, was later a senior foreign policy advisor to Democratic presidents from Truman to Johnson. In 1954, he was elected New York governor, but was defeated for reelection in 1958 by Nelson Rockefeller.

106. Ibid., 83, 86, 96.

107. "Robert Horton to Talk to Advertising Club," *WP*, September 25, 1940, 30.

108. Horton to Rear Admiral Ben Moreell, Chief of the Bureau of Yards and Docks, September 19, 1940. Folder: 020 Executive Depts (*sic*)of U.S., Box 1.

109. Miss [Laura Ann] Hatfield (Clerk-Stenographer) to Mrs. [Elizabeth] Seakar (Photo Editor), memo, October 8, 1940, n.t.; Robert Straus, Special Assistant to the Director, to Alfred Palmer, October 30, 1940. Folder: Still Pictures Sect[ion], Box 15. Straus became Horton's longtime assistant director, with the two staying together for nearly all of Horton's federal career. In 1947, the *Chicago Tribune* smeared Straus for involvement in a Communist front organization and for supporting Henry Wallace's left-leaning disenchantment with Truman's hard line toward the Soviet Union (William Moore, "Wallace Talk Sponsor Hit as Red Front Unit," June 15, 1947,

3). Late in life, Straus became an early environmental activist ("Robert Ware Straus, Conservationist, Dies," *WP*, August 27, 1991, B6). A nonprofit organic farm on the Potomac in Maryland is named after him. It is "a model for farming for the future," based on proximity to an urban area and poor soil conditions (http://accokeekfoundation.org/visit/education/stewardship/). Straus's brother was Michael W. Straus, a former Chicago reporter who became press secretary to Interior Secretary Harold Ickes and later became commissioner of reclamation. Michael Straus briefly worked under his brother at DOI in early 1942 as the head of the Production Drive's PR (US CSC, *Official Register, 1942*, 21).

110. Epstein, 4.

111. Steele also suggested that the fall of France in mid-1940 had a significant impact on Hollywood's Jewish executives ("Great Debate," 75).

112. Herbert Morgan, MGM Short Subjects, to Horton, August 6, 1940. Folder: Metro-Goldwyn-Mayer, Box 5.

113. "Supplemental List," Margaret Holmead, Chief, NDAC Personnel Section, to Horton, memo, July 20, 1940, n.t., 3. For a short period, Rosten was carried on the payroll of NDAC's Consumer Protection Division (memo to Miss Holmead, July 24, 1940, n.t., n.a. [probably from Ruth Bledsoe, DOI office manager], 3). Both in Folder: Personnel Regulations, Box 9. Rosten, a Ph.D. in political science from University of Chicago, had written his dissertation on the Washington press corps. It was published by University of Chicago Press in 1937. He then moved to LA to write about the movie industry (published in 1941). Later, he became a screenwriter and popular author, most remembered for *The Joys of Yiddish.*

114. Steele, "Great Debate," 74 nn. 17–18.

115. Rosten to Horton, memo, September 13, 1940, n.t. Folder: Radio, Box 5; George McMillan to Straus, memo, October 10, 1940, Subject: Work for Leo Rosten. Folder: Personnel Action 40–41–42, Box 15.

116. Harmon, 703.

117. Arch Mercey and Robert Collyer to Horton, memo, August 27, 1940, Subject: Newsreel and Topical Motion Picture Program. Folder: Newsreel (Miscellaneous), Box 5.

118. John Bridgeman, National Youth Authority, to Horton, September 30, 1940; Karl Borders, Executive Assistant, National Youth Authority, to Sidney Sherwood, Assistant Secretary, NDAC, September 30, 1940. Both in Folder: Personnel Regulations. Box 9.

119. Hartley, "Sight and Sound," 225; "America Builds Ships," *Defense* 1:2 (September 6, 1940): 4.

120. December 4, 1940, n.a., n.t. (probably DOI's FY1942 budget request to BOB), ellipses in original. Horton's parenthetical "of the Commission" was misleading and inaccurate. The original law would have meant a reference to the *council.* Folder: Information Div., Box 13.

121. Hechler, *Division of Information,* 176. Hechler later became a congressman (D-WV).

122. Ibid., 181.

123. Attachment, Horton to Sidney Sherwood (NDAC Assistant Secretary), June 26, 1940. Folder: Personnel Regulations, Box 9.

124. Margaret Holmead, Chief, NDAC Personnel Section, to Horton, memo, July 20, 1940, n.t. Folder: Personnel Regulations, Box 9. Holmead was the daughter of White House assistant and NDAC secretary William McReynolds.

125. Ruth Bledsoe (Horton's administrative assistant) to Miss Whelan, memo, August 14, 1940, n.t. Folder: Personnel Regulations, Box 9. The memo names fourteen, but not Rosten, who technically was on another division's payroll.

126. Horton to Sherwood, memo and attachment, October 23, 1940, n.t. Folder: Personnel Regulations, Box 9.

127. Sherwood to Horton, June (probably a typo, should be July) 2, 1940. Folder: Personnel Regulations, Box 9.

128. Sherwood to Horton, July 1, 1940. Folder: Memos–Sherwood, Box 7.

129. Form designating an office manager for each NDAC subunit, July 12, 1940, signed by Horton. Folder: Personnel Regulations, Box 9.

130. Sherwood to Horton, memo, October 21, 1940, n.t., underlining in original. Folder: Personnel Regulations, Box 9. Sherwood and Holmead may come across as fussy bureaucrats more concerned about paperwork than an agency's substantive mission. Still, whatever their motivation, they were protecting the agency politically. FDR's alphabet agencies were often subject to hostile congressional investigations (by members of the conservative coalition), by penny-pinching appropriations subcommittees and the General Accounting Office. Congressional requests for full personnel records were common. Sherwood and Holmead wanted to keep NDAC paperwork in order prevent headlines of congressional claims of mismanagement, administrative chaos, incomplete records, illegal payments of salaries, and violations of civil service regulations.

131. Lee, *Congress*, 84–97.

132. Page 52. The reference librarians at OGR's US Information Service compiling the *Manual* were diligent about accuracy. It is unlikely that this listing of Horton's title was an error. Nearly simultaneously, a newsmagazine still listed him as "Director of Public Relations" ("Personnel of the Advisory Defense Commission," *Business Week*, July 6, 1940, 24).

133. US Information Service, OGR, "Contact Guide—National Defense Program," mimeograph, July 25, 1940, 3.

134. US NDAC, *Numbered Document File*, Document 112, cover page.

135. Horton to Shannon Allen, Director, Radio Section, Department of the Interior, August 6, 1940. Folder: Radio, Box 5.

136. Elliot, "Consumer Representation," 15, 38.

137. US NDAC, *Handbook*, iii, iv, 3.

138. US NDAC, *Minutes*, 76; "National Defense Advisory Commission," *Defense* [1:1] (August 30, 1940): 4.

139. Horton to Sherwood, memo, September 20, 1940, n.t. Folder: Memos–Sherwood, Box 7.

140. Paul Mallon, "Hitler Marks Sept. 15 for Final Victory," *HC* (August 30, 1940): 3.

Chapter Three

1. It was almost always accompanied by the condition "except in case of attack," but he omitted the qualification in the most-covered speech of his campaign, thinking it was unnecessary and obvious (Burns, 448–49). That gave rise to the long-running Republican criticism that he had lied to the voters to win the election.

2. Payne, *Franco and Hitler*, 63.

3. Roosevelt, *Press Conferences*, 16:372.

4. Frank Kluckhohn, "President Names a Four-Man Board for Defense Drive," *NYT*, December 21, 1940, 1.

5. US NDAC, *Minutes,* PR-348.

6. "Defense Information Lack Arouses Suspicion of Byrd," *CSM,* December 16, 1940, 1.

7. "Dirksen Calls for Inquiry on Arms Lag," *WP,* December 21, 1940, 2.

8. Administrative order: 3 *CFR 1938–1943 Comp* 1320–21. Executive order: Roosevelt, 1969, 9:689–92.

9. US NDAC, PR-344.

10. Examples of references to Horton or DOI as part of OPM, rather than NDAC: *Internal document:* Frank Bane, Director, NDAC Division of State and Local Cooperation [NDAC] to Horton, memo, February 7, 1941, n.t. Folder: B (alphabetical series), Box 9. *Newspaper:* Pearson and Allen, "Washington Merry-Go-Round," *(Reno) Nevada State Journal,* February 19, 1941, 4; AP, "Defense Setup Is Complicated," *(Phoenix) Arizona Republic,* March 9, 1941, sec. 2, p. 3. *Publication:* Junior Bar Conference, *Reports and Program,* 10.

11. Document, n.a. (almost certainly Horton), n.t., n.d., begins with "The law creating the Commission," 3 (Folder 1–1, Box 9).

12. Ibid., 1.

13. Ibid., 4.

14. Ibid., 2.

15. For a listing of the titles of those releases, see US National Archives, *Pamphlet Accompanying Microcopy No. 185,* 24–37.

16. See, for example, PR-254, November 15, 1940: "Release Friday Afternoon Papers" (US NDAC, *Press Releases*).

17. George McMillan to Straus, memo, February 10, 1941, Subject: Timing of press releases. Folder: McMillan, Box 14.

18. See, for example, PR-258, radio address by Donald Nelson, November 18, 1940: "Not to be released before 10:30 p.m. E.S.T." (US NDAC, *Press Releases*).

19. See, for example, PR-276, November 28, 1940, ibid.

20. See, for example, PR-293, December 6, 1940, ibid.

21. Document, n.a., n.t., December 4, 1940, begins with "We are submitting herewith justification of the budget estimate," 2. Folder: Information Div., Box 13.

22. US NDAC, *Press Releases,* PR-262, 334.

23. Ibid., PR-278.

24. Ibid., PR-344. Cooke had an extraordinary career in public administration, including a working relationship with Frederick Taylor, founder of scientific management, and a pioneering study of municipal public reporting (Schachter, *Frederick Taylor;* Lee, "History," 459–60, 472 n. 51).

25. US NDAC, *Press Releases,* PR-307.

26. Robert Collyer to Horton, memo, November 22, 1940, Subject: Progress on newsreels, stills and television, 1. Folder: Newsreel (Miscellaneous), Box 5.

27. Ibid., 1–2.

28. Straus to Robert Collyer, memo, January 21, 1941, Subject: Functions of Picture Office. Folder: Still Pictures Sect., Box 15.

29. US NDAC, *Functions and Activities.*

30. US NDAC, *Press Releases,* PR-323, 1, emphasis added.

31. Sayre, "Radio," 681, emphasis added.

32. The other two stories apparently included: Chesly Manly, "Knudsen Stand Forced on Him, His Friends Say," *CT*, December 23, 1940, 1; AP, "C.I.O. Unionist's Plane Speedup Plan Rejected," *CT*, January 2, 1941, 28. Horton had likely been contacted by Early or Mellett.

33. US NDAC, *Minutes*, 133.

34. Horton was listed on the program of the American Political Science Association's thirty-sixth annual conference in Chicago as copresenting a paper on December 30, 1940, titled "Public Opinion and National Defense" (Cosgrove, "Thirty-Sixth Annual Meeting," 129). Horton's copresenter was Edward Bernays, the leading practitioner of private-sector PR. I was unable to locate a copy of his talk at the National Archives or the Bernays Papers at the Library of Congress (e-mail from Jeffrey Flannery, Head, Reference & Reader Services, Manuscript Division, July 3, 2010, author's files). Six months later, Bernays presented a talk on government PR at the Army Industrial College (Bernays, *Public Relations*). Given the similarities of topics, it is likely that Bernays's planned paper at APSA (whether delivered or not, whether in cooperation with Horton or not) would have been similar to the Army lecture.

The APSA session was one of two on "Public Opinion and Propaganda" organized and chaired by Princeton professor Harwood Childs, the founding managing editor of *Public Opinion Quarterly* in 1937. The panelists included a who's who of government PR. Besides Horton, they included Arch Mercey, Cedric Larson, and Harold Graves (Cosgrove, "Thirty-Sixth," 120, 129). Childs later published an article on federal wartime PR (H. Childs, "Public Information").

35. Secretary to Commissioners, Heads of Offices and Members of the Staff, Memorandum No. 9, January 14, 1941. Folder: Memos–Sherwood, Box 7.

36. AP, "Prepare Plans to Farm Out Defense Work," *CT*, January 29, 1941, 23; AP, "Major Defense Contractors Urged to Help Small Plants," *LAT*, January 29, 1941, 9.

37. US NDAC, *Minutes*, 138.

38. The entire run of *Defense* (renamed *Victory* after Pearl Harbor) is online: www.archive.org.

39. US NDAC, *Numbered Document File*, Document 20b.

40. Ibid. Horton showed bureaucratic deftness in the "debate" with Bane. He let Bane go first, giving Horton a chance to rebut Bane's arguments. Horton submitted his letter the day before the commission meeting, too late for a surrebuttal by Bane.

41. US NDAC, *Minutes*, 132–33.

42. After the commission's decision for Horton, Bane became quite snippy in contacts with DOI. A week after losing the showdown, Bane complained in writing to Horton about DOI supposedly releasing news that should have been shared with the appropriate state defense council in advance (US NDAC, *Press Releases*, PR-336). His insinuation was that Horton either was deliberately undermining Bane or that DOI was incompetent in clearing press releases before issuing them. A few weeks later, he complained that DOI had not done enough to encourage press coverage of speeches by OPM/NDAC officials at a meeting of the Council of State Governments in Washington. Straus, Horton's deputy, replied in an equally short tone that Bane had informed DOI in advance of the meeting that no publicity arrangements needed to be made (Bane to Horton, January 9, 1941; Straus to Bane, February 27, 1941; Folder: B [alphabetical series], Box 9).

43. Straus to Shane MacCarthy, memo, April 9, 1941, n.t. Folder: "Mc" (alphabetical series), Box 9.

44. Pearson and Allen, "Washington Merry-Go-Round," *(Reno) Nevada State Journal*, February 19, 1941, 4.

45. The *Post* also took something of an indirect potshot at Horton and his bureaucracy in a photo spread and article about the supposed poor management of moving DOI and other defense agencies to a new building. It included a picture of an "information division" secretary surrounded by boxes of supplies but no desk. Another was a secretary (identified by name but not by her DOI affiliation) trying to answer four phones while in an otherwise empty room (Alfred Friendly, "Defense Efforts All Out—Out in Street—Moving: Bottlenecks in OPM," *WP*, January 31, 1941, 32).

46. "Defense Publicity Plan," *Newsweek*, January 13, 1941, 10.

47. US NDAC, *Numbered Document File*, Document 20b, 1.

48. "Information Division," n.a., n.d. ("1940" pencil marking), 1. Folder: Information Div., Box 13. This document was apparently an early and partial draft for either a report on DOI's work in 1940 and/or for the FY1942 budget request documentation.

49. McMillan to Straus, memo, January 10, 1941, Subject: Press Digest. Folder: McMillan, Box 14. In a handwritten postscript, McMillan noted: "In rereading this I discover we've made no provision for the Merry-Go-Round. We could get [the] Times-Herald just for this column." This was an indication of how influential the Pearson and Allen column was to Washington officialdom. (The column shifted to the *Post* in August 1942.)

50. Lee, *First*, 87–90, 92–94.

51. It is also possible that Horton chafed at being viewed as under Mellett's informal supervision and sought autonomy—an almost inexorable bureaucratic imperative.

52. Robert Collyer to Horton, memo, November 22, 1940, Subject: Progress on newsreels, stills and television, 3. Folder: Newsreel (Miscellaneous), Box 5.

53. Straus to Robert Collyer, memo, January 21, 1941, "Functions of Picture Office." Folder: Still Pictures Sect., Box 15.

54. McMillan to Straus, memo, February 15, 1941, Subject: Pictures. Folder: McMillan, Box 14, emphasis in original.

55. Devine, "Films," 686. This office was different from the Washington-based Film Unit that focused on in-house productions.

56. A newspaper columnist reported in January that "for some time" Horton's Hollywood branch office included a dollar-a-year man whose job was "to arrange for production of patriotic pictures and also prevent the screening of films which might be objectionable" (Ray Tucker, "Washington," *Reno [NV] Evening Gazette*, January 21, 1941, 4). This was probably a garbled reference to Rosten, who was not an *employee* of DOI, but rather was paid as a consultant on a per-diem basis. The lack of a *salary* for Rosten may have confused the reporter and led him to conclude that Rosten was a dollar-a-year man.

57. Horton to Rosten, February 12, 1941. Folder: R (alphabetical series), Box 9.

58. McDonald, "Films," 128–29.

59. US Office of Education, *3434 U.S. Government Films*, 189–90.

60. L. C. Larson and Lloyd Evans, "New Films of the Month, As they Look to a Teacher Committee," *Educational Screen* 21:2 (February 1942): 76.

61. Doherty, *Projections of War*, 304; US Office of Education, *3434*, 144. Some sources confuse *TVA* with *Power for Defense*. However, they were released about two months apart and had different lengths (Larson, "Publicity for National Defense," 250).

62. In late 1941 (but before Pearl Harbor), the South experienced some power shortages, largely

due to the electrical needs of defense production. DOI worked on a campaign to promote reductions in consumer consumption and prepare the citizenry for continuing shortages (Straus to George H. Lyon, memo, November 3, 1941, Subject: S. E. Power Shortage. Folder: O.C.D., Box 15).

63. US NDAC, *Minutes,* 139.

64. Ibid., 148. *Power for Defense* generated enough buzz that at least one movie house felt it was worth listing in its newspaper advertising (*Moberly [MO] Monitor-Index and Democrat,* March 20, 1941, 2).

65. Larson and Evans, "New Films of the Month", 74, 76.

66. The short on ships, mentioned briefly in the preceding chapter, was a two-reel documentary produced by the MC (after Horton left for NDAC), but available through DOI. It was released in the winter of 1940–41 ("Screen News Here and in Hollywood," *NYT,* February 6, 1941, 25). Confusingly, it was sometimes referred to as *America Builds Ships* (*Defense* 1:2 [September 6, 1940]: 4), the same title as a different short DOI released in June 1941. Compounding the confusion was that the 1941 version of *America Builds Ships* was sometimes referred to as *Men and Ships* ("They Now Know the Meaning of 'Lower Away'" [caption], *WP,* June 23, 1941, 14).

67. Robert Collyer to Horton, memo, November 22, 1940, Subject: Progress on newsreels, stills and television, 3. Folder: Newsreel (Miscellaneous), Box 5.

68. McMillan to Straus, memo, December 30, 1940, n.t. Folder: McMillan, Box 14.

69. Friedrich, *Controlling Broadcasting,* 20. However, Friedrich's morale comment related to government radio programming, which Horton also did before Pearl Harbor (see chap. 5).

70. US NDAC, *Press Releases,* PR-348.

71. "Message to Those Who Man Defense Plants" (caption), *NYT,* January 14, 1941, 10.

72. "Letter from William Knudsen to manufacturers and text of the poster to be displayed," *Defense* 2:2 (January 14, 1941): 4, emphasis in original.

73. Calculations are difficult partly because DOI grew so significantly during FY1941. The fiscal year began on July 1, 1940, a month after Horton was hired, and the unit consisted of only a handful of people. When FY1941 ended on June 30, 1941, DOI was a major entity. Another likely reason for the limited documentation is that the White House sought to minimize the transparency of spending data by DOI and other administration PR activities because they would likely become targets of intense political and press attacks. My calculation is based on projecting DOI's annualized salary base (for the last third of FY1941) as a proportion of total spending. The annualized payroll was about $140,000 (President Roosevelt to William H. McReynolds, February 28, 1941. Folder: Horton, Box 7). For its FY1942 budget request, payroll was about 75 percent of DOI's budget (US House, *Second Deficiency Appropriation Bill,* hearings, 672). If that ratio was roughly the same in the preceding fiscal year, then the division's annualized budget for FY1941 would have been roughly about $186,000.

74. "Transfer to New Quarters of the Office of Production Management," *Defense* 2:5 (February 4, 1941): 2.

75. Document, n.t., December 4, 1940, begins with, "We are submitting herewith justification of the budget estimate," 3. Folder: Information Div., Box 13.

76. *November 1940 (28):* Organization chart and list of employees, attachment to memo from Mr. Olson to Miss Ruth Bledsoe, January 3, 1941. Folder: Personnel Recommendations, Box 9. *Early 1941 (170):* Division of Information, OEM [staff directory], January 1, 1941. Binder: Functions and Operations of DOI, 1941–42, Box 13.

77. Jerry Kluttz, "Federal Diary," *WP,* January 30, 1941, 15.

78. John R. Kennedy, Editor, *Federal Register,* to Horton, August 15, 1940. Folder: Personnel Regulations, Box 9.

79. Permission and paperwork were also needed for transfers of employees from one NDAC division to another. "Request for Inter-Division Transfer of Personnel" (NDAC form), October 10, 1940. Folder: Personnel Regulations, Box 9.

80. Mr. Olson, Chief, NDAC Classification Section, to All Division Office Managers, memo, December 31, 1940, 2. Folder: Personnel Regulations, Box 9.

81. Position description for Photographic Editor, Information Division, (handwritten notation: "approved 12–5–40"). Folder: Washington Information Specialists (Descriptions), Box 8.

82. US Civil Service Commission Classification Sheet, for Davis W. Snow, January 17, 1941, 1. Folder: Washington Information Specialists (Descriptions), Box 8.

Chapter Four

1. Roosevelt, *Public Papers,* 8:309, emphasis added.

2. Brownlow, 425.

3. With both OGR and DOI in EOP, a clarification about their respective missions: OGR was the president's PR agency for the civilian portion of the entire executive branch excluding, theoretically, OEM. DOI was the president's PR agency for OEM. Nonetheless, there was some duplication and overlap, especially concerning public inquiries.

4. Lee, *First,* 67–79.

5. "Propaganda Aim Seen in New Bill," *NYT,* February 23, 1941, 23.

6. For example, the president's FY1942 budget request listed NDAC as allocated $4.5 million for FY1941 from the president's emergency funds (US BOB, *Budget . . . for the Fiscal Year Ending June 30, 1942,* 44). This was, of course, an estimate. FY1941 was only half over when the president submitted to Congress his FY1942 budget request.

7. A reminder that McReynolds was also was one of the six administrative assistants to the president. Beginning in the fall of 1940, OGR's Mellett was another.

8. President Roosevelt to William McReynolds, Liaison Officer for Emergency Management, February 28, 1941, 2. Folder: Horton, Box 7. The letter also created a Division of Central Administrative Services in OEM (the same status as DOI) and redirected funds previously allocated by the president to NDAC. With the creation of OPM (unofficially in December, officially in January), NDAC was largely defunct, or at least no longer an operational entity. It is also worth noting that in the letter Roosevelt did not create DOI; rather he authorized another official to establish it. This semantic difference would permit the president, if necessary, to respond to potential congressional or press attacks on DOI by claiming that *he* had not created DOI.

9. Koppes and Black doubly err, identifying the president's February letter as a March executive order (*Hollywood,* 52).

10. The Executive Office of the President itself had no director, or even a liaison officer. All EOP entities reported directly to the president.

11. Moving fast, Mellett's OGR incorporated the organizational changes of FDR's February 28 letter into the next edition of the *US Government Manual* (March 1941): 69–70, 593.

12. McReynolds to Horton, memo, n.t., n.d. Folder: Horton, Box 7. March 5, 1941, per Gosnell, (26).

13. Catton, 53.

14. US NDAC, *Press Releases,* PR-160.

15. Using databases of historical newspapers, I could not find any newspaper that carried the release. Horton's trick of burying news by releasing it on Friday afternoon became common in Washington in the 1990s because, similarly, the Friday-night TV news audience was the smallest of the week, as was the readership of Saturday newspapers. So that no one could accuse him of hiding the news, he also reprinted the release on the front page of *Defense* ("Defense Agency Reorganization," 2:11 [March 19, 1941]:1).

16. Paul Mallon, "Italy Masks Movement of Nazi Troops," *HC,* March 15, 1941, 3. Nine months later, another reporter flagged the oddity that most OEM agencies were created by an executive order, but DOI only by a presidential letter (Blair Bolles, "Federal Bureau Collects, Dispenses Defense News," *HC,* November 30, 1940, A20).

17. US House, *Second Deficiency Appropriation,* hearings, 672–83.

18. US National Archives, *Pamphlet Accompanying Microcopy No. 185,* 37. Occasionally, it issued releases on Saturdays, rarely on Sundays.

19. The PM series started in mid-January after OPM was formally created. Although the PM series partially overlapped with the period covered in chapter 4, it entirely covered the ten months examined in this chapter. For simplicity purposes, the PM series is therefore discussed in this chapter instead of in the preceding one.

20. US OEM, [*Press Releases*]. This calculation is based on the (incomplete) collection of bound DOI press releases in Princeton University's library. The two volumes extend from PM-144 on March 10, 1941, to PM-3563 on June 8, 1942. In that compilation, the first post–Pearl Harbor release is PM-1728. Hence, the conclusion of 1,727 releases from the beginning of the PM series to Pearl Harbor. The catalogued title was *[Press Releases] March 10, 1941–June 8, 1942,* and authorship recorded as US Office for Emergency Management.

PM-142 was located in a separate source (US OPM, *Numbered Document File,* Document 18[4]) along with and five others: PM-365 (Doc. 27a), PM-389 (Doc. 19b), PM-532 (Doc. 41c) and PM-605 (Doc. 22b). Also US National Archives, *Pamphlet Accompanying Microcopy No. 195.*

21. Straus to Shane MacCarthy, memo, April 9, 1941, n.t., 2. Folder: M (alphabetical series), Box 9. Brewer stated that DOI "churned out between ten and twenty press releases a day" (93).

22. This figure includes releases mailed to newspapers around the country, not just handed out in the press room ("Industrial News from Washington," *Paper Mill News* 64:44 [November 1, 1941]: 23).

23. Jerry Kluttz, "Federal Diary," *WP,* September 23, 1941, 17.

24. Clarke Beach, "OPM, Two-Fisted Glamor [*sic*] Boy," *Galveston (TX) Daily News,* August 17, 1941, 19.

25. McMillan to Straus, memo, March 28, 1941, Subject: Speeches. Folder: McMillan, Box 14.

26. Beginning in mid-June, Assistant Director Straus submitted to Horton two weekly confidential documents called "Weekly Round Up" and "Box Score." The quotes are from, respectively, the second "Weekly Round Up" (n.d., but probably June 15, 1941) and July 7, 1941, [Doc.] 4891. Binder: Weekly Round Ups/Box Score, Box 13.

27. US DOI, *Transcript: Priorities Division,* 15.

28. "Breaking the News Gently," *Business Week,* August 30, 1941, 7.

29. Memo (for reporters), "Office for Emergency Management," March 7, 1941, [Doc.] 745. Folder: Information Div., Box 13.

30. Pearson and Allen, "Washington Merry-Go-Round," *(Reno) Nevada State Journal,* April 17, 1941, 4.

31. McMillan to Straus, memo, April 23, 1941, n.t. Folder: McMillan, Box 14.

32. "Division of Information," n.a. (almost certainly Horton), n.d., 1–2. Binder: Functions and Operations of DOI, 1941–42, Box 13. March 14, 1941, per Gosnell (80).

33. US OEM, *[Press Releases],* PM-629, 12–13.

34. Catton, 66–67.

35. Ibid., 57, 77.

36. "Propaganda," *Tide* 15:16 (August 15, 1941): 13.

37. AP, "Kellogg Says There Will Be No Power Shortage in U.S.," *CSM,* June 3, 1941, 17.

38. "OPM Disavows Kellogg Stand on Power," *WP,* June 6, 1941, 7.

39. "Kellogg Resigns OPM Power Post," *NYT,* June 24, 1941, 11.

40. McMillan also wrote an article in *Public Opinion Quarterly* about federal PR activities in mid-1941, including DOI ("Government Publicity," 392–95).

41. McMillan to Straus, memo, June 9, 1941, Subject: Radio news coverage. Folder: McMillan, Box 14.

42. Cover letter "Dear Sir" to radio stations, June 28, 1941. Folder: O.C.D., Box 15.

43. Radio News Release, For Release Wednesday, July 2, 1941, n.t. Folder: O.C.D., Box 15.

44. Frances Knight to Straus, memo, July 16, 1941, n.t. Folder: O.C.D., Box 15.

45. Herbert Harris to Paul Porter, memo, n.d. (probably late August or early September, 1941), Subject: Foreign Language Press and Radio, 1. Binder: Day Book, DOI, D. King, Aug. 1941–Jan. 1942, Box 13.

46. The production of foreign-language materials led DOI to have some modest dealings with William Donovan, the coordinator of information (COI), who was in charge of short-wave news and propaganda broadcasts aimed at audiences in Europe (Horton to Donovan, memo, July 31, 1941, n.t. Folder: Publicity–Donovan, Box 11; Henry Paynter to Straus, memo, November 6, 1941, Subject: Short Wave Info for COI. Folder: Paynter, Box 10). COI became the Office of Strategic Services, then the CIA.

DOI's press release and information dissemination activities also led to some interactions with another international OEM agency. Nelson Rockefeller's office focused on improving relations with Latin America. Given Horton's centralization philosophy, he naturally recommended that the Rockefeller staffer handling economic news work alongside DOI staffers *at DOI headquarters* rather than where Rockefeller was located (Horton to Frank Jamieson, Office of the Coordinator of Inter-American Affairs, memo, November 14, 1941, Subject: Latin America–Economic Defense Information, 2. Folder: Washington Information Specialists [Descriptions], Box 8).

47. US DOI, *Transcript: Priorities Division,* 15, emphasis added.

48. US OEM, *Defense: One Year.*

49. Straus to James Secrest, memo, April 21, 1941, Subject: Anniversary. Folder: Secrest, Box 12, Box 15.

50. US OEM, [*Press Releases*], PM-427.

51. William Nelson to Straus, memo, May 14, 1941, Subject: Picture Service in connection with anniversary. Folder: Still Pictures Sect., Box 15.

52. Bernard Schoenfeld to Horton, memo, April 21, 1941, Subject: Anniversary Defense Program, 1. Folder: Schoenfeld, Box 12.

53. OPM, *Listing of Major War Department Supply Contracts.*

54. "State Industries Get 70 Millions More War Work," *Oakland (CA) Tribune,* September 16, 1941, 16.

55. "War Against Waste" series: http://digitalcollections.smu.edu/cdm4/item_viewer.php?CISOROOT=/hgp&CISOPTR=605&CISOBOX=1&REC=6. For published version, see *Piqua (OH) Daily Call,* October 27, 1941, 5; October 28, 1941; 8; October 30, 1941, 6; October 31, 1941, 3.

56. McMillan to Straus, memo, October 18, 1941, n.t. Folder: McMillan, Box 14.

57. http://memory.loc.gov/master/pnp/cph/3c00000/3c02000/3c02200/3c02222u.tif.

58. Roy Jackson to Straus, memo, July 25, 1941, Subject: Progress Reports, 1. Folder: J (alphabetical series), Box 9.

59. For an early example, see "Defense Progress," *Defense* 2:31 (August 5, 1941): 1.

60. US OEM, *[Press Releases],* PM-181.

61. Ibid., PM-362.

62. Farley, "School Public-Relations Broadcasting," 151.

63. US OEM, *[Press Releases],* PM-1147; Transcript, October 27, 1941, *Voice of Firestone* weekly radio program. Folder: Horton, Box 7.

64. "Radio Time Donated for Defense Information," *Defense* 2:48 (December 2, 1941): 29.

65. "Division of Information," n.a. (almost certainly Horton), n.d., 6, emphasis added. Binder: Functions and Operations of DOI, 1941–42, Box 13. March 14, 1941, per Gosnell (80).

66. See, for example, the bibliographic credits for the 1941 documentaries *Army in Overalls* (WorldCat Accession No. 47739283) and *Bits and Pieces* (WorldCat Accession No. 47739413), emphasis added.

67. WorldCat accession No. 47739413, emphasis added. Also: www.imdb.com/title/tt0186949/.

68. Reflecting the critical condition of the United Kingdom, Roosevelt dramatically signed the bill ten minutes after a courier delivered it from Capitol Hill and then immediately released military supplies to Great Britain and Greece (Turner Catledge, "Final Step Swift," *NYT,* March 12, 1941, 1, 3).

69. McMillan to Straus, memo, March 7, 1941, Subject: A Plan for Promotion of our Subcontracting Program, 1, emphasis added. Folder: McMillan, Box 14.

70. "Division of Information," n.a. (almost certainly Horton), n.d., 1, emphasis added. Binder: Functions and Operations of DOI, 1941–42, Box 13.

71. Schoenfeld to William Donovan, Straus, and Horton, memo, July 30, 1941, Subject: Radio and Civilian Morale. Folder: Publicity-Donovan, Box 11.

72. Subject: Memorandum on Speakers' Policy, n.a., n.d. (handwritten notation: 10/2/1941), 1, emphasis added. Folder: Speakers Data–Tom Wilson, Box 12.

73. Schoenfeld to Straus, memo, October 22, 1941, Subject: Jergen Program. Folder: Schoenfeld, Box 12.

74. US OPM, *Minutes,* 36.

75. Ibid., 37. The "minuteman" reference was to CPI's World War I program of volunteer public speakers (also called four-minute men), who gave short talks before a movie began. The term was from the militia in the early part of the American War of Independence who were ready to fight at a moment's notice.

76. F. & L. S. to Horton, memo, August 22, 1941, 1. Binder: Functions and Operations of DOI, 1941–42, Box 13. I was unable to identify the authors based on these initials. The memo also characterized OPM's leadership as "scared green" regarding the upcoming supply and market problems, a variation on being "green around the gills," that is, feeling nauseated.

77. Ibid., 3, underlining in original. This was the penultimate sentence of the memo.

78. "A Program for the Division of Information: A New Victory Program," October 18, 1941, n.a. (probably Horton). Folder: V (alphabetical series), Box 9. The document surmised there were three reasons underlying the apparent civic apathy about events in Europe:

1. The great residual distrust of the British Empire.
2. The hatred of Soviet Russia that exists among many large and important groups.
3. Anti-semitism. (6)

Pre-Holocaust, there was "chronic anti-Semitism" among many of the WASP elite, Progressive reformers, nativists, Prohibitionists, and the KKK (Okrent, 239). It was common to have "restricted" hotels and country clubs barring Jews and blacks, as well as residential real estate titles prohibiting sales to them.

79. US DOI, *Guns Not Gadgets,* inside front cover.

80. US DOI, *Dollars for Democracy,* 1; *Materials for Defense,* inside front cover.

81. "Used Aluminum Collection Campaign," *Defense* 2:26 (July 1, 1941): 15; "State Plans Are Pressed," *NYT,* July 15, 1941, 12.

82. AP, "Some 'Jump Gun' on Aluminum Program," *Portsmouth (OH) Times,* July 4, 1941, 1.

83. "Scrap Metal Campaign Is Big Success," *Hagerstown (MD) Daily Mail,* July 25, 1941, 2.

84. A July 7 status update confessed that while a "no holds barred" effort would be made, nonetheless, "still no program announced" (Binder: Weekly Round Ups/Box Score, Box 13). That same day, Horton sent a frantic telegram to the film industry's liaison office asking it to announce a *postponement* of the dates of the collection (Horton to Francis Harmon, Coordinator, Motion Picture Committee Cooperating for National Defense, telegram. Folder: H [alphabetical series], Box 9). According to Gosnell, the conflicting public directives about the aluminum collection campaign made by OCD officials were "extremely irritating to an information man who sees public good-will dissipated by administrative blunders" (59). Writing after the war, and in typical melodramatic fashion, Catton said it was a flop because "the Army's production men coldly pointed out that scrap aluminum was no good for airplanes—they had to have virgin metal. The let-down was bad, especially since no arrangements had been made for getting the scrap to the smelters after it had been collected" (78).

85. Doherty, 304.

86. Another follow-up in March 1942, on the results of the aluminum campaign, documented that generally pots and pans were made from an inferior category of aluminum that could not be used for airplanes. However, the smelted aluminum was used for other military items that could be manufactured with them (AP, "Inquiry over Aluminum," *NYT,* March 14, 1942, 10). FDR's critics sometimes belittled such campaigns (paper, fat, tires, etc.), claiming they were not used or needed, but instead were phony efforts to promote support for the war.

87. Shale, 22.

88. US OEM, [*Press Releases*], PM-563.

89. "Propaganda for War" (editorial), *Zanesville (OH) Times Recorder,* June 21, 1941, 4.

90. Lee, *First; Congress.*

91. US House, *Second Deficiency Appropriation Bill for 1941,* hearings and H. Rep. 849.

92. *CR* 87:5 (June 25, 1941): 5500.

93. Ibid., 5507–8. These DOI criticisms were mild compared to the ferocious attacks on OGR. This bill also included FY1942 funding for OGR. Republicans made strenuous efforts in committee and through floor amendments to defund or reduce OGR funding. At other times, congressional Republicans compared OGR and Mellett to Stalin's KGB (then called OGPU) and to Goebbels (Lee, *First,* 70, 100–101, 109).

94. United Press, "Lend-Lease Aid Passes Billion-Dollar Figure," *LAT,* November 24, 1941, 7.

95. Paul Mallon, "Italy Masks Movement of Nazi Troops," *HC,* March 15, 1941, 3.

96. Pearson and Allen, "Washington Merry-Go-Round," *(Reno) Nevada State Journal,* April 17, 1941, 4.

97. "Propaganda Chief," editorial, *Zanesville (OH]) Times Recorder,* April 25, 1941, 6A.

98. Peter Edson, "In Washington" (syndicated column), *Racine (WI) Journal-Times,* May 14, 1941, 10.

99. "Propaganda," *Tide* 15:16 (August 15, 1941): 13.

100. "Government Envelopes," editorial, *Iola (KS) Register,* September 27, 1941, 4.

101. Frank Kent, "Great Game of Politics" (syndicated column), *HC,* October 13, 1941, 2.

102. James Reston, "Defense Picture Given to World in All Media by Federal Agencies," *NYT,* October 27, 1941, 36. This was the first of a two-part series. The second article, on October 29, did not mention DOI.

103. "Too Much Government Publicity," editorial, *Ames (IA) Daily Tribune,* October 28, 1941, 4.

104. George Morgenstern, "Onward March the Brigades of War Ballyhoo," *CT,* November 7, 1941, 17.

105. "Press Front Lend-Lease," *Newsweek,* November 17, 1941, 61; "Publicity," *United States News,* November 7, 1941, 18.

106. Blair Bolles, "Federal Bureau Collects, Dispenses Defense News," *HC,* November 30, 1940, A20.

107. Roscoe Drummond, "U.S. to Bridge Sea with Ships," *CSM,* March 17, 1941, 17.

108. Having both served in the Wilson administration, Creel and FDR were friendly. Early in FDR's presidency, Creel and *Collier's* were pro-FDR, and Creel's writings were viewed as representing Roosevelt's thinking (Shesol, 155–56).

109. George Creel, "The Truth Shall Make You Free," *Collier's,* November 1, 1941, 28. He probably meant more press agents than *reporters* in Washington, but even that claim was probably wrong when including reporters for specialized publications.

110. "More Writers Than Readers," editorial, *Collier's,* December 6, 1941, 86.

111. Blair Bolles, "Washington, Capital of Confusion," *American Mercury* 53:212 (August 1941): 159.

112. "This Is Where You Come In: The Box Score," n.a., n.d. (handwritten notation: 8/1/41). Binder: Functions and Operations of DOI, 1941–42, Box 13.

113. Carl J. Friedrich, "The Poison in Our System," *Atlantic Monthly,* June 1941, 670. As mentioned in the introduction, beginning in 1932, Friedrich advocated for vigorous PR as inherent to the democratic responsibility of public administration.

114. D. A. Saunders, "The Failure of Propaganda," *Harper's*, November 1941, 649.

115. Steele, *Propaganda*.

116. LaGuardia remained mayor while heading OCD.

117. Roosevelt, *Public Papers*, 10:163.

118. Roosevelt, *Press Conferences*, 17:327.

119. Catton, 78.

120. Lawrence Davis, "LaGuardia Warns of Aid to Enemy by Lack of Unity," *NYT*, May 29, 1941, 1, 4.

121. For example, in a speech to fire chiefs in August, LaGuardia spoke exclusively about the role of fire departments in civilian defense, not about the morale of the population or justifying the president's emergency mobilization (LaGuardia, *Civilian Defense*).

122. Masthead, *Defense* 2:30 (July 29, 1941): 1. A few months later, a reporter counted seventeen (Blair Bolles, "Federal Bureau Collects, Dispenses Defense News," *HC*, November 30, 1940, A20).

123. Troy, 121.

124. Horton to Wayne Coy (OEM liaison officer), memo, June 6, 1941, Subject: Printing for OEM; and Coy to Heads of OEM Agencies, draft memo, Subject: Establishment of a Printing Control Unit, DOI, July 1, 1941 (effective date). Both in Folder: Printing Control, Box 8. Coy to Heads of [OEM] Agencies, administrative memo, n.d. (probably about July 1, 1941), Subject: Preparation of printed materials and distribution procedures for the Office for Emergency Management; and James Brewbaker to all OEM Information Specialists, memo, Subject: Publications Procedure, n.d. (probably about July 1, 1941). Both in Folder: Publications Procedure, Box 6.

125. US House, *Second Deficiency*, hearings, 677.

126. "Purpose," n.a. (probably Horton), n.d. (about August 1941, based on reference to DOI's fifteen months), 4. Binder: Functions and Operations of DOI, 1941–42, Box 13.

127. Ibid., 5. This looked like a something of a power-grab impinging on the agency of Horton's patron, Mellett. In the context of *publications*, this is odd, because OGR already focused almost exclusively on distributing the pamphlets of other agencies (Lee, *First*, 90–92). It is possible that there was a cooling of the relationship between the two in 1941. Another hint of an estrangement came during Horton's congressional testimony in June. First, he said there was no relationship between DOI and OGR "that I know of." Second, regarding OGR's activities, he said, "I am not entirely familiar with them" (US House, *Second Deficiency*, hearings, 674). It is possible that Horton was merely engaging in a standard strategy by testifiers of saying as little as possible and being highly legalistic and narrow in responses to questions. That helped muffle extended arguments with hostile committee members. It could also be that as DOI grew (eventually becoming larger than OGR), Horton chafed at any continuing impression that he was subservient to Mellett.

128. "A Program for the Division of Information: A New Victory Program," October 18, 1941, n.a. (probably Horton), 1, emphasis in original. Folder: V (alphabetical series), Box 9.

129. Ibid., 2, emphasis added.

130. US House, *Second Deficiency*, H. Rep. 849, 11, emphasis added.

131. One of the reasons the congressional recommendation had little to no effect was due to an unusual legislative situation. Usually, agencies treat recommendations contained in committee reports (especially for appropriations bills) as virtually the same as a law. In this case, the report language was not compulsory in the conventional sense because the bill itself was an unrestricted appropriation of national defense funds to OEM to be allocated at the president's

discretion. Therefore, there were no appropriations *as such* to OEM agencies. This also meant no future accountability on implementation of committee recommendations at the following year's budget hearings.

132. LaGuardia was also running for reelection in 1941. He narrowly won. FDR publicly endorsed him for reelection against Tammany's Democratic nominee. This gave rise to the speculation that the OCD appointment was largely to help LaGuardia win reelection by showing the voters that their mayor was a national figure. This seems unlikely. FDR wanted a public dynamo who could use the platform of OCD to influence public opinion in favor of the defense effort. That LaGuardia would ultimately fail as OCD director was neither obvious nor predictable.

133. W. N. Nelson to W. B. Phillips, memo, November 14, 1941, Subject: Waste Paper. Folder: Still Pictures Sect.; and Straus to George H. Lyon, memo, November 27, 1941, Subject: Radio man for Youth Section of OCD. Folder: O.C.D; Box 15.

134. James Brewbaker to George Lyon, memo, November 27, 1941, Subject: Distribution of Bill of Rights poster. Folder: Bill of Rights Day, Box 13.

135. Straus to George Lyon, OCD, memo, September 3, 1941, Subject: Printing. Folder: O.C.D., Box 15.

136. December 3, 1941, n.t. (Text begins: "The time allowed for putting on Civilian Defense Week"), n.a., 1–2. Folder: O.C.D., Box 10. Confirming these in-house observations, a *Times* article reported that New Jersey officials received about forty thousand posters more than they needed ("OCD Floods Jersey Areas with Posters," *NYT,* November 20, 1941, 29). For a copy of the poster, see *Defense* 2:45 (November 12, 1941): 23. Not all DOI offices had a negative experience with OCD regarding Civilian Defense Week. Radio chief Schoenfeld reported that he considered the radio aspect successful, including four series that were broadcast on four hundred radio stations, covering most of the country (Schoenfeld to Horton et al., memo, November 22, 1941, Subject: Final Poll of Civilian Defense Week Radio. Folder: Schoenfeld, Box 12).

137. Eleanor Roosevelt, "Our Bill of Rights Deserves Thought" ("My Day" column), *Atlanta Constitution,* November 29, 1941, 14. In the mid-1930s, Roosevelt's opponents promoted observances of Constitution Day to highlight their insinuation that his policies were a threat to Constitutional government (Shesol, 167–68). Slyly, a few years later, the administration began promoting observances of Bill of Rights Day, perhaps partly as a progressive counterweight.

138. "Mrs. Roosevelt to Appear on 'Keep 'em Rolling' Today," *Jefferson City (MO) Sunday News and Tribune,* November 16, 1941, 7.

139. George Lyon to Mrs. Roosevelt, memo, October 2, 1941, Subject: Information Program for Division of Voluntary Participation. Folder: O.C.D., Box 15; Straus to Mrs. Roosevelt, memo, October 30, 1941, n.t. (about spreading defense work throughout the country). Folder: R (alphabetical series), Box 9.

140. George Lyon to Straus, memo, November 28, 1941, Subject: Mayris Chaney, Dance Director, [OCD] Physical Fitness Program. Folder: O.C.D., Box 15. Chaney, a friend of Mrs. Roosevelt's, quickly became subject of a short-lived scandal, with congressional criticism that she was a fan dancer, implying striptease. While a mischaracterization, it was too good for the press and FDR's opponents to let go of. Chaney resigned (Lee, *First,* 120, 226 n. 22).

141. Horton to LaGuardia, draft memo, July 31, 1941, Subject: Facts and Figures. Folder: Publicity–O.C.D., Box 11; Proposed Publications of the U.S. Office of Civilian Defense, n.a., n.d. (handwritten notation: 8/14/41) and George Lyon to LaGuardia, memo, September 12, 1941, Subject: Information Program for O.C.D. Binder: Day Book, DOI, D. King, Aug. 1941–Jan. 1942,

Box 13; Memo from Lyon to Straus, September 10, 1941, Subject: Information Program for OCD. Folder: O.C.D., Box 15; Lyon to Mrs. Eleanor Roosevelt, memo, October 6, 1941, Subject: Information Program for OCD. Folder: O.C.D., Box 15; Straus to DOI Staff, memo, October 14, 1941 (re: PR plan for Civilian Defense Week). Folder: Civilian Defense Week, Box 13.

142. S. Howard Evans to Straus, memos, October 31, 1941, Subject: Cooperative Relationships, and draft memorandum of understanding, October 31, 1941. Both in Folder: O.C.D., Box 15.

143. An organization chart of federal units engaged in housing construction for the defense effort listed a dozen agencies (OEM, How Defense Housing Is Built [chart], May 1, 1941, [Doc.] 36796. Folder: Housing, Box 15).

144. Dana Doten (DOI staffer attached to Housing Coordinator's Office) to Horton, memo, November 8, 1941, Subject: 6 Weeks' Progress Report-Defense Housing, 1. Folder: Housing, Box 15.

145. Jerry Kluttz, "Federal Diary," *WP*, November 24, 1941, 17.

146. C. F. Palmer to Staff, memo, November 19, 1941, Subject: Appointment of Howard Acton, emphasis added. Folder: Personnel Action 40–41–42, Box 15.

147. Straus to Palmer, memo, November 25, 1941, Subject: Howard Acton position. Folder: Personnel Action 40–41–42, Box 15.

148. "Howard Acton Appointed Special Assistant to Palmer," *Defense* 2:48 (December 2, 1941): 29.

149. Sidney Sherwood, Assistant [OEM] Liaison Officer, to Horton, memo, November 29, 1941. Folder: Housing, Box 15.

150. Sidney Sherwood from Horton, memo, December 2, 1941, n.t. Folder: Housing, Box 15.

151. The issue continued after Pearl Harbor (see chap. 7).

152. "Miss Elliott Quits OCD Consumer Post for College Place," *WP*, December 11, 1941, 10.

153. Bucher, *Preliminary Inventory*, 2.

154. Roosevelt, *Public Papers*, 10:426.

155. Carlisle Bargeron, "Harmony in U.S. Handouts," *Nation's Business*, December 1941, 48–50, 78–79.

156. MacLeish to Horton, November 5, 1941. Folder: Mc (alphabetical series); and Horton to MacLeish, November 24, 1941. Folder: M (alphabetical series), Box 9.

157. MacLeish to Horton, November 25, 1941. Folder: Mc (alphabetical series), Box 9.

158. US BOB, *United States at War*, 215.

159. Catton, 78. For a contemporaneous review of OFF's work by one of its officers, see Kane ("The O.F.F."). For a historical perspective, see Girona and Xifra ("Office of Facts and Figures"). After OFF and OWI, McLeish returned to work full-time as Librarian of Congress. When his term expired at the end of 1944, he planned to leave Washington. But, after being reelected to his fourth term, FDR nominated him for a new subcabinet position, assistant secretary of state for public and cultural relations. This reinvolved MacLeish in government PR (Lee, "Public Affairs Enters the US President's Subcabinet"). At the same time, FDR nominated Stettinius (from the production effort) as secretary of state.

Chapter Five

1. Putnam, *Bowling Alone.*

2. Junior Bar Conference of the American Bar Association, *—for a More Perfect UNION*, leaflet, n.d. (probably early 1941). Folder: McMillan, Box 14.

3. Junior Bar Conference, *Reports and Program,* 10. Lewis Powell Jr. chaired it and, decades later, became a US Supreme Court justice.

4. Straus to Horton, memo, March 13, 1941, n.t.

5. Arch Mercey, OGR, to Straus, memo, May 20, 1941, Subject: Junior Chamber of Commerce. Folder: M (alphabetical series), Box 9.

6. Morale, n.d. (probably August 1941), n.a. Folder: Publicity-Donovan, Box 11.

7. Weekly Roundup for September 29, 1941. Binder: Weekly Round Ups/Box Score, Box 13.

8. Weekly Roundup for November 24, 1941. Binder: Weekly Round Ups/Box Score, Box 13.

9. Memorandum on Speakers' Policy, n.a., n.d. (handwritten notation: 10/2/41), 2. Folder: Speakers Data–Tom Wilson, Box 12.

10. Horton, n.t. (summary of DOI activities), October 4, 1941, [Doc.] 10533, 3. Folder: Oct. 4, 1941 DOI, Box 15.

11. DOI, *Defense Program: A Handbook for Speakers.*

12. Lyon to Straus, memo, September 10, 1941, Subject: Information Program for OCD, 3. Folder: O.C.D., Box 15.

13. McMillan to Straus, memo, September 29, 1941, Subject: Sample speeches. Folder: McMillan, Box 14.

14. Horton, n.t. (summary of DOI activities), October 4, 1941, [Doc.] 10533, 3. Folder: Oct. 4, 1941 DOI, Box 15. OCD's *Bureau* of Facts and Figures should not to be confused with the *Office* of Facts and Figures established a few weeks later.

15. Memorandum on Speakers' Policy, n.a., n.d. (handwritten notation: 10/2/41), 3. Folder: Speakers Data–Tom Wilson, Box 12.

16. "Division of Information" (summary of visual materials distributed by DOI), n.a., March 15, 1941, 1. Binder: Functions and Operations of DOI, 1941–42, Box 13. For each agency, getting public credit was of major import. In their struggle to survive, grow, and gain autonomy, agencies wanted the public to know what *they* did, figuring it helped increase their positive image with voters and, as a result, with Congress.

17. Another shorthand was the in-house moniker for the photo office: Still Pix (Weekly Roundup for October 27, 1941. Binder: Weekly Round Ups/Box Score, Box 13).

18. William M. Nelson to Straus, memos: May 14, 1941, Subject: Picture Service in connection with anniversary; May 22, 1941, Subject: Picture Distribution in Connection with Anniversary. Folder: Still Pictures Sect., Box 15.

19. "New Photographs Available," *Defense* 2:18 (May 6, 1941) 24; Weekly Roundup for August 11, 1941. Binder: Weekly Round Ups/Box Score, Box 13. One of the pictures distributed nationally was the defense information quintet, consisting of Mellett and Horton, along with the information directors of the Army, Navy and State Department. "Picture News," *Ogden (UT) Standard-Examiner,* April 26, 1941, 6.

20. Weekly Roundup for October 6, 1941. Binder: Weekly Round Ups/Box Score, Box 13.

21. "New Photographs Available," *Defense* 2:18 (May 6, 1941): 24.

22. Horton, n.t. (summary of DOI activities), October 4, 1941, [Doc.] 10533, 2. Folder: Oct. 4, 1941 DOI, Box 15.

23. Many DOI photos from this period are on the Library of Congress's website. Example include: manufacturing by a subcontractor (May 1941): www.loc.gov/pictures/item/oem2002001759/PP/); defense housing construction (July 1941): www.loc.gov/pictures/item/oem2002000833/PP/; shipbuilding at Newport News (October 1941): www.loc.gov/pictures/

item/oem2002010385/PP/; and civilian defense (October 1941): www.loc.gov/pictures/item/oem2002010152/PP/.

24. William Nelson to Straus, memo, August 2, 1941. Subject: British Press Service Photos. Folder: Still Pictures Sect., Box 15.

25. Horton to Donovan, memo, July 31, 1941, n.t., 3. Folder: Publicity–Donovan, Box 11.

26. F. & L. S. to Horton, memo, July 30, 1941, 1. Folder: Publicity–Donovan, Box 11. I was unable to identify the authors based on these initials. Films in production included defense plant security and eating healthy foods (AP, "Plant Guards Make the Movies," *Hutchinson [KS] News*, August 15, 1941, 6; "Motion Picture to Portray Sound Nutrition," *Defense* 2:48 [December 2, 1941]: 29).

27. Larson, "Official Information," 74–75.

28. "Workshops for Defense," *Air Youth Horizons* 2:6 (June–July 1941): 4.

29. Perhaps indicating that he had a greater degree of involvement in this short than others, Horton was listed in the credits (WorldCat accession No. 47739283).

30. *Food for Freedom* was released on December 9, 1941, so it is considered here as a pre–Pearl Harbor production.

31. For example, its screenings were widely reported. The *NYT* film column "Of Local Origin" mentioned its showings three times: November 6, 1941, 27; March 30, 1942, 21; November 9, 1942, 27. Other coverage of screenings: Nelson Bell, "Frank Lloyd All at Sea in 'This Woman Is Mine'" (local entertainment column), *WP*, October 17, 1941, 10; "Music Held Builder of Civilian Morale," *NYT*, November 30, 1941, D5; "Museum Showing Films on Defense," *Baltimore Sun*, January 25, 1942, SM11.

32. Excerpts of Sandburg's script were used as captions in a photo spread of stills from the movie ("Bomber," *U.S. Camera*, January 1942, 56–57).

33. Nelson Bell, "Success as Breadwinner Oddly Went to His Feet" (local entertainment column), *WP*, October 16, 1941, 22.

34. Leonard Lyons, "New York Calling!" (entertainment column), *WP*, October 30, 1941, 9.

35. "Building of a Bomber," *HC*, October 29, 1941, 5.

36. Horton to Wayne Coy, memo, October 22, 1941, n.t. (request for additional positions), 3. Binder: Functions and Operations of DOI, 1941–42, Box 13.

37. Larson, "Publicity for National Defense," 250.

38. WorldCat accession No. 1179749. I was unable to obtain it.

39. Rosten to Horton, Mellett, Mercey, and Herbert Harris, memo, May 15, 1941, Subject: Government Films. Folder: R (alphabetical series), Box 9.

40. Division of Information (summary of activities), March 1, 1941, 2. Binder: Functions and Operations of DOI, 1941–42, Box 13.

41. Before his academic career, Ruch was vice president of the Opinion Research Corporation, giving him professional expertise in survey research (Ruch, "The Problem of Measuring Morale," 228).

42. "Films' Warmongering Refuted by U. of So. Calif. Poll on 'Propaganda,'" *Variety*, August 6, 1941, 4; "Press Okays Hays' Pix Stand," *Film Daily*, August 6, 1941, 8. The research was sponsored by the Committee for National Morale, a national group of anti-isolationist faculty, so these *initial* results could be subject to criticism as not impartial. Ruch served on the committee's executive committee (Ruch, "Problem," 228).

43. Mimeographed excerpts from both articles. Folder: Newsreel (Miscellaneous), Box 5.

44. That the *final* survey results were later published in a peer-reviewed journal strengthened their credibility.

45. Isolationist senators Burton Wheeler (D-MT) and Gerald Nye (R-ND) were frequently quoted in the press as critical of President Roosevelt's leanings to help Great Britain.

46. Ruch, "Problem," 224–25. The article did not break out the "No" from "Don't know" answers. Given the rough parallel with the preliminary August results, it is a fair assumption that the "Don't know" answers were relatively minor, perhaps in single digits. Presumably, if "Don't know" had been more than that, peer reviewers would have insisted it be listed separately.

47. Ruch also asked an identical question about *feature* films. Were audiences concerned about pro-war propaganda subtly or overtly in them? The accusation from isolationists was that the (impliedly Jewish-dominated) Hollywood was sneaking warmongering messages in putative entertainment. Results were even more lopsidedly in the negative than for shorts and newsreels: 16 percent "Yes," 77 percent "No," and 7 percent "Don't know."

48. Marion Sabatini to W. B. Phillips, memo, November 22, 1941, Subject: It Takes Both Barrels (poster). Folder: Posters, Box 10. Larson estimated the print run for posters as up to 100,000 ("Official Information," 73).

49. Bird and Rubenstein, 24, 29.

50. "Division of Information," n.a. (almost certainly Horton), n.d., 5. Binder: Functions and Operations of DOI, 1941–42, Box 13. March 14, 1941, per Gosnell (80).

51. Ibid.

52. Masthead, *Defense* 2:12 (March 25, 1941): 1.

53. PM-339 was listed in a compilation index prepared by OGR's Statistics Section, but I was unable to locate it (US OGR, *Index of Press Releases,* 1).

54. Ellipsis in original.

55. The background was blue, the wording white, and the logo red, white, and blue. For a black-and-white version, see AP, "New Poster for Defense Plants," *NYT,* May 17, 1941, 7.

56. *Defense* 2:17 (April 29, 1941): 1.

57. Horton to Sidney Sherwood, memo, May 28, 1941, n.t. Folder: Personnel Regulations; and Sherwood to Horton, memo, June 16, 1941, Subject: Project P-NDC-25-Defense Plant Poster Campaign. Folder: DOI Memos, Box 9. Horton asked for $41,265, and BOB approved it, indicating a consensus about the importance of industrial posters.

58. *Defense* 2:26 (July 1, 1941): 1.

59. Ibid., 24; "Production for Victory," *United States News,* November 7, 1941, 11.

60. Three are in "OEM 'Keeps 'em Posted,'" *WP,* September 6, 1941, 10.

61. "Keep 'em Rolling!" *Defense* 2:29 (July 22, 1941): 24.

62. US OEM, [*Press Releases*], PM-896. Also AP, "Defense Plants Urged to Display OPM Signs," *CSM,* August 9, 1941, 3.

63. *Defense:* "Don't Let Him Down!" 2:36 (September 9, 1941): 24; "United We Stand," 2:40 (October 7, 1941): 24.

64. Marion Sabatini to W. B. Phillips, memo, November 22, 1941, Subject: It Takes Both Barrels. Folder: Posters, Box 10.

65. Initial version: "Two Words Different," *WP,* January 10, 1942, 10. Post–Pearl Harbor version: *Victory* 3:3 (January 20, 1942): 32.

66. "Division of Information," n.a. (almost certainly Horton), n.d., 4. Binder: Functions and Operations of DOI, 1941–42, Box 13. March 14, 1941, per Gosnell (80).

67. Horton, n.t. (summary of DOI activities), October 4, 1941, [Doc.] 10533, 2. Folder: Oct. 4, 1941 DOI, Box 15.

68. US DOI, *Priorities and Defense.*

69. US OEM, [*Press Releases*], PM-302.

70. US DOI, *Situation in Steel.*

71. US OPM, *Ships for Freedom.* Also "Booklet Describes Ship Labor Stabilization Agreement," *Defense* 2:48 (December 2, 1941): 27. DOI's logo is on p. 23.

72. US DOI, *Guns Not Gadgets.*

73. US DOI, *Materials for Defense.*

74. US DOI, *Dollars for Democracy.*

75. "'Dollars for Democracy' Pamphlet Released by OEM," *Defense* 2:42 (October 21, 1941): 11. Also US OEM, [*Press Releases*], PM-1366.

76. Schoenfeld to Horton, memo, November 18, 1940, n.t. Folder: Radio; Schoenfeld, Progress Report of the Radio Section since Its Inception in March 1941, n.d. (probably January 1942). Folder: Radio Section Reports, Box 5.

77. Sayre, *Analysis of the Radiobroadcasting,* 33.

78. "Division of Information," n.a. (almost certainly Horton), n.d., 10. Binder: Functions and Operations of DOI, 1941–42, Box 13. March 14, 1941, per Gosnell (80).

79. Schoenfeld to Straus, memo, October 2, 1941, Subject: Progress Report–September, 1941. Folder: Schoenfeld, Box 12.

80. Schoenfeld to Horton and Straus, memo, May 28, 1941, n.t. Folder: Schoenfeld, Box 12.

81. Horton, n.t. (summary of DOI activities), October 4, 1941, [Doc.] 10533, 2. Folder: Oct. 4, 1941 DOI, Box 15. This statistic probably included rebroadcasts of network programs by local stations (Claire Korman, Radio Section, to Ruth Bledsoe, memo, November 3, 1941, Subject: Transcriptions for the month of October. Folder: Radio, Box 5).

82. Division of Information," n.a. (almost certainly Horton), n.d., 10. Binder: Functions and Operations of DOI, 1941–42, Box 13. March 14, 1941, per Gosnell (80).

83. Farley, "School," 151.

84. Schoenfeld, "Commentary," 358.

85. Ibid., 359, emphasis in original.

86. "OEM to Broadcast Report of Year's Progress in Defense," *Defense* 2:20 (May 20, 1941): 2.

87. "OEM to Present Two Radio Plays July 4," *Defense* 2:26 (July 1, 1941): 2.

88. "OEM to Present Paul Muni," *Defense* 2:27 (July 9, 1941): 24.

89. "Two Radio Programs Portray Defense Housing Progress," *Defense* 2:29 (July 22, 1941): 21.

90. OEM, [*Press Releases*], PM-1547.

91. Kozlenko, *One Hundred:* Lewis Jacobs, "Prague Is Quiet: An Experimental Fantasy," 151–55; Bernard Schoenfeld, "What We Defend: Experimental Fantasy," 304–13, and "Independence Hall: A Historical Drama," 497–504; ad, *NYT Book Review,* October 19, 1941, 37.

92. Horton to Wayne Coy, memo, October 22, 1941, n.t. (request for additional positions), 2. Binder: Functions and Operations of DOI, 1941–42, Box 13.

93. Miller, *You Can't.*

94. Round Up for November 24, 1941. Binder: Weekly Round Ups/Box Score, Box 13; "Radio Program Sets Record," *Victory* 3:15 (April 14, 1942): 27.

95. Bill of Rights Day occurred on December 15, 1941, a week after Pearl Harbor.

96. "Roosevelt Proclaims Bill Of Rights Day," *Hamilton (OH) Journal,* November 29, 1941, 1.

97. James Brewbaker to George Lyon, memo, November 27, 1941, Subject: Distribution of Bill of Rights poster. Folder: Bill of Rights Day; and Lyon to Horton, August 26, 1941, memo, Subject: Poster Distribution (re: Legion's general interest in helping distribute OCD posters). Binder: Day Book, DOI, D. King, Aug. 1941–Jan. 1942, Box 13.

98. "'I'm an American' to Be More Than Song Tomorrow," *CT,* May 17, 1941, 8; "I'm an American! City to Shout It at Rally Today," *CT,* May 18, 1941, 14.

99. "Speed Armament Program! Knudsen Urges Patriot Rally," *CT,* May 19, 1941, 2. Speech text: "Knudsen tells what it is to be an American," *Defense* 2:20 (May 20, 1941): 3.

100. "Knudsen Urges Middle West to Put Shoulder to Arms Program," *CT,* May 19, 1941, 30.

101. Arthur Stringer, National Association of Broadcasters, to All Broadcast Station Executives, memo, June 27, 1941, Subject: Here are the Plans to Build Morale This 4th of July. Folder: Schoenfeld, Box 12.

102. *WP,* July 4, 1941, 1.

103. *NYT,* July 5, 1941: Frank Kluckhohn, "Roosevelt Urges US to Pledge Lives As Well As Work to Human Freedom"; "Solemn Hush Here"; "Leading the Nation in Pledge of Allegiance."

104. "Roosevelt Talk Stops Times Square Traffic," *WP,* July 5, 1941, 3.

105. Ibid.

106. Jerry Kluttz, "Federal Diary," *WP,* September 23, 1941, 17.

107. Horton, n.t. (summary of DOI activities), October 4, 1941, [Doc.] 10533, 3. Folder: Oct. 4, 1941 DOI, Box 15.

108. Thomas W. Wilson to Donald M. Nelson, memo, September 2, 1941, Subject: Conservation Information Program. Folder: S.P.A.B. [Supply, Priorities and Allocations Board], Box 12.

109. Harriet Elliot, Associate Administrator, Office of Price Administration and Civilian Supply, memo, June 18, 1941, Subject: Campaign for Summer Buying and Storage of Coal; Charles Coltman to Mr. Trussell, memo, August 15, 1941, Subject: "Buy Now" Campaign. Both in Folder: C (alphabetical series), Box 9. Also US OEM, *[Press Releases],* PM-548.

110. J. D. Secrest to Straus, memo, August 13, 1941, Subject: Waste paper salvage campaign. Folder: Secrest, Box 12.

111. T. W. Wilson Jr. to Horton et al., memo, November 27, 1941, n.t. Folder: R (alphabetical series), Box 9.

112. George Lyon to Straus, memo, December 5, 1941, Subject: Promotion Plans for the Volunteer Office. Folder: O.C.D., Box 15. Separately, in the spring of 1941, DOI did the PR for the State and Local Cooperation Division effort to recruit citizens to volunteer as air-raid spotters for the Army Air Force (US OEM, *[Press Releases],* PM-318, 394).

113. T. W. Wilson Jr. to Presidents of the Federal Reserve Banks, memo, n.d. (probably February or March 1941), Subject: Local Publicity, [Doc.] 115. Folder: F (alphabetical series), Box 9.

114. McMillan to Straus, memo, March 7, 1941, Subject: Plan for Promotion of our Subcontracting Program, 1. Folder: McMillan, Box 14.

115. Doherty, 304. Section 179.6 of the Records of the War Production Board (RG 179) includes the film (at National Archives II).

116. *Short Version:* Division of Information (summary of activities), March 1, 1941, 2. Binder: Functions and Operations of DOI, 1941–42, Box 13. It is also referred to in US NDAC, 1946, 148.

Long version: "Defense Business Checklist," *Business Week*, May 17, 1941, 30; "Urge Use of Subcontractors," *National Municipal Review* 30:6 (June 1940): 361.

117. US OPM, *Defense Contract Service;* "'Farming Out Methods' released—Fifth Bulletin in Series," *Defense* 2:15 (April 15, 1941): 5.

118. DOI stills for print media use included six from the movie *Bits and Pieces:* www.loc.gov/pictures/item/2004667542/; and one from a small lathe shop: www.loc.gov/pictures/item/oem2002001759/PP/.

119. Lewis, "Subcontracting," 405–6.

120. Dewey Fleming, "Small Firms Will Be Given Defense Work," *Baltimore Sun*. September 5, 1941, 1, 11.

121. Horton to Floyd B. Odlum, memo, September 27, 1941, Subject: Information Program for Division of Contract Distribution. Folder: N (alphabetical series), Box 9.

122. Odlum to Horton, October 11, 1941, n.t. Folder: D (alphabetical series), Box 9.

123. "Defense Officials to Interview 30,000 Small Manufacturers in Tour for Contracts," *Defense* 2:43 (October 28, 1941): 7; "Three Special Trains Begin Tour to Help Manufacturers Get Defense Work," *Defense* 2:46 (November 18, 1941): 22.

124. "3 'Defense Specials' Leave Here with Officials Seeking Out More Plants and Tools for Arms," *WP*, November 11, 1941, 11.

125. The Library of Congress collection includes eighteen photos taken inside the trains before departing Union Station: http://lccn.loc.gov/2004668585. One is online: www.loc.gov/pictures/item/oem2002011746/PP.

126. AP, "OPM's Defense Train Visits Wilmington for Clinic," *WSJ*, November 12, 1941, 11; "'Defense Train' Shown," *NYT*, November 13, 1941, 25; "OPM's Special Attracts 604 Visitors in S[alt] L[ake]," *Salt Lake City (UT) Tribune*, November 18, 1941, 13, 19; Havens Wilber, "OPM Special Train Here," *Madison (WI) Capital Times*, November 28, 1941, 1, 6; "Contracts Fixed on Defense Train," *NYT*, November 29, 1941, 23; Norman Hoefer, "Defense Special Inspection Found Helpful by Some," *Freeport (IL) Journal Standard*, December 3, 1941, 22. Other coverage included "How Government Takes Its Needs Direct to Businessmen," *LAT*, November 28, 1941, A1–A2; and "It Happened in Texas," *CSM*, December 20, 1941, 21. In advance of its stop in Jackson, Mississippi, the local electric utility placed a newspaper ad urging local manufacturers to attend ("Opportunity Presented to Mississippi," *Greenville [MS] Delta Democrat-Times*, December 2, 1941, 5).

127. December 21, 1941: AP, "Trains with Exhibits Help Convert Peace Firms to Arms Plants," *Baltimore Sun*, 8; "11,000 Small Firms Rally for Work," *NYT*, 9.

128. "Defense Officials to Interview 30,000 Small Manufacturers in Tour for Contracts," *Defense* 2:43 (October 28, 1941): 7; "Penalizing Laws on Prices Sought," *NYT*, December 2, 1941, 15.

129. *CT*, October 23, 1941: Lloyd Norman, "Firms Besiege Arms Clinic in Hunt for Work," 31; "At Arms Clinic," 34.

130. "Defense Production Clinics Acclaimed as Meetings End," *LAT*, November 19, 1941, 1, 3.

131. Charles Egan, "Defense Officials Hold 'Brokers' Unnecessary," *NYT*, December 7, 1941, E8.

132. Straus to Thomas Wilson, memo, July 15, 1941, Subject: Civilian and National Defense Exposition of America. Folder: Wilson, Thos. W., Box 12.

133. "National Defense Exposition," n.a., n.d. (probably about July 1941). Folder: E (alphabetical series), Box 9.

134. I was unable to locate total attendance figures. *NYT* coverage included: "Children Frolic

at Defense Show," September 22, 1941, 6; "Gas Chamber Gives Civilians a Big Thrill," September 23, 1941, 16; "Defense Show near End," October 12, 1941, 42.

135. "Defense Contracts Speeded by Clinic Here," *NYT*, September 25, 1941, 14.

136. "Exhibits" (summary of meeting), August 4, 1941, n.a. Folder: E (alphabetical series); Straus to Major Frank McCabe, War Department, August 6, 1941. Folder: Mc (alphabetical series), Box 9.

137. Straus to all Employees, Information Division, memo, November 7, 1941, n.t. Folder: Memos-Straus, Box 7. Carlu also designed several DOI posters.

138. Larson put it at 18' x 40' ("Official Information," 70). It is possible that DOI produced several sizes to tour the country.

139. In 1942, DOI published the photomontage in a folded-leaf format: *The 4 Freedoms and the Arsenal of Democracy,* GPO 16–23967–2. It is in the collection of the UCLA Library, Barcode A0011348588; also WorldCat accession No. 320222378.

140. "Photo Murals Dedicated in Defense Square," *WP*, November 8, 1941, 13. In 1939, DAR had famously refused to permit opera singer Marian Anderson to hold a concert at DAR Hall because she was African American. This became a cause célèbre. As a substitute, Eleanor Roosevelt arranged for her to have an outdoor concert in front of the Lincoln Memorial.

141. A collection of sixty-one photos of the murals are in the Library of Congress catalogue: http://lccn.loc.gov/2004667544. Two are online: www.loc.gov/pictures/item/oem2002003492/PP/ and www.loc.gov/pictures/item/oem2002001786/PP/.

142. Grover Theis, *Miami Herald,* to Carlton Skinner, Acting Director of Information, US MC, February 17, 1941; Horton to Mellett, draft memo, February 21, 1941. Both in Folder: M (alphabetical series), Box 9.

143. Straus, DOI (summary of activities), n.d. (handwritten on file copy: 3/1/41), 3. Folder: Information, 1941–42, Box 13.

144. Regional Information Specialist, classification position description, signed by Richard Custer, Classification Investigator, and approved by Richard W. Cooper, Chief, Classification Section, April 9, 1941. Folder: Regional Information Specialists, Box 8.

145. Regional Information Officer (staff directory), July 8, 1941. Folder: Regional Information Specialists, Box 8.

146. J. D. Secrest to Straus, memo, July 2, 1941, Subject: Advance Notice on Press Release to Field Men. Folder: Secrest, Box 12.

147. Schoenfeld to Straus, Secrest, and Laura Schopper, memo, June 24, 1941, Subject: Iowa state broadcasting. Folder: Schoenfeld, Box 12.

148. Davis Snow, Director of Information, Defense Housing Coordination, to Dean Jennings, Regional Information Officer, form letter, San Francisco, May 27, 1941; cover note from Snow to Straus seeking approval of the form letter (and handwritten note on file copy of Straus's OK, May 28, 1941). Both in Folder: Housing, Box 15.

149. J. D. Secrest to Straus, memo, June 6, 1941, n.t. Folder: Secrest, Box 12.

150. "OEM Opens Regional Office in N.Y.," *WSJ,* June 21, 1941, 4; "Call for Wardens Gets Big Response," *NYT*, June 21, 1941, 8.

151. "Regional Information Offices Established in 10 Cities," *Defense* 2:32 (August 12, 1941): 23.

152. *Atlanta Constitution:* "Consumer Work to Be Discussed," November 9, 1941, 13A; W. M. Hines, "City Apathetic toward Civilian Defense Program," November 16, 1941, 13; "At Federal Offices," December 2, 1941, 11.

153. "Over 12 Million Allotted for Texas Defense Housing," *Galveston (TX) Daily News,* June 19, 1941, 3; "S[an] A[ntonio] Housing Plan Vetoed," *San Antonio (TX) Light,* July 3, 1941, 10-B; AP, "State Defense Set-Up Praised," *Albuquerque (NM) Journal,* July 12, 1941, 1.

154. "Business Heads View OPM Train," *San Antonio (TX) Light,* December 3, 1941, 4-A.

155. After returning from a trip to California, Labor Division head Sidney Hillman sent Horton a complimentary letter about DOI's regional PIO in San Francisco, Dean Jennings: "If the rest of your men are nearly as competent and cooperative as Mr. Jennings, you certainly have a fine set-up" (October 10, 1941. Binder: Day Book, DOI, D. King, Aug. 1941–Jan. 1942, Box 13).

Hillman's high regard for Jennings was evidently widely shared. After Congress defunded OWI's regional offices for FY1944, Jennings became a freelance writer. The next year, Edward Banfield (later a noted political scientist), PIO for the federal Farm Security Administration's western region, replied to a Jennings request for background information on wartime Mexican labor in California. In his cover letter, Banfield said he'd like to meet Jennings because "I'd like to see what a guy with your reputation looks like" (Banfield to Jennings, April 11, 1944, Farm Security Administration Papers).

156. "Defense Official on Survey Trip," *Helena (MT) Independent,* August 29, 1941, 6.

157. William Nelson to Straus, memo and attachment, August 11, 1941, Subject: Picture File. Attachment, Photographic Unit, General Description of Photographs in OEM Picture File (Aug. 5, 1941). Folder: Still Pictures Sect., Box 15.

158. Consumer Division, OPACS, Preliminary Press Manual for Field Staff, n.d. (handwritten note: 8/14/41), 1. Binder: Day Book, DOI, D. King, Aug. 1941–Jan. 1942, Box 13.

159. Straus to Leigh Plummer, memo, August 15, 1941, Subject: Changes in your 8/13/41 Preliminary Press Manual for Field Staff. Binder: Day Book, DOI, D. King, Aug. 1941–Jan. 1942, Box 13.

160. Paul Jordan to Straus, October 7, 1941. Folder: Personnel Regulations, Box 9.

161. McMillan to Straus, memo, September 5, 1941, n.t. Folder: McMillan, Box 14; Straus to Horton, memo, September 5, 1941, Subject: Government agencies having field offices. Binder: Day Book, DOI, D. King, Aug. 1941–Jan. 1942, Box 13.

162. Straus to Wayne Coy, memo and attachment, October 23, 1941, n.t. Folder: Information Division (Per[sonnel]), Box 8. When the original Boston regional information officer was replaced in late 1941, his successor was newspaperman E. Bigelow Thompson. Four months earlier, Thompson's daughter married the son of Senator Harry Byrd Sr., who had been so critical of FDR and Horton about airplane production figures. In 1964, the son, Harry Byrd Jr., succeeded his father in the Senate.

163. J. D. Secrest to John Jago, memo, October 28, 1941, n.t. Folder: Information Division (Per[sonnel]), Box 8.

164. Weekly Round Up for June 30, 1942. Binder: Weekly Round Ups/Box Score, Box 13.

165. Weekly Round Up for July 14, 1942. Binder: Weekly Round Ups/Box Score, Box 13.

166. Stephen Fitzgerald to Horton, Straus, and Secrest, memo, October 13, 1941, Subject: New England and other places, 2. Folder: V (alphabetical series), Box 9.

167. Straus to All Regional Information Offices, draft of form memo, August 23, 1941, n.t. Binder: Day Book, DOI, D. King, Aug. 1941–Jan. 1942. The weekly report on September 2, 1941, noted, "Field boys are making a survey of civilian morale" (Weekly Round Up for September 2, 1942. Binder: Weekly Round Ups/Box Score, Box 13).

168. Lee, *First,* 86.

169. Peter Edson, "In Washington," *Racine (WI) Journal Times,* May 14, 1941, 10.

170. McMillan to Straus, memo, April 19, 1941, Subject: Monthly Report, 4. Folder: McMillan, Box 14.

171. Schoenfeld [to Straus?], memo, April 14, 1941, n.t. Folder: Schoenfeld, Box 12.

172. Horton to Staff, DOI, memo, August 15, 1941, n.t. Binder: Day Book, DOI, D. King, Aug. 1941–Jan. 1942, Box 13.

173. The House Appropriations Committee report on the omnibus bill funding all OEM agencies for FY1942 made the same point: "In arriving at a determination of the amount [to be funded], there is no comparative previous experience to act as a guide" (US House, *Second Deficiency,* H. Rep. 849, 10).

174. US House, *Second Deficiency,* hearings, 672.

175. Larson, "Official Information," 69.

176. Blair Bolles, "Federal Bureau Collects, Dispenses Defense News," *HC,* November 30, 1940, A20.

177. "Division of Information," 1 (handwritten). Folder: Lecture Materials 1941–42, Box 1, Fred S. Siebert Papers. Siebert was a professor of journalism at University of Wisconsin–Madison and a few months later authored an article in *Journalism Quarterly* on organizational structure of federal wartime information. James Reston used the same figure in "Defense Picture Given to World in All Media by Federal Agencies," *NYT,* October 27, 1941, 36.

178. George Morgenstern, "Onward March the Brigades of War Ballyhoo," *CT,* November 7, 1941, 17. He reported that DOI had just requested "an additional $122,400 for press releases" above its $750,000 current budget.

179. Frank Kent, "Great Game of Politics," *Baltimore Sun,* October 13, 1941, 2.

180. Sherwood to Horton, memo, June 16, 1941, Subject: Project P-NDC-25-Defense Plant Poster Campaign. Folder: DOI Memos, Box 9.

181. US House, *Second Deficiency,* hearings 672.

182. Bolles, "Federal Bureau Collects."

183. "Publicity," *United States News* 11:19 (November 7, 1941): 18; "Press Front Lend-Lease," *Newsweek,* November 17, 1941, 61; Reston, "Defense Picture Given to World."

184. Larson, "Official Information," 69.

185. Peter Edson, "In Washington," *Dunkirk (NY) Evening Observer,* October 8, 1941, 6. He lists 210 employees in Washington and 30 field staffers.

186. Siebert lecture notes.

187. US Congress, *Reduction of Nonessential Federal Expenditures,* Part 5, 2037.

188. DOI, Budget Estimate, October 20, 1941. Folder: Information Division (Per[sonnel]), Box 8.

189. However, holding a civil service position was not a *guarantee* of a job, only first call for vacancies. After World War II, many civil servants were "RIFed" (Reduction in Force).

190. Straus to Staff, memo, October 13, 1941, n.t. Folder: Memos–Straus, Box 7.

191. Principal Information Specialist, classification position description, signed by Donald Wilson, Classification Investigator, and approved by Richard Cooper, Chief, Classification Section, August 1, 1941. Folder: Washington Information Specialists (Descriptions), Box 8.

192. Onslow, "Personnel Problems," 1.

193. "U.S. Seeks More Writers," *NYT,* September 22, 1941, 7; "U.S. Hunting for Specialists in Many Fields," *WP,* September 22, 1941, 22; Jerry Kluttz, "Federal Diary," *WP,* October 3, 1941, 25.

194. L. A. Moyer, CSC Executive Director and Chief Examiner, to OEM, June 5, 1941. Folder: Poster Artists, Box 8.

195. "A Program for the Division of Information: A New Victory Program," October 18, 1941, n.a. (probably Horton). Folder: V (alphabetical series), Box 9. The potshot at intellectuals is obscure, but the timing suggests a likely interpretation. The memo was issued six days before Roosevelt released the executive order creating OFF. Presumably, Horton had been tipped off by a White House source, including that OFF's director would be Archibald MacLeish. As the Librarian of Congress and a well-known poet, MacLeish was viewed as something of an egghead. The people he subsequently hired for OFF had a similar bent. Horton's comment might have been a preemptive attack on the kind of PR he expected from OFF, implying that it would fail because the OFF intellectuals would not know how to communicate effectively with the average citizen. The "Victory Program" terminology was also being used in a slightly different context in Washington in late 1941 before Pearl Harbor. It was the informal term for OEM's incipient plans to expand military production in 1942. Press coverage usually placed it in quotation marks to indicate an unofficial title.

196. Catton to Straus, memo, December 1, 1941, n.t. , 1. Binder: Functions and Operations of DOI, 1941–42, Box 13.

197. Catton was the PIO to the head of the production effort, while Fitzgerald managed DOI's Production Branch, the staff who worked with OEM agencies involved in the production effort.

198. Fitzgerald to Horton and Straus, memo, December 1, 1941, Subject: 1942 Program for Production Branch and Information Division, underlining in original. Binder: Functions and Operations of DOI, 1941–42, Box 13.

199. Leigh Plummer to Straus, memo, November 25, 1941, n.t., 1. Binder: Functions and Operations of DOI, 1941–42, Box 13.

200. Dana Doten to Mr. Palmer (Defense Housing Coordinator), memo, October 16, 1941, Subject: Information Program (For Six Months Period–October 15, 1941 to April 15, 1942). Folder: P (alphabetical series), Box 9.

201. Okrent, 18.

Chapter Six

1. Wohlstetter, *Pearl Harbor.* At a White House meeting on Thursday, November 25, the president said the Japanese might attack as soon as Monday, November 29 (Current, "How Stimson Meant," 67). His prediction was likely based on the same intelligence that prompted the military's November 27 war warning.

2. Nelson, 183.

3. Ketchum, "Interview with Robert Wyman Horton," December 30, 1987, 6. Papers of Richard Ketchum.

4. Catton, 82.

5. Arthur Kurlan, "Director Looks Back," *NYT,* February 1, 1942, 10X.

6. Ketchum, "Interview with Robert Wyman Horton."

7. Nelson, 182.

8. Eugene Duffield, "U.S. Industry's Sole Objective," *WSJ,* December 8, 1941, 1.

9. "Nelson Says Nazis Caused the Attack," *NYT*, December 8, 1941, 4, emphasis added.

10. Based on Germany's treaty with Japan, Hitler declared war on the United States a few days later. This prompted Roosevelt to send a written message to Congress asking it to reciprocate, which it did.

11. "People of the Week," *United States News*, December 19, 1941, 51.

12. AP, "Remember Pearl Harbor Is New Slogan of OPM," *HC*, December 11, 1941. For example, December 12, 1941, press release by the Transportation Division (US OEM, [*Press Releases*], PM-1789).

13. "Immortal War Slogans," *NYT Sunday Magazine*, January 11, 1942, 25. While the slogan initially was popular, it gradually faded from use.

14. Straus to Turner Rose, memo, December 11, 1941, Subject: New name for weekly publication (magazine). Folder: T. Rose, Box 11.

15. Masthead, *Victory, formerly Defense* 2:50 (December 16, 1941).

16. US OEM, *[Press Releases]*, PM-1722, PM-1734, T-102, PM-1795.

17. "War Poster," *Victory* 3:1 (January 6, 1942): 31.

18. Horton to All Employees, memo, December 11, 1941, n.t. Folder: Horton, Box 7. The memo refers to "what happened in Hawaii and the Philippines last Sunday," suggesting that the Japanese attack on US planes in Philippine bases was initially viewed as important as Pearl Harbor. This dual focus has faded from historical memory.

19. Horton to the Staff, memo, December 30, 1941, n.t. Folder: Memos–Straus, Box 7.

20. US OEM, [*Press Releases*], PM-2000.

21. DOI July 1941–June 1942, 5. Binder: DOI Report July 1941–June 1942, Box 14.

22. Folder: OEM 1942, Box 1, Siebert Papers.

23. Gosnell, 83.

24. Horton insisted that DOI writers use newspaper-style plain English. An exception was a May 16, 1942, release listing the consumer products that would be affected by the latest WPB decision as "homeric" (US OEM, [*Press Releases*], PM-3299, lowercase in original).

25. Ibid., PM-3390.

26. Ibid., PM-3267. The other one percent came from Africa.

27. Ibid., PM-3391.

28. Ibid., WPB-787, 932.

29. "Our Part," *Mining World* 4:1 (January 1942): 1; "Business-Paper Editors and Publishers Ready to Help in Nation's War Effort," *Victory* 2:52 (December 30, 1941): 25.

30. WPB, *Converting Industry*, 2. Also "Conversion of Industry to War Production," *Bulletin of the American Ceramic Society* 21:3 (March 15, 1942): 39–40.

31. "Labor Press Praised by U.S. Leaders for Support of Nation's War Effort": *Bridgemen's Magazine* 42:5 (May 1942): 267; *Railroad Telegrapher* 59:5 (May 1942): 304. Horton's statement was not included in the *Times*' coverage, which instead noted that he had called for "fair relations between labor and management if the war is to be won" ("W. H. Davis Asks Labor Press to Work for Non-Stop Production," *NYT*, May 10, 1942, 33).

32. Horton to Staff Members, memo, April 18, 1942, Subject: Releasable Information, [Doc.] X-631, 2. Folder: Staff Memos, Box 12.

33. Childs, *I Write from Washington*, 278.

34. "Hacks vs. Minnows," *Newsweek*, May 4, 1942, 32.

35. Damon Runyon, "The Brighter Side" (syndicated column), *Charleston (WV) Gazette*, June 6, 1942, 6. Later in the column, he reverted to the usual journalist's viewpoint, complaining about too many releases and too much flackery in government.

36. US OEM, [*Press Releases*], PM-1998.

37. Ibid., R-16.

38. *Defense Review No.* 2 and *No.* 3. Based on: www.imdb.com/title/tt0186950/ and www.imdb.com/title/tt0186951/.

39. US OEM, *OEM Handbook*.

40. US DOI, *Gadgets to Guns;* US WPB, *Production Goes to War.*

41. "America from Dunkirk to Pearl Harbor: The Story of 599 Days," December 20, 1941, n.a. (probably Horton), 4. Folder: America from Dunkirk to Pearl Harbor, Box 14. The document has a control number (X 1546), indicating circulation to an in-house audience. It was laid out in a publication-ready format, including a title page and a quote from the president on the first inside page, suggesting it was intended for publication.

42. Brands, *American Dreams,* 22.

43. DOI July 1941–June 1942, 7. Binder: DOI Report, July 1941–June 1942, Box 14.

44. AP, "Attacks Union 'Hotheads,'" *Baltimore Sun,* May 10, 1942, 7.

45. Bernard Schoenfeld, "Battle of the Ether Waves!" *Radio Daily* 19:63 (June 26, 1942): 8.

46. Lee, *Congress,* chap. 8. A month after Pearl Harbor, *Life* magazine published a feature on the new wartime Washington, including criticism of government PR. It placed quotation marks around the term "information services" and concluded with a snide condemnation: "Phrases, phrases, phrases, and the citizens of Pocatello, Idaho and Punxsutawney, Pa. are still in the dark, still wondering what's going on. Churchill's heroic statement that 'never before in history have so many owed so much to so few' applies to Washington: 'Never before in history have so few kept so much from so many'" (Milton Mayer, "Washington Goes to War," *Life,* January 5, 1942, 59).

47. *CR* 88:8 (February 6, 1942): A414; (February 9, 1942): A488; (March 2, 1942): A788.

48. "Information Services of the Government," *CR* 88:2 (February 23, 1942): 1513.

49. This appalling accusation and Vandenberg's endorsement of it helps correct the romantic myth of American unity and solidarity during World War II. Roosevelt's partisan and ideological opponents simply shifted to new nomenclature. They said they supported the war effort, but just were shocked by how Roosevelt was bungling it. This is also a reminder that the brutal political rhetorical used by Republicans, talk radio, and Fox News against Presidents Clinton and Obama is *not* a new phenomenon. One modest mitigating factor to understand such a fantastical enmity for government PR is that in those days propaganda was thought of as an irresistible power, akin to fears of brainwashing in the 1950s. Propaganda was viewed as omnipotent, able to convince anyone of anything, and with no antidote. Once used, resistance was futile, these congressional conservatives and FDR opponents feared.

50. *CR* 88:1 (January 22, 1942): 549.

51. F. R. Kent Jr., "Senator Taft Assails War by Publicity," *Baltimore Sun,* February 14, 1942, 1, 7. In his columns, Kent often criticized Horton and DOI.

52. AP, "Sen. Byrd Calls Federal Travel Costs 'Scandal,'" *CT,* May 2, 1942, 13.

53. Robert De Vore, "Senate Report Scores Federal Publicity Flood," *WP,* May 31, 1942, 11. Also: Chesly Manly, "U.S. Propaganda for Week Would Fill 7½ Tribunes," *CT,* May 31, 1942, 8;

"Official 'Deluge' of News Assailed," *NYT*, May 31, 1942, 33. I was unable to locate the original press release from DOI.

54. *CR* 88:4 (May 28, 1942): 4684. For the context of Tydings's attack, see Lee, *Congress*, chap. 8. Tydings's seeming acceptance of government PR by "old established orthodox bureaus or divisions" was likely a reference to USDA's extensive information activities. He would not have wanted his remarks to look like an attack on something his farmer constituents liked. Note also that he disassociated himself the justification for the war: "We are told" (by the president, presumably) that the Axis threatens civilization, but Tydings wasn't agreeing.

55. Editorials: "Words Will Win the War," *El Paso (TX) Herald-Post*, May 22, 1942, 4; "Those Rare Coins" and "The Item of Cost," both in *Charleston (WV) Daily Mail*, June 4–5, 1942, 6; "Patriots and Papsuckers," *Massillon (OH) Evening Independent*, June 8, 1942, 4; "Insult to Children," *Miami (OK) News-Record*, June 11, 1942, 8.

56. "Mrs. America and Defense" (DOI column), *Ukiah (CA) Redwood Journal*, June 15, 1942, 3.

57. "The Home Front" (DOI column), *(Greene) Iowa Recorder*, June 3, 1942, 3.

58. "Here's How to Spend the Weekend," *WP*, June 27, 1942, 12. The coverage was an excuse for cheesecake photos.

59. "Have Your Vacation Even without a Car," *HC*, May 10, 1942, C8.

60. US Office of Education, *3434*, 160, 98.

61. "'He's Watching You,'" *Victory* 3:26 (June 30, 1941): 19. The poster was prepared by DOI, but not released until two weeks after it was merged into OWI.

62. Harper, *Catalogue: War, Revolution and Peace*, 30–31.

63. Bird and Rubenstein, 28.

64. Roosevelt, *Public Papers*, 11:54–56.

65. Later, largely forced by a bill passed by Congress, Roosevelt named James Byrnes as virtually the assistant president overseeing the economy.

66. Catton later helped ghostwrite Nelson's war memoir. Also Lee, "Origins."

67. Gosnell, 35.

68. Nelson to WPB Staff Members, memo, February 3, 1942, n.t. Folder: WPB-ID Responsible for Information Work, Box 6.

69. Organization charts: "Nelson Reveals Setup for Powerful War Production Board," *CT*, January 22, 1942, 3; "Organization under War Production Board, January 20," *Victory* 3:4 (January 27, 1942): 5. Photos: "Experts Fill Posts in War Production Board Setup Created by Nelson," *Hutchinson (KS) News*, February 14, 1942, 3; "Associated Press News in Pictures," *High Point (NC) Enterprise*, February 1, 1942, 8A.

70. Fesler et al., 238.

71. Nelson, 204.

72. *US Government Manual*, Spring 1942 (January 31, 1942): 575.

73. Henderson to Wayne Coy, OEM liaison officer, February 28, 1942. Folder: Consumer Personnel, Box 8. Signaling its importance, entertainment columnist Leonard Lyons mentioned a rumor of Horton's takeover ("Words to the Wise," *WP*, January 22, 1942, 9).

74. Leo Crowley, Alien Property Custodian, to Horton, May 12, 1942; Horton to Crowley, also May 12, 1942. Folder: A (alphabetical series), Box 13; Milton Eisenhower, Director, War Relocation Authority, to Horton, May 16, 1942; Horton to Eisenhower, May 18, 1942. Folder: War Relocation Authority, Box 6.

Eisenhower was a longtime USDA information official whom Roosevelt trusted. Eisenhower's brother, Dwight, was at that time an obscure Army general. A few months earlier, at the president's request, Milton Eisenhower had reviewed all wartime information services and recommended reorganizing them (Lee, *First*, chap. 8). The War Relocation Authority was the government agency that implemented the forcible removal of Japanese from the Pacific states to concentration camps in the western desert. Eisenhower briefly headed it. According to Eisenhower, Horton had "pressed hard" to appoint DOI as its PR provider rather than the agency creating its own in-house PR office. Eisenhower later claimed he acceded to Horton's lobbying because Eisenhower wanted the Relocation Authority to get as little publicity as possible. Given his lack of faith in Horton's model, Eisenhower later rationalized that contracting with DOI for PR services was one way to assure a low public profile for the Relocation Authority (Gosnell, 78). This post-hoc explanation strains credulity, given the thousands of press releases issued by DOI.

75. DOI [summary], n.a., June 1, 1942, [Doc.] X-1237, 2. Folder: X-1237–June 1, 1941, DOI, Box 14.

76. OCD had been under constant attack from the congressional conservative coalition as a boondoggle, including supposedly silly activities and appointment of incompetents. On January 8, 1942, the House approved a bill transferring OCD to the War Department. The next day, FDR replaced LaGuardia with Landis, thereby deflating that political balloon and maintaining OCD as a presidential agency. The Senate never took it up (Gosnell, 66–67).

77. Ibid., 68–69.

78. Straus to DOI Staff, memo, February 7, 1942, Subject: Changes within DOI. Folder: Memos–Personnel, Box 8; AP, "OCD Publicity Plan," *CSM*, February 9, 1942, 3; Peter Edson, "Behind the News in Washington," *Pampa (TX) News*, February 10, 1942, 4. At a February 11 press conference, Landis said he wanted OCD to have its own information service (*Victory* 3:7 [February 17, 1942]: 31).

79. US Congress, *Reduction of Nonessential*, Part 3, 1085–87.

80. Acton to Straus, January 7, 1942. Folder: Personnel Action 40–41–42, Box 15.

81. W. H. Lawrence, "President Merges Housing Agencies," *NYT*, February 25, 1942, 24; "Housing Office Abolished," *OEM News: Employee Publication* 1:3 (March 5, 1942): 1–2. In a face-saving gesture, Roosevelt said Palmer had done a "splendid job" and sent him to study British wartime housing.

82. Horton to John Blandford Jr., National Housing Administrator, memo, March 4, 1942, n.t. Folder: B (alphabetical series), Box 9.

83. Ruth Bledsoe to Jim Culhane, memo, January 2, 1942, Subject: Transfer of Personnel; Pearl [Morris] to Ruth [Bledsoe], memo, February 4, 1942, n.t.; Frankie Keyser to Miss Thelma Willoughby, memo, February 18, 1942, Subject: Transfer of Files. All in Folder: Memos-Personnel, Box 8.

84. "Information Division Tells U.S. about OEM's Management of War," *OEM News: Employee Publication* 1:2 (February 19, 1942): 3.

Chapter Seven

1. Harlow, *Public Relations in War and Peace*, 199.

2. Turner Rose (to Straus?), memo, December 30, 1941, Subject: VICTORY Magazine. Folder: T. Rose, Box 11.

3. "Of Local Origin," *NYT,* March 30, 1942, 21.

4. "All Industry Meeting in Chicago Opens May 11," *Refrigerating Engineering* 43:5 (May 1942): 301, uppercase in original.

5. "Dr. Vande Bogart Addresses Local Rotary Club," *Havre (MT) Daily News,* June 26, 1942, 2.

6. "The Crisis in Rubber," *Town Meeting* 8:7 (June 15, 1942) 3–18.

7. AP, "Government May Buy Private Cars," *Joplin (MO) Globe,* June 12, 1942, 12A. Never one to let material be used only once, Horton reconfigured the broadcast text into an article (Horton and Scott, "Rubber").

8. "Hero of Post 'Parasite' Probe Is Writer Who Admits He's One," *WP,* February 1, 1942, 1, 8.

9. Dewey Fleming, "29 Field Offices Of the OEM Spraying Country with 'News,'" *Baltimore Sun,* February 19, 1942, 6.

10. Peter Edson, "Nation's Capital News," *Altoona (PA) Mirror,* February 7, 1942, 8; Paul Mallon, "News behind the News," *Dunkirk (NY) Evening Observer,* March 15, 1942, 6.

11. Jerry Kluttz, "Federal Diary," *WP,* February 26, 1942, 17.

12. "So They Say!" *Wisconsin Rapids Daily Telegram* (July 1, 1942): 4.

13. Thomas Pryor, "Of Films and the War," *NYT,* December 14, 1941, 6X.

14. Leonard Lyons, "Departmental Memos" (syndicated column), *WP,* February 3, 1942, 16.

15. "Flicker Phiz Cops Top Billing in OCD Pressagentry Turkey," *WP,* February 3, 1942, 1. As a joke, the article was written in the style of Hollywood journalism. It described Horton as a "gray-maned, personable straight man."

16. "Advertisers, Agencies, Stations," *Billboard,* May 30, 1942, 8.

17. John Earle, "Pictures for Defense," *Popular Photography,* April 1942, 19–21, 44–45, 94–95.

18. DOI July 1941–June 1942, 5. Binder: DOI Report July 1941–June 1942, Box 14.

19. Gosnell, 87.

20. Doherty, 304–5.

21. The subtitle of the short was "A Defense Report on Film," so it could be also be considered part of DOI's film-based public reporting.

22. Richard Coe, "Now It Seems That Dr. Kildare Has Gotten Himself a Protege," *WP,* January 16, 1942, 8.

23. Doherty, 155.

24. "Orson Welles in U.S. Film," *NYT,* January 25, 1942, 12. Like the bomber documentary, the first version was one-reel (ten minutes) and then was rereleased as a two-reeler (twenty minutes) titled *Building a Tank.*

25. Gosnell, 90. To save paper, poster sizes were reduced (AP, "War Poster Size Cut," *CSM,* February 16, 1942, 7).

26. Appendix A: List of Posters, Report of Publications and Graphics Section, April 1941–June 1942. Binder: DOI Report July 1941–June 1942, Box 14.

27. "Genius, Brawn and Valor Smash the Axis," *Cumberland (MD) Evening Times,* January 27, 1942, 13.

28. Appendix A: List of Posters, Report of Publications and Graphics Section, April 1941–June 1942, 2.

29. "Conservation," *Victory* 3:2 (January 13, 1942): 24.

30. "A Warning," *Victory* 3:7 (February 17, 1942): 16.

31. "*U.S. Camera* Announces," *U.S. Camera,* February 1942, 36–37; "A Call to Photographers," *U.S. Camera,* March 1942, 64; "Camera Comment," *CSM,* January 15, 1942, 21; J. D., "Notes of the Cam-

era World," *NYT*, February 1, 1942, XX 5; J. D., "Notes of Camera World," *NYT*, March 1, 1942, XX 5.

32. For the initial winning submissions from professionals and amateurs, see *U.S. Camera*, April 1942, 10–11, 48–49. Steichen's title was now Navy Reserve Lieutenant Commander.

33. "Printed in Camera Magazine," *Alton (IL) Evening Telegram*, July 23, 1942, 3.

34. Broughton, "Government Agencies and Civilian Morale," 174.

35. DOI July 1941–June 1942, 5; and Appendix B: List of Publications, Report of Publications and Graphics Section, April 1941–June 1942. Binder: DOI Report July 1941–June 1942, Box 14.

36. "WPB Booklet Gives Ideas to Increase Plant Efficiency," *Brick & Clay Record* 100:6 (June 1942): 29; US WPB, *Priorities Orders in Force*.

37. US DOI, *Conversion*.

38. US WPB, *Converting Industry*.

39. US WPB, *Local Government and the War*.

40. Gosnell, 89.

41. DOI (summary submitted to OFF), January 26, 1942, 5. Folder: January 26, 1942 DOI, Box 15.

42. The 850 figure is from "Radio Program Sets Record," *Victory* 3:15 (April 14, 1942): 27.

43. Transcription Programs, July 1, 1941–June 30, 1942, n.a. (probably Schoenfeld), n.d. Folder: Radio–Wright Patman, Box 6. Excerpts from the program on sugar rationing, the third episode of *Three Thirds of the Nation*, and *You Can't Do Business with Hitler* are in Dryer, *Radio in Wartime*, chap. 9.

44. DOI July 1941–June 1942, 5. Binder: DOI Report July 1941–June 1942, Box 14.

45. Miller, *You Can't*.

46. "Radio Program Sets Record," *Victory* 3:15 (April 14, 1942): 27.

47. US OEM, [*Press Releases*], R-15; Transcription Programs, July 1, 1941–June 30, 1942, n.a. (probably Schoenfeld), n.d., 1. Folder: Radio–Wright Patman, Box 6.

48. DOI's initial twelve episodes: www.archive.org/details/OTRR_You_Cant_Do_Business_With_Hitler_Singles. OWI continued the series: http://radiogoldindex.com/cgi-local/p2.cgi?ProgramName=You+Can%27t+Do+Business+With+Hitler. Photos of a rehearsal: www.loc.gov/pictures/item/2005675141/.

49. "Roosevelt to Hear Nation on Records," *NYT*, January 29, 1942, 17; "Radio Log," *Charleston (WV) Gazette*, May 5, 1942, 11; Transcription Programs, July 1, 1941–June 30, 1942, n.a. (probably Schoenfeld), n.d., 2. Folder: Radio–Wright Patman, Box 6.

50. The Production Drive was headed by Michael Straus, brother of DOI assistant director Robert Straus (US CSC, 1942, 21).

51. Performance measurement is something of a management fad in public administration in the first decades of the twenty-first century. The numeric targets for the production drive demonstrate that performance measurement and public reporting of the results were practiced a half century earlier (Lee, "Is There Anything New").

52. "Nelson Opens Great War Production Drive" (text of radio address), *Victory* 3:10 (March 10, 1942): 1, 6–7.

53. US BOB, *United States at War*, 212; Gosnell, 37–39; MacLeish to Nelson, February 7, 1942; MacLeish to Horton, February 9, 1942; The Production Drive (plan, probably written by DOI), February 13, 1942; Nelson to Roosevelt, February 19, 1942. All in Folder: Production Drive, Box 8. Also DOI July 1941–June 1942, 41. Binder: DOI Report July 1941–June 1942, Box 14.

54. Transcription Programs, July 1, 1941–June 30, 1942, n.a. (probably Schoenfeld), n.d., 2. Folder: Radio–Wright Patman, Box 6.

55. Appendix B: List of Publications, Report of Publications and Graphics Section, April 1941–June 1942, 7. Binder: DOI Report July 1941–June 1942, Box 14.

56. US BOB, *United States at War,* 212.

57. Charles Egan, "June War Output 3 Times November's," *NYT,* July 26, 1942, 1, 27. It was even praised in Congress (United Press, "Production Gains Acclaimed," *NYT,* July 27, 1942, 17). Nelson followed up with a second monthly report covering July (AP, "Text of Nelson Statement on War Production," *NYT,* August 23, 1942, 35).

58. There is an incomplete archival record about plans to move or reorganize DOI's Campaign Branch. A January memo stated, "Inasmuch as it appears the Campaign Branch set-up remains at status quo, I am returning two files on the subject" (Marion Sabatini to Miss [Ruth] Bledsoe, memo, January 28, 1942, n.t. Folder: Campaigns Branch Personnel, Box 8).

59. Secrest to Straus, memo, December 24, 1941, n.t. Folder: S (alphabetical series), Box 9.

60. "Rumors Cause Tire Ration Troubles," *San Antonio (TX) Light,* January 9, 1942, 3-B.

61. "The Home Front," *(Smithport, PA) McKean County Democrat,* March 12, 1942, 8.

62. AP, "Guns, Bayonets Guard Welders in Shipyards," *CT,* December 23, 1941, 11; AP, "Strike Ban Plan Offered Welders Quit," *HC,* December 23, 1941, 2; "Want Navy to Run Shipyards in West," *NYT,* December 24, 1941, 35.

63. AP, "U.S. Seizes 10,000 Tons of Scrap Metal from Single Farm in Ohio," *CSM,* April 14, 1942, 19.

64. "Named Public Relations Head," *Piqua (OH) Daily Call,* January 19, 1942, 2; United Press, "Oklahoman Appointed," *Lubbock (TX) Morning Avalanche,* February 27, 1942, 6; "Teague Named to Information Branch Office," *HC,* May 17, 1942, 6.

65. DOI July 1941–June 1942, 47. Binder: DOI Report July 1941–June 1942, Box 14.

66. "Scenarist in New Post," *LAT,* March 14, 1942, 5; AP, "Pauline Bates Brown to Handle Publicity," *Tucson (AZ) Daily Citizen,* May 2, 1942, 6. However, she was not a salaried DOI employee. Rather, she was a dollar-a-year-(wo)man, while simultaneously holding her previous position as PR director for the state's civilian defense council.

67. "OEM Information Division field offices," *Victory* 3:15 (April 14, 1942): 27.

68. Ruth Bledsoe to Charles Wills, memo, January 30, 1942, n.t.; William Dougherty to Samuel Slotky, Regional Information Consultant, memo, February 5, 1942, Subject: Personnel Training. Both in Folder: Memos–Personnel, Box 8. Secrest to Field Information Officers, memo, February 9, 1942, Subject: CAS (Central Administrative Services, a division of OEM). Folder: Memos–General, Box 7.

69. Dewey Fleming, "29 Field Offices of the OEM Spraying Country with 'News,'" *Baltimore Sun,* February 19, 1942, 1, 6.

70. DOI July 1941–June 1942, 47. Binder: DOI Report July 1941–June 1942, Box 14.

71. "Many Can Get Sub-Contracts on War Work," *Charleston (WV) Gazette,* March 1, 1942, 3.

72. AP, "Scrap Metal Drive Opens," *Indiana (PA) Evening Gazette,* January 27, 1942, 5.

73. AP, "Sugar Instructions," *Gettysburg (PA) Times,* April 23, 1942, 1–2; "Gas Rationing Starts Today As Registration of Motorists Ends," *Lebanon (PA) Daily News,* May 15, 1942, 1.

74. "Maximum Price Rules Available at Office Merchants Association," *Burlington (NC) Daily Times-News,* May 5, 1942, 3; "Queries and Answers on Price Regulations," *Salt Lake City (UT) Tribune,* May 18, 1942, 9, 13.

75. "'Bachelor's Friend' Guaranteed Sox Available for Fall Season," *Atlanta Constitution,* July 27, 1942, 6.

76. AP, "City, County Defense Units Hold Discussion," *Ogden (UT) Standard-Examiner,* January 5, 1942, 3.

77. "For Defense," *(Madison) Wisconsin State Journal,* January 12, 1942, 8.

78. Transcription Programs, July 1, 1941–June 30, 1942, n.a. (probably Schoenfeld), n.d., 3. Folder: Radio–Wright Patman, Box 6.

79. DOI July 1941–June 1942, 48. Binder: DOI Report July 1941–June 1942, Box 14.

80. J. D. Secrest to Straus, memo, January 8, 1941 (typo, should be 1942), Subject: Radio assistants, and attachment (excerpts from reports by regional officers to Secrest on need for radio staffers); Schoenfeld to Straus, memo, February 18, 1942, Subject: Need for Radio Field Men. Both in Folder: Radio activities, Box 8.

81. AP, "Pauline Bates Brown to Handle Publicity," *Tucson (AZ) Daily Citizen,* May 2, 1942, 6.

82. Gosnell, 89.

83. "Radio Program Sets Record," *Victory* 3:15 (April 14, 1942): 27.

84. William Spire to Secrest, Schoenfeld et al., memo, June 3, [1942], Subject: Report of OEM Radio Field Operations. Folder: Reports of Radio Activities, DOI Field Offices, Box 12.

85. "Announcement of Competition for Pictures to Record Defense and War Activities," *O.E.M. Art Bulletin No. 1,* n.d., [Doc.] 16894. Folder OEM Art Bulletin No. 1, Box 6. Contreras's date is December 15, 1941 (*Tradition and Innovation in New Deal Art,* 234 n. 67).

86. Thomas Linn, "U.S. Offers Artists a Way to Serve Their Country," *NYT,* December 21, 1941, D7; Ada Rainey, "Eben Comins Presents Valuable Collection to Wellesley College," *WP,* December 21, 1941, L7; Eleanor Jewett, "Government to Buy Paintings of War Effort," *CT,* December 28, 1941, H2; Arthur Millier, "War to Force Numerous Changes on World of Art," *LAT,* December 28, 1941, C7; Jane Watson, "News and Comment," *Magazine of Art* 35:1 (January 1942): 32–33.

87. Stanley, "Lively Poster Arts," 19.

88. DOI (summary of activities submitted to OFF), January 26, 1942, 6. Folder: January 26, 1942 DOI, Box 15. However, in a press release a week later, DOI stated that 2,582 entries had been received (US OEM, 1941–42, PM 2394). The report to OFF was probably a rough estimate for use in an in-house document.

89. Olin Dows, Consultant, OCD, to Horton, memo, February 2, 1942, n.t. Folder: OEM Art Bulletin No. 1, Box 6. The memo also refers to Horton as having *participated* in the selection of the finalists, even though he was not publicly listed as a member of the jury. He probably wanted a final say to assure no politically embarrassing finalists.

90. "Defense Activity Displayed in Art," *NYT,* March 19, 1942, 26.

91. Olin Dows, Consultant, OCD, memo, to Horton, February 2, 1942.

92. Clark, *Forbes Watson,* 159.

93. Ada Rainey, "War Art Show Opens," *WP,* February 8, 1942, L4.

94. "War Art on View Today," *NYT,* March 14, 1942, 18; "Museum of Modern Art Opens Small Exhibition of Art in War by Civilians," press release 42313–18, n.d.: http://moma.org/docs/press_archives/778/releases/MOMA_1942_0020_1942-03-13_42313-18.pdf.

95. American Artists' Record of War and Defense, Past Exhibitions, National Gallery of Art: www.nga.gov/past/data/exh5.shtm.

96. US OFF, *How the Populace.*

97. US OFF, *People's Attitudes.*

98. Horton to MacLeish, letter and two-page attachment, "Questions for Proposed Roper Poll," March 14, 1942. Folder: Mc (alphabetical series), Box 9.

99. The lack of publicly disclosed budget data seems at least partly deliberate. For example, in late September, the president sent a message to Congress with a proposed budget for OWI for the remainder of FY1943. It provided no baseline information on the spending levels of its OEM predecessors in FY1942 (US House, *Supplemental Estimate of Appropriations . . . Office of War Information*).

100. US House, *Second Supplemental,* hearings, 423.

101. Gosnell, 4. Bishop and Mackay reported 520 (6). Gosnell's figure is used here because he had access to original sources (including BOB working files), had interviewed some of the participants, and wrote his report in 1944.

102. US House, *Second Supplemental,* hearings, 423.

103. US CSC, *Official Register . . . 1941,* 13.

104. US CSC, *Official Register . . . 1942,* 21–22.

105. Jerry Kluttz, "Federal Diary," *WP,* December 12, 1941, 25.

106. Straus to DOI Staff, memo, December 30, 1941, n.t. Folder: Straus, Box 7.

107. Straus to DOI Staff, memo, February 13, 1942, n.t. Folder: Straus, Box 7.

108. Horton to DOI Staff, memo,February 16, 1942, Subject: Annual Leave, underlining in original. [Doc.] X127. Folder: Horton, Box 7.

109. Jerry Kluttz, "Federal Diary," *WP,* February 26, 1942, 17.

110. Horton to DOI Employees, memo, April 27, 1942, Subject: Annual Leave. [Doc.] X-725. Folder: Horton, Box 7.

111. Richard Cooper, Chief, OEM Classification Section, to Horton, memo, February 4, 1942, Subject: Approval of Classification Sheets; Reply memo from Horton to Cooper, February 9, 1942. Folder: Memos–General, Box 7.

112. Information Division Departmental [Directory], n.d.; and handwritten cover note attachment, April 22, 1942. Folder: Civil Service Status of Information Division Departmental Personnel, Box 8.

Chapter Eight

1. Gosnell, 101.

2. "Duplication of Effort, Heavy Expense Cause of Adverse Criticism," *Washington Evening Star,* March 30, 1942. Reprinted in *CR* 88:8 (March 31, 1942): A1284.

3. For example: "President Plans Single News Unit," *NYT,* April 4, 1942, 18; Pearson and Allen, "Washington Merry-Go-Round," *Charleston (WV) Gazette,* May 8, 1942, 6.

4. Lee, *First,* 122–34, 149–57.

5. Horton to Employees, memo, May 26, 1942, n.t. [Doc.] X-1127. Folder: Horton, Box 7. The meeting was scheduled to *start* at 6:00 p.m., an indication of the long hours DOI staff routinely worked.

6. Landry, "Commentary," 34. Landry was *Variety*'s radio editor. This comment was considered newsworthy by the *Chicago Tribune:* Larry Wolters, "A Year of War Sharpens Radio Edge as Weapon," December 6, 1942, N6.

7. Childs, "Public Information," 61.

8. Lee, *First,* 138.

9. Winkler, 22.

10. Again, Catton got the date wrong, stating the OWI executive order was announced on June 12, 1942 (186).

11. It also received the above-board foreign informational activities of Coordinator of Information William Donovan. The remaining below-board responsibilities became the Office of Strategic Services (later, the CIA). After a fierce behind-the-scenes bureaucratic turf war, Rockefeller retained his informational role vis-à-vis Latin America.

12. Roosevelt, *Public Papers*, 11:275, 277.

13. The *Times'* front-page story did not catch the significance of that detail. The AP did ("Elmer Davis Is Named Chief of All U.S. War Information," *WP*, June 14, 1942, 9), as did the *Wall Street Journal* ("New War Information Office," June 15, 1942, 2).

14. U.S. Congress, *Reduction,* Part 5, 912, 915–16. Based on those statistics, OGR did the worst, with 30 percent. OFF did well with 63 percent. The best was the Coordinator of Information, at 78 percent, mostly because its overseas work didn't overlap with any of the other pre-OWI agencies.

15. Mackay, "Domestic Operations," 67.

16. Jerry Kluttz, "In Defense of Government Press Agents," *WP*, June 21, 1942, B4.

17. "A Job for Elmer Davis," *New Republic,* June 22, 1942, 847.

18. "Information Please," *Life,* July 27, 1942, 37.

19. Crider, *Bureaucrat,* 142.

20. US Congress, *Reduction,* Part 5, 2040.

21. "Tie in with the 10th Observance of National Maritime Day, May 22, 1945," Division of Public Relations, US MC, WorldCat accession No. 78645722. Also "Maritime Day Publicity," *Victory Fleet* 3:36 (March 5, 1945): 1.

22. "Maritime Day," *Victory Fleet* 3:40 (April 9, 1945): 1–4 and insert.

23. http://digital.library.northwestern.edu/wwii-posters/img/ww1645-76.jpg.

24. "Speakers and Posters," *Victory Fleet* 3:46 (May 14, 1945): 1.

25. "The Nation Salutes the Merchant Marine," *Victory Fleet* 3:49 (June 4, 1945): 1.

26. Margaret Morris Pinet, *Jefferson City (MO) News and Tribune,* December 10, 1944, 1; *Ogden (UT) Standard-Examiner,* December 8, 1944, 5A.

27. *Lumberton (NC) Robesonian,* January 29, 1945, 5; *Brown Alumni Monthly,* January–February 1945, 135.

28. "*SS Joshua A. Leach* Makes Fine War Record," *Brotherhood of Locomotive Firemen and Enginemen's Magazine* 120:1 (January 1946): 8.

29. "Selling Marine Surpluses," *Victory Fleet* 4:3 (July 16, 1945): 3, emphasis in original.

30. Douglas Larsen, "Government Publicity Agent," *Sandusky (OH) Register Star-News,* August 18, 1945, 4.

31. Catton, 189.

32. *NYT,* April 20, 1947, 16 X; April 27, 1947, 14 X.

33. "Robert Horton," obituary, *Addison County (VT) Independent,* September 20, 1993.

34. "News Commentator to Lecture Monday," *HC,* February 8, 1948, A9.

35. Horton, "Thanks to a Burglar."

36. Horton, *To Pay or Not to Pay;* Center for the Study of Democratic Institutions, *Broadcasting and Government Regulation* and *Relation of the Writer to Television.*

37. "The Economic Squeeze on Mass TV," *Reporter* 22 (April 28, 1960): 14–20.

38. Ickes's diary recounted secondhand a 1941 incident about Horton. At a party hosted by Interior Deputy Secretary Abe Fortas, Horton began talking about the failures and inadequacies of OPM, and then, allegedly, "had actually broken down and cried about it" (December 27, 1941, Reel 4, 6154). If the account is accurate, it reflects the pressures Horton was under and that his emotional reactions to his work cut so deep that he was close to the breaking point.

39. Catton to Horton, October 6, 1948. Folder: Correspondence, 1948, 1949, 1952; Box 9, Bruce Catton Collection.

40. My conclusion based on not locating any response by Horton in Catton's archived files.

41. Charles Morrissey, "Additional Notices of Vermont Books," *Vermont History* 42:3 (Summer 1974): 250.

42. I was unable to locate any living relatives of Horton in Vermont.

43. Ketchum, "Note" preceding "Interview with Robert Wyman Horton," December 30, 1987, 1.

44. "Robert Horton," obituary.

Conclusion

1. Lee, "Government Public Relations during Herbert Hoover's Presidency."

2. Arthur Krock, "The Workings of the New Deal Publicity System" ("In the Nation" column), *NYT,* August 28, 1940, 18. While the column was perceptive and analytic, Krock by this time was a consistent conservative critic of FDR and the column reflected that. During Roosevelt's first term, Krock had been sympathetic to the New Deal, and his columns during that period were interpreted in Washington as representing the president's personal thinking on issues (Shesol, 209).

3. US NDAC, *Minutes,* 104.

4. Mansfield, *Short History of OPA,* 317.

5. Article II, Section 1.

6. Article II, Section 2.

7. Rosenbloom, *Building a Legislative-Centered Public Administration.*

8. Lee, *Congress.*

9. Rich, *Greatest Story.*

10. Ervin, *Whole Truth,* 5.

11. Lee, "Public Affairs Enters."

12. Ibid., 190.

13. The speech received routine coverage, but no commentary on Sargeant doing something inappropriate. A few days later, Sargeant gave a speech of his own that also had political implications, defending the administration's record on the Korean War (United Press, "More Gained Than Lost in Korea, Official Says," *Pacific Stars & Stripes,* October 25, 1952, 5).

14. Catton, 54.

15. Krock, *Memoirs,* 202.

16. Lee, *Congress,* chap. 1.

17. Weinberg, "What to Tell America," 74.

18. Gosnell, 103–5.

19. While Horton was a New Dealer, he was no progressive on race. A 1941 syndicated column contained this racist story, clearly supplied by Horton:

> Robert Horton, office of production management publicist, recently told an amusing story about Dr. Charles F. Kettering. As chief research man for General Motors, Dr. Kettering is an associate of Mr. Horton's boss—William S. K[n]udsen.
>
> Dr. Kettering, according to Mr. Horton, was setting up an extremely complicated bit of apparatus with the aid of a Negro employee when the scientist was summoned from the laboratory. On his return, he found that the mechanism had been constructed perfectly. Dr. Kettering asked: "George, did you do that?"
>
> "Yes, sir."
>
> "Well, how did you know how to do such a difficult job?"
>
> "Well," replied George, "we colored folks has to use our heads sometimes!" (Ray Tucker, "Washington," *Reno (NV) Evening Gazette,* April 1, 1941, 4)

On the other hand, DOI's exhibition of wartime paintings (personally judged by Horton) included several paintings depicting African Americans contributing to the war effort, with at least one of them painted by an African American artist ("Negro Subjects in War Art Show," *Atlanta Daily World,* April 7, 1942, 6).

20. Catton, 189.

21. "Advertising Clubs," *Tide* 16:22 (November 15, 1942): 14.

22. Koppes and Black, 52.

23. Winkler, 22,

24. Bishop and Mackay, 6 n. 15, quoting BOB.

25. Gosnell, 10.

26. MacCann, 124.

27. Erwin Canham, "Down the Middle of the Road," *CSM,* November 28, 1941, 24.

28. Catton, 189.

29. Bishop and Mackay, 20.

30. Furman, *Washington By-Line,* 296.

31. Pearson and Allen, "Washington Merry-Go-Round," *(Reno) Nevada State Journal,* February 19, 1941, 4.

32. During his brief tenure at OWI, an incident highlighted Horton's hot personality and tensions with his former mentor, Lowell Mellett. OWI film czar Mellett had invited several hundred PIOs and their wives to a semi-social event to screen some new war-related shorts and newsreels. After the screening, Horton "lit into" the newsreels with his usual "hard-hitting" style. Newsreel staffers argued back. Mellett was embarrassed by Horton's behavior and tried to smooth things over (Jerry Kluttz, "Federal Diary," *WP,* July 16, 1942, 21).

33. Brands, *Traitor,* 819.

34. Merry, *Country of Vast Designs,* 473.

35. Hart, "National Administration," 31.

36. Lee, *First,* 159.

37. Catton, 180.

38. Nelson, xii–xiii.

39. Okrent, 293.

40. Davies, *No Simple Victory,* 34.

BIBLIOGRAPHY

Primary Sources

ARCHIVAL SOURCES

Catton, Bruce, Collection. American Heritage Center, University of Wyoming, Laramie.

Division of Information, Office for Emergency Management. File: General Correspondence and Other Records, Entry 576A, Office of War Information, Record Group 208, National Archives II, College Park, MD.

Early, Steven T., Papers of. Roosevelt Presidential Library, Hyde Park, NY.

Farm Security Administration, Western Region. File: P.R. & Inf. 12-1-43 (2), Box 5, General Correspondence 1943-1945, Farmers Home Administration, Record Group 96, Pacific Regional Archives of the National Archives, San Francisco.

Ickes, Harold L. *Diary*. Microfilm. Manuscript Division, Library of Congress, Washington, DC.

Ketchum, Richard M. "Interview with Robert Wyman Horton, Dec. 30, 1987." Box: *The Borrowed Years*, Ketchum Papers, Research Collections, Bailey/Howe Library, University of Vermont, Burlington.

Mellett, Lowell, Papers of. Roosevelt Presidential Library, Hyde Park, NY.

Siebert, Fred S., Papers. Wisconsin Historical Society, Madison.

Wallace, Henry Agard, Papers of. *The Diary of Henry Wallace, January 18, 1935–September 19, 1946*. Glen Rock, NJ: Microfilming Corporation of America, 1977. Special Collections Department, University of Iowa Libraries, Ames.

GOVERNMENT DOCUMENTS

Allison, Graham T., Jr. "Public and Private Management: Are They Fundamentally Alike in All Unimportant Respects?" In *Setting Public Management Research Agendas: Integrating the Sponsor, Producer and User.* Washington, DC: Office of Personnel Management, 1980.

Bernays, Edward L. *Public Relations*. Short Course No. 2, April–July, 1941, AIC 54(6/26/41)16 gew. Mimeograph. Washington, DC: Army Industrial College, 1941.

Bucher, Betty R. *Preliminary Inventory of the Records of the Information Department of the Office of Price Administration [Record Group 188]*. Washington, DC: National Archives, 1959.

Fesler, James W., et al. *Industrial Mobilization for War: History of the War Production Board and Predecessor Agencies, 1940–1945*. Vol. 1, *Program and Administration*. 1947. Reprint, New York: Greenwood, 1969.

Gosnell, Harold F. *Division of Information of the Office for Emergency Management*, Administrative Histories of World War II Civilian Agencies No. 52. Typescript on microfilm. Washington, DC: Committee on War Records, BOB, 1944.

Hechler, Kenneth W. *Division of Information*, Administrative Histories of World War II Civilian Agencies No. 52. Typescript on microfilm. Washington, DC: Committee on War Records, BOB, 1942[?].

Horton, Robert W., and Jack Garrett Scott. "Rubber: Basis of Today's Warfare." *Foreign Commerce Weekly* 8 (July 4, 1942): 8, 41.

Mansfield, Harvey C., and Associates. *A Short History of OPA*, General Publication No. 15, Historical Reports on War Administration. Washington, DC: Office of Temporary Controls, OPA, 1948.

Onslow, Walton. "Personnel Problems in Federal Information Service." *[Interior Department] Personnel Bulletin* 1 (August 1941): 1–4.

Troy, Thomas F. *Donovan and the CIA: A History of the Establishment of the Central Intelligence Agency*. [Langley, VA]: Center for the Study of Intelligence, CIA, 1981.

US Bureau of the Budget. *Budget of the United States Government for the Fiscal Year Ending June 30, 1940*. Washington, DC: GPO, 1939.

———. *Budget of the United States Government for the Fiscal Year Ending June 30, 1942*. Washington, DC: GPO, 1941.

———, War Records Section. *The United States at War: Development and Administration of the War Program by the Federal Government*, Historical Reports on War Administration No. 1. 1946. Reprint, New York: Da Capo, 1972.

US Civil Service Commission. *Official Register of the United States, 1941*. Washington, DC: GPO, 1941.

———. *Official Register of the United States, 1942*. Washington, DC: GPO, 1942.

———. *Official Register of the United States, 1943*. Washington, DC: GPO, 1943.

US Congress. Joint Committee on Reduction of Nonessential Federal Expenditures. *Reduction of Nonessential Federal Expenditures*, Part 3. 77th Cong., 2nd sess., 1942. Public hearings.

———. Part 5. 78th Cong., 1st sess., 1943. Public hearings.

US Division of Information. *Conversion: America's Job*, Arsenal of Democracy Series. Washington, DC: DOI, OEM, 1942.

———. *The Defense Program: A Handbook for Speakers*. Washington, DC: GPO, 1941.

———. *Dollars for Democracy*. Washington, DC: DOI, OEM, 1941.

———. *Gadgets to Guns*. Washington, DC: DOI, OEM, 1942.

———. *Guns Not Gadgets*. Arsenal of Democracy Series. Washington, DC: DOI, OEM, 1941.

———. *Materials for Defense*. Arsenal of Democracy Series. Washington, DC: DOI, OEM, 1941.

———. *Priorities and Defense: A Handbook on the Operation of the Priorities System*. Washington, DC: GPO, 1941.

———. *The Situation in Steel: Transcript of the Meeting of Iron and Steel Industry with the Iron and Steel Branch, Office of Production Management, Tuesday, November 11, 1941*. Washington, DC: DOI, OEM, 1941.

———. *Transcript: Priorities Division Conference with Trade Magazines and Newspapers, August 26, 1941*. Washington, DC: GPO, 1941.

US House. Committee on Appropriations. *Independent Offices Appropriation Bill for 1941*, Part 1. 76th Cong., 3rd sess., 1940. Public hearings.

———. *National War Agencies Appropriation Bill for 1944*, Part 1. 78th Cong., 1st sess., 1943. Public hearings.

———. *Second Deficiency Appropriation Bill for 1941*. 77th Cong., 1st sess., 1941. Public hearings.

———. *Second Deficiency Appropriation Bill, 1941*. 77th Cong., 1st sess., 1941. H. Rep. 849.

———. *Second Supplemental National Defense Appropriation Bill for 1943*. 77th Cong., 2nd sess., 1942. Public hearings.

US House. *Supplemental Estimate of Appropriations, Office for Emergency Management, Office of War Information*. 77th Cong., 2nd sess., 1942. House Doc. 862.

US Maritime Commission. *America Builds Ships: The Program of the United States Maritime Commission: Travel and Ship under the American Flag*. Washington, DC: Maritime Commission, 1940.

———. *American Flag Services: In Foreign Trade and with United States Possessions as of April 1, 1939*. Report 1500–8-A. Washington, DC: GPO, 1940.

———. *General Information on the United States Maritime Service*. Washington DC: Maritime Commission, 1939.

———. *General Information on the United States Maritime Service*, Revised January 1940. Washington DC: Maritime Commission, 1940.

———. *New Ships for the Merchant Marine: A Description, with Principal Characteristics, of the Types of Ships Being Built in the Construction Program*. Washington, DC: GPO, 1940.

US National Archives. *Pamphlet Accompanying Microcopy No. 185: Press Releases of the Advisory Commission to the Council of National Defense, June 3, 1940–January 15, 1941*. Washington, DC: National Archives, 1957.

———. *Pamphlet Accompanying Microcopy No. 195: Numbered Document File of the Council of the Office of Production Management, December 21, 1940– January 14, 1942*. Washington, DC: National Archives, 1957.

US National Defense Advisory Commission. *Handbook of the Advisory Commission to the Council of National Defense*. Washington DC: Office of the Assistant Secretary, NDAC, 1940.

———. *Minutes of the Advisory Commission to the Council of National Defense: June 12, 1940, to October 22, 1941*. Historical Reports on War Administration, WPB, Documentary Publication No. 1. Washington, DC: GPO, 1946.

———. *National Defense Advisory Commission: Functions and Activities*. Washington, DC: GPO, 1940.

———. *Numbered Document File of the Advisory Commission to the Council of National Defense, 1940–41; File Microcopies of Records in the National Archives: No. 187*. Microfilm. Washington, DC: National Archives, 1950.

———. *Press Releases of the Advisory Commission to the Council of National Defense, June 3, 1940–January 15, 1941; File Microcopies of Records in the National Archives: No. 185*. Microfilm. Washington, DC: National Archives, 1950.

US Office for Emergency Management. *Defense: One Year*. Washington, DC: GPO, 1941.

———. *OEM Handbook: Functions and Administration*. Washington, DC: GPO, 1942.

———. *[Press Releases] March 10, 1941–June 8, 1942*. (*Note:* Two bound volumes of DOI releases, at the Princeton University Library.)

US Office of Education. *3434 U.S. Government Films*, Bulletin 1951, No. 21. Washington, DC: GPO, 1951.

US Office of Facts and Figures. *How the Populace Regards the Government's Handling of War News*. Report No. 4A. Mimeograph. Washington, DC: Polling Division, Bureau of Intelligence, OFF, 1941.

———. *People's Attitudes toward the Government's Information Policy*. Mimeograph. Washington, DC: Polling Division, Bureau of Intelligence, OFF, 1942.

US Office of Government Reports, Statistics Section. *Index of Press Releases Issued by the Office for Emergency Management by General Classification, October 4, 1940 through Feb. 28, 1942* (handwritten strikethrough and new date). Mimeograph. Washington, DC: OGR, 1942.

US Office of Production Management. *Listing of Major War Department Supply Contracts by State, June 1940 through September 1941*. Washington, DC: DOI, 1941.

———. *Minutes of the Council of the Office of Production Management: December 21, 1940, to January 14, 1942*, Documentary Publication No. 2, Historical Reports on War Administration. Washington, DC: GPO, 1946.

———. *Numbered Document File of the Council of the Office of Production Management, December 21, 1940–January 14, 1942; File Microcopies of Records in the National Archives: No. 19*. Microfilm. Washington, DC: National Archives, 1951.

———. *Ships for Freedom: The Story of the Stabilization Program in the Shipbuilding Industry*. Washington, DC: DOI, 1941.

———, Production Division. *Defense Contract Service: An Appeal to Every American Manufacturer*. Washington, DC: GPO, 1941.

US War Production Board. *Converting Industry: Turning a Nation's Production to War; Transcript of Conference of Business-Paper Editors and Publishers with War Production Board Officials, Washington, D. C., February 13, 1942.* Washington, DC: DOI, WPB, 1942.

———. *Local Government and the War: Transcript of War Production Board Conference of County Officials, Washington, D.C., March 9 and 10, 1942.* Washington, DC: DOI, WPB, 1942.

———. *Priorities Orders in Force: An Alphabetical Listing of All Priorities Orders in the M, P, E, and L Series.* Washington, DC: DOI, OEM, 1942.

———. *Production Goes to War.* Washington, DC: DOI, WPB, 1942.

MEMOIRS

Brownlow, Louis. *A Passion for Anonymity: The Autobiography of Louis Brownlow; Second Half.* Chicago: University of Chicago Press, 1958.

Catton, Bruce. "Handwriting on the Wall." In *America's 85 Greatest Living Authors Present: This Is My Best; In the Third Quarter of the Century,* edited by Whit Burnett. Garden City, NY: Doubleday, 1970.

———. *The War Lords of Washington.* 1948. Reprint, New York: Greenwood, 1969.

Childs, Marquis W. *I Write from Washington.* New York: Harper and Brothers, 1942.

Ervin, Sam J., Jr. *The Whole Truth: The Watergate Conspiracy.* New York: Random House, 1980.

Furman, Bess. *Washington By-Line: The Personal History of a Newspaperwoman.* New York: Knopf, 1949.

Krock, Arthur. *Memoirs: Sixty Years on the Firing Line.* New York: Funk and Wagnalls, 1968.

Land, Emory S. *Winning the War with Ships: Land, Sea and Air—Mostly Land.* New York: McBride, 1958.

Miller, Douglas. *You Can't Do Business with Hitler.* Boston: Little, Brown, 1941.

Nelson, Donald M. *Arsenal of Democracy: The Story of American War Production.* New York: Harcourt, Brace, 1946.

Roosevelt, Franklin D. *Complete Presidential Press Conferences of Franklin D. Roosevelt.* New York: Da Capo, 1972.

———. *The Public Papers and Addresses of Franklin D. Roosevelt,* 13 vols. 1938–1950. Reprint, New York: Russell and Russell, 1969.

Secondary Sources

Axelrod, Alan. *Selling the Great War: The Making of American Propaganda.* New York: Palgrave Macmillan, 2009.

Baldasty, Gerald J. *E. W. Scripps and the Business of Newspapers.* Urbana: University of Illinois Press, 1999.

Berry, Jeffrey M. *A Voice for Nonprofits.* 2003. Reprint, Washington, DC: Brookings Institution, 2005.

Bird, William L., Jr., and Harry R. Rubenstein. *Design for Victory: World War II Posters on the American Home Front.* New York: Princeton Architectural Press, 1998.

Bishop, Robert L., and LaMar S. Mackay. "The Federal Government Reports on Defense, 1939–1942." In *Mysterious Silence, Lyrical Scream: Government Information in World War II,* Journalism Monograph No. 19, edited by Robert L. Bishop and LaMar S. Mackay. Lexington, KY: Association for Education in Journalism, 1971.

Brands, H. W. *American Dreams: The United States since 1945.* New York: Penguin, 2010.

———. *Traitor to His Class: The Privileged Life and Radical Presidency of Franklin Delano Roosevelt.* New York: Doubleday, 2008.

Brewer, Susan A. *Why America Fights: Patriotism and War Propaganda from the Philippines to Iraq.* New York: Oxford University Press, 2009.

Broughton, Philip S. "Government Agencies and Civilian Morale." *Annals of the American Academy of Political and Social Science* 220 (March 1942): 168–77.

Burns, James MacGregor. *Roosevelt: The Lion and the Fox.* 1956. Reprint, New York: Smithmark, 1996.

Center for the Study of Democratic Institutions. *Broadcasting and Government Regulation in a Free Society* (proceedings of panel discussion). Santa Barbara, CA: Center for the Study of Democratic Institutions, 1959.

———. *The Relation of the Writer to Television* (proceedings of panel discussion). Santa Barbara, CA: Center for the Study of Democratic Institutions, 1960.

Childs, Harwood L. "Public Information and Opinion." *American Political Science Review* 37 (February 1943): 56–68.

Clark, Lenore. *Forbes Watson: Independent Revolutionary.* Kent, OH: Kent State University Press, 2001.

Contreras, Belisario R. *Tradition and Innovation in New Deal Art.* Lewisburg, PA: Bucknell University Press, 1983.

Cosgrove, Kenneth. "Thirty-Sixth Annual Meeting of the American Political Science Association." *American Political Science Review* 35 (February 1941): 114–41.

Crider, John H. *The Bureaucrat.* Philadelphia: Lippincott, 1944.

Current, Richard N. "How Stimson Meant to 'Maneuver' the Japanese." *Mississippi Valley Historical Review* 40 (June 1953): 67–74.

Davies, Norman. *No Simple Victory: World War II in Europe, 1939–1945.* New York: Viking, 2007.

Devine, John. "Films." *Public Opinion Quarterly* 4 (December 1940): 684–86.

Doherty, Thomas. *Projections of War: Hollywood, American Culture, and World War II.* New York: Columbia University Press, 1993.

Downing, David. *Sealing Their Fate: The Twenty-Two Days That Decided World War II.* Cambridge, MA: Da Capo, 2009.

Dryer, Sherman H. *Radio in Wartime.* New York: Greenberg, 1942.

Elliott, Harriet. "Consumer Representation on the National Defense Advisory Commission." In *The Consumer and Defense,* edited by Frances Hall. Ann Arbor, MI: Edwards, 1940.

Ellul, Jacques. *Propaganda: The Formation of Men's Attitudes.* 1965. Reprint, New York: Vintage, 1973.

Epstein, Edward Jay. *The Big Picture: The New Logic of Money and Power in Hollywood.* New York: Random House, 2005.

Farley, Belmont. "School Public-Relations Broadcasting." In *Education on the Air: Twelfth Yearbook of the Institute for Education by Radio,* edited by Josephine H. MacLatchy. Columbus: Ohio State University, 1941.

Fellows, Erwin W. "'Propaganda': History of a Word." *American Speech* 34 (October 1959): 182–89.

Friedrich Carl J. *Controlling Broadcasting in Wartime: A Tentative Public Policy,* Monograph No. 2, Studies in the Control of Radio. 1940. Reprint, New York: Arno, 1971.

Friedrich, Carl J., and Taylor Cole. *Responsible Bureaucracy: A Study of the Swiss Civil Service.* 1932. Reprint, New York: Russell and Russell, 1967.

Friel, Brian. "Toot Your Horn?" ("Management Matters" column). *Government Executive* 42 (February 2010): 37–38.

Fulbright, J. William. *The Pentagon Propaganda Machine.* New York: Vintage, 1971.

Girona, Ramon, and Jordi Xifra. "The Office of Facts and Figures: Archibald MacLeish and the 'Strategy of Truth.'" *Public Relations Review* 35 (September 2009): 287–90.

Halper, Emanuel B. "Supermarket Use and Exclusive Clauses, Part 3—Horrendous World War Remolds the American Supermarket." *Real Property, Probate and Trust Journal* 40 (Fall 2005): 403–75.

Harlow, Rex F. *Public Relations in War and Peace.* New York: Harper and Brothers, 1942.

Harmon, Francis S. "The Motion Picture Industry and National Defense." In *The 1941 Film Daily Year Book of Motion Pictures,* edited by Jack Alicoate, 23rd ed. New York: Film Daily, 1941.

Harper, Paula. *Catalogue: War, Revolution and Peace: Propaganda Posters from the Hoover Institution Archives, 1914–1945.* Stanford, CA: Hoover Institution on War, Revolution, and Peace, 1970.

Hart, James. "National Administration." *American Political Science Review* 37 (February 1943): 25–34.

Hartley, William H. "Sight and Sound in Social Studies." *Social Education* 5 (March 1941): 224–30.

Horton, Robert W. "Thanks to a Burglar." *Yankee,* May 1959, 46–49.

———. *To Pay or Not to Pay: A Report on Subscription Television.* Santa Barbara, CA: Center for the Study of Democratic Institutions, 1960.

———. "Tomorrow's Merchant Fleet." In *American Merchant Marine Conference Proceedings, 18th Annual Meeting, New York, October 18–20, 1944,* vol. 10. New York: Propeller Club of the United States, 1945.

Jackson, Bud. "Earned Media." In *Political Communication: The Manship School Guide*, rev. ed., edited by Robert Mann and David D. Perlmutter. Baton Rouge: Louisiana State University Press, 2011.

Jensen, Oliver, ed. *Bruce Catton's America: Selections from His Greatest Works.* Garden City, NY: American Heritage, 1979.

Junior Bar Conference of the American Bar Association. *Reports and Program: Eighth Annual Meeting, Indianapolis, Indiana, September 28–30, 1941.* [Baltimore: Lord Baltimore Press], 1941.

Kane, R. Keith. "The O.F.F." *Public Opinion Quarterly* 6 (Summer 1942): 204–20.

Kennett, Lee. *For the Duration . . . The United States Goes to War: Pearl Harbor–1942.* New York: Scribner's, 1985.

Ketchum, Richard M. *The Borrowed Years, 1938–1941: America on the Way to War.* 1989. Reprint, New York: Anchor, 1991.

Koppes, Clayton R., and Gregory D. Black. *Hollywood Goes to War: How Politics, Profits, and Propaganda Shaped World War II Movies.* New York: Free Press, 1987.

Kosar, Kevin R. "The Executive Branch and Propaganda: The Limits of Legal Restrictions." *Presidential Studies Quarterly* 35 (December 2005): 784–97.

Kozlenko, William, ed. *One Hundred Non-Royalty Radio Plays.* New York: Greenberg, 1941.

Krieghbaum, Hillier. "The Office of War Information and Government News Policy." *Journalism Quarterly* 19 (September 1942): 241–50.

Kumar, Martha Joynt. *Managing the President's Message: The White House Communication Operation.* 2007. Reprint, Baltimore: Johns Hopkins University Press, 2010.

LaGuardia, Fiorello. *Civilian Defense: An Address Delivered at the Sixty-Ninth Annual Conference of the International Association of Fire Chiefs Held at Boston, August 19–20–21–22, 1941.* [Quincy, MA?]: International Association of Fire Chiefs, 1941.

Lamme, Margot Opdycke, and Karen Miller Russell. "Removing the Spin: Toward a New Theory of Public Relations History." *Journalism & Communication Monographs* 11 (Winter 2010): 281–362.

Land, Emory S. "Building an American Merchant Marine." *Annals of the American Academy of Political and Social Science* 211 (September 1940): 41–48.

Landry, Robert J. "Commentary" (after chapter 1). In Dryer, *Radio in Wartime.*

Lane, Frederic C. *Ships for Victory: A History of Shipbuilding under the U.S. Maritime Commission in World War II.* 1951. Reprint, Baltimore: Johns Hopkins University Press, 2001.

Larson, Cedric. "Official Information for America at War." *Print* 2 (October–December 1941): 66–86.

———. "Publicity for National Defense—How It Works." *Journalism Quarterly* 18 (September 1941): 245–55.

Lee, Mordecai. "A Case Study of Congressional Hostility to Agency Public Relations: The Federal Reserve and Senator Heflin, 1922." *Public Relations Review* 35 (September 2009): 291–93.

———. "Clara M. Edmunds and the Library of the United States Information Service, 1934–1948." *Libraries & the Cultural Record* 42 (2007): 213–30.

———. *Congress vs. the Bureaucracy: Muzzling Agency Public Relations*. Norman: University of Oklahoma Press, 2011.

———. "Congressional Controversy over the Federal Prohibition Bureau's Public Relations, 1922." *Public Relations Review* 34 (September 2008): 276–78.

———. *The First Presidential Communications Agency: FDR's Office of Government Reports*. Albany: State University of New York Press, 2005.

———. "Government Public Relations during Herbert Hoover's Presidency." *Public Relations Review* 36 (March 2010): 56–58.

———. "The History of Municipal Public Reporting." *International Journal of Public Administration* 29 (2006): 453–76.

———. "Intersectoral Differences in Public Affairs: The Duty of Public Reporting in Public Administration." *Journal of Public Affairs* 2 (May 2002): 33–43.

———. "Is There Anything New under the Sun? Herbert Simon's Contributions in the 1930s to Performance Measurement and Public Reporting of Performance Results." *Public Voices* 6, no. 2–3 (2003): 73–82.

———. "Origins of the Epithet 'Government by Public Relations': Revisiting Bruce Catton's *War Lords of Washington*, 1948." *Public Relations Review* 35 (November 2009): 388–94.

———. "Public Affairs Enters the US President's Subcabinet: Creating the First Assistant Secretary for Public Affairs (1944–1953) and Subsequent Developments." *Journal of Public Affairs* 8 (August 2008): 185–94.

———. "The Return of Public Relations to the Public Administration Curriculum?" *Journal of Public Affairs Education* 15 (Fall 2009): 515–33.

Lee, Mordecai, Grant Neeley, and Kendra Stewart, eds. *The Practice of Government Public Relations*. Boca Raton, FL: CRC Press, 2012.

Lewis, Howard T. "Subcontracting: The Current Problem." *Harvard Business Review* 19 (Summer 1941): 405–18.

Lobdell, George H. "Frank Knox, 11 July 1940–28 April 1944." In *American Secretaries of the Navy*, vol. 2, 1913–1972, edited by Paolo E. Coletta. Annapolis, MD: Naval Institute Press, 1980.

MacCann, Richard Dyer. *The People's Films: A Political History of U.S. Government Motion Pictures*. New York: Hastings House, 1973.

Mackay, Lamar Seal. "Domestic Operations of the Office of War Information in World War II." PhD diss., University of Wisconsin–Madison, 1966.

Maltese, John Anthony. *Spin Control: The White House Office of Communications and the Management of Presidential News*. 2nd ed. Chapel Hill: University of North Carolina Press, 1994.

McDonald, John. "Films." *Public Opinion Quarterly* 5 (March 1941): 127–29.

McMillan, George E. "Government Publicity and the Impact of War." *Public Opinion Quarterly* 5 (Autumn 1941): 383–98.

Merry, Robert W. *A Country of Vast Designs: James K. Polk, the Mexican War, and the Conquest of the American Continent.* New York: Simon and Schuster, 2009.

Miller, Lee G. *The Story of Ernie Pyle.* New York: Viking, 1950.

Okrent, Daniel. *Last Call: The Rise and Fall of Prohibition.* New York: Scribner, 2010.

Patterson, James T. *Congressional Conservatism and the New Deal: The Growth of the Conservative Coalition in Congress, 1933–1939.* 1967. Reprint, Westport, CT: Greenwood, 1981.

Payne, Stanley G. *Franco and Hitler: Spain, Germany, and World War II.* New Haven: Yale University Press, 2008.

Plant, Jeremy F. "Carl J. Friedrich on Responsibility and Authority." *Public Administration Review* 71 (May/June 2011): 471–82.

Putnam, Robert D. *Bowling Alone: The Collapse and Revival of American Community.* New York: Simon and Schuster, 2000.

Rich, Frank. *The Greatest Story Ever Sold: The Decline and Fall of Truth in Bush's America.* New York: Penguin, 2007.

Rosenbloom, David H. *Building a Legislative-Centered Public Administration: Congress and the Administrative State, 1946–1999.* Tuscaloosa: University of Alabama Press, 2000.

Ruch, Floyd L. "The Problem of Measuring Morale." *Journal of Educational Sociology* 15 (December 1941): 221–28.

Safire, William. *Safire's Political Dictionary.* New York: Oxford University Press, 2008.

Sayre, Jeanette. *An Analysis of the Radiobroadcasting [sic] Activities of Federal Agencies,* Monograph No. 3, Studies in the Control of Radio. 1941. Reprint, New York: Arno, 1971.

———. "Radio." *Public Opinion Quarterly* 4 (December 1940): 680–84.

Schachter, Hindy Lauer. *Frederick Taylor and the Public Administration Community: A Reevaluation.* Albany: State University of New York Press, 1989.

Schoenfeld, Bernard C. "Commentary" (after chapter 9). In Dryer, *Radio in Wartime,*

Shale, Richard. *Donald Duck Joins Up: The Walt Disney Studio during World War II.* 1976. Reprint, Ann Arbor, MI: UMI Research Press, 1982.

Shesol, Jeff. *Supreme Power: Franklin Roosevelt vs. the Supreme Court.* New York: Norton, 2010.

Siebert, Fredrick S. "Federal Information Agencies–An Outline." *Journalism Quarterly* 19 (March 1942): 28–33.

Sproule, J. Michael. *Propaganda and Democracy: The American Experience of Media and Mass Persuasion.* New York: Cambridge University Press, 1997.

Stanley, Eliot H. "The Lively Poster Arts of Rockwell Kent." *Journal of Decorative and Propaganda Arts* 12 (Spring 1989): 6–31.

Steele, Richard W. "The Great Debate: Roosevelt, the Media, and the Coming of the War, 1940–1941." *Journal of American History* 71 (June 1984): 69–92.

———. *Propaganda in an Open Society: The Roosevelt Administration and the Media, 1933–1941.* Westport, CT: Greenwood, 1985.

Walton, Douglas. *Media Argumentation: Dialectic, Persuasion, and Rhetoric.* New York: Cambridge University Press, 2007.

Weinberg, Sydney. "What to Tell America: The Writers' Quarrel in the Office of War Information." *Journal of American History* 55, no. 1 (June 1968): 73–89.

Weiss, Janet A. "Public Information." In *The Tools of Government: A Guide to the New Governance,* edited by Lester M. Salamon. New York: Oxford University Press, 2002.

Wills, Garry. *A Necessary Evil: A History of American Distrust of Government.* New York: Simon and Schuster, 1999.

Winfield, Betty Houchin. *FDR and the News Media.* 1990. Reprint, New York: Columbia University Press, 1994.

Winkler, Allan M. *The Politics of Propaganda: The Office of War Information, 1942–1945.* New Haven: Yale University Press, 1978.

Wohlstetter, Roberta. *Pearl Harbor: Warning and Decision.* Stanford: Stanford University Press, 1962.

INDEX